AMERICA'S PUBLIC HOLIDAYS

AMERICA'S *H*OLIDAYS PUBLIC

1865-1920

ELLEN M. LITWICKI

SMITHSONIAN INSTITUTION PRESS
WASHINGTON AND LONDON

FOR MY PARENTS, JEAN AND ROY LITWICKI

EDITOR: Ruth G. Thomson
DESIGNER: Amber Frid-Jimenez

LIBRARY OF CONGRESS CATALOGING-IN-PUBLICATION DATA
Litwicki, Ellen M.
America's public holidays, 1865–1920 / Ellen M. Litwicki
  p.   cm.
  Includes bibliographical references (p.) and index.
  ISBN 1-56098-863-0 (alk. paper)
  I. Holidays—United States—History. I. Title.
GT4803.L57   2000
394.26973—DC21 99-462086

BRITISH LIBRARY CATALOGUING-IN-PUBLICATION DATA AVAILABLE

MANUFACTURED IN THE UNITED STATES OF AMERICA
07 06 05 04 03 02 01 00   5 4 3 2 I

∞ The paper used in this publication meets the minimum
requirements of the American National Standard for Information
Sciences—Permanence of Paper for Printed Library Materials
ANSI Z39.48-1984.

CONTENTS

ACKNOWLEDGMENTS

This book began more than ten years ago with a question about why and how various Americans sought to establish a unifying national culture at the turn of the twentieth century. By sheer happenstance, the first in a series of topics I intended to examine was the holidays created in this period. As is so often the case in scholarship, I found such a wealth of information on this subject, and it so clearly addressed the issues in which I was interested, that it became the focus of the dissertation, which has, after extensive revision, become this book. Many individuals and institutions have assisted me on this long journey, and it is my great pleasure to acknowledge their contributions.

Dorothy Ross and Joseph Kett not only guided the dissertation but also have provided advice and encouragement as I have labored to transform it into a publishable manuscript. John Bodnar, Colleen McDannell,

Deborah Welch, Bill Graebner, Wilbur Zelinsky, Bill Beezly, and Dirk Raat have all read portions of the manuscript at various stages, and it has benefited immensely from their insights. I wish to thank as well the anonymous referees who read the manuscript for Smithsonian Institution Press. Their criticisms and comments helped me to sharpen my analysis at critical junctures.

A number of institutions provided invaluable research assistance along the way. The National Endowment for the Humanities supported a precious six months of research in the wonderful collections at the Winterthur Library, which enabled me to begin the process of revising the dissertation, and a grant from the Virginia Historical Society enabled me to strengthen my analysis of Confederate Memorial Day. Librarians and archivists at Winterthur, the Virginia Historical Society, the Arizona Historical Society, the Chicago Historical Society, the Arizona State Archives, the Chicago Park District, the Chicago Public Library, the Newberry Library, the University of Virginia's Alderman Library, and the Library of Virginia expertly assisted me in tracking sources and photographs. I also wish to thank the wonderful people at the Smithsonian Institution Press who have done so much to help make this book a reality; I am especially grateful to my acquisition editor, Mark Hirsch, and my copy editor, Ruth Thomson.

The State University of New York College at Fredonia has furnished crucial institutional support for the book, including grants that enabled me to complete the research, to find the photographs for the book, to pay for photographic permissions, and to complete the manuscript revisions. The women of the interlibrary loan office at Reed Library have helped me adapt to the painful absence of a research library. Maggie Bryan-Peterson and Cathe Kilpatrick of the college's Research Services Office have cheerfully supplied essential support at various stages of the manuscript preparation. I wish to extend special thanks to Paul Schwartz, dean of arts and humanities at Fredonia, who graciously provided funding for photographs. Finally, I thank Sylvia Peterson and my colleagues in the history department for their advice and encouragement along the way.

The assistance of these fine individuals and institutions has made this book immeasurably stronger. Any remaining errors, of course, are solely my own.

I cannot close without thanking my friends and family for their unstinting support and encouragement over the course of this project. Without the spiritual and social sustenance they provided, I literally could not have completed the book. They never complained about my obsession with holidays, although I am sure they wearied of hearing about them. I wish in particular to thank Lynda Coon, Elisabeth Sommer, Kathy Haldane, Jena Gaines, Candice Bredbenner, Manny Avalos, Deb Welch, Nancy Gee, Jenny Dyck, Janice Peterson, Nancy Boynton, Chris Borycki, Bea and Stephen Hardy, Dolly Rauh, Andrea Herrera, Arlene Hibschweiler, and Jane Romal. I am especially thankful for the many hours of conversation about cultural history I have shared with Jeannette Jones, Colleen McDannell, Kasey Grier, Mary Corbin Sies, and Ann Smart Martin. I am grateful to my aunts, Kay and Irene Hackett, who furnished shelter and good companionship on many research trips to Chicago. Finally, I want to thank my family, without whom I would not be here. My sister Carol has been my friend, sparring partner, and confidante all my life. She and her husband, Doug Copp, along with my other siblings and their spouses, Jay Litwicki and Mary Lynn Sheldon, Mark Litwicki and Juliana Morales, Vince and Mary Alionis, and Tom and Darcie Litwicki, have extended their love and support in more ways than I can count. I thank Jessica and Jackie Copp, and Ben, Shelby, and Megan Litwicki for bringing such joy to my life. And last, but certainly not least, I thank my parents, Jean and Roy Litwicki, for always encouraging me to create my own path in life. To them I dedicate this book.

INTRODUCTION

ETWEEN 1865 AND 1920 Americans invented more than twenty-five holidays.[1] Some, such as Memorial and Labor Days, became a permanent part of the nation's holiday calendar, while others, such as Constitution and Bird Days, never really caught on. Some holidays, such as Confederate Memorial Day, remained regional. Still others, such as Tadeusz Kosciuszko's Birthday or Emancipation and Haymarket Martyrs' Days, remained particular to ethnic, racial, or ideological groups. In addition to creating these new holidays, Americans in this period breathed new life into older ones, including the Fourth of July, Washington's Birthday, and St. Patrick's Day. What was behind this frenzy of holiday creativity? The trauma of the Civil War and its aftermath, the joys of emancipation, the vast immigration of Europeans, and the struggles of American labor all added new holidays to the American calendar in the decades following the war. So did the increasing ethnic diversity of urban populations, explosive class conflict, and perceptions of urban disorder, which spurred both self-styled civic elites and progressive reformers at the turn of the century to create or to revive "national" celebrations to bring order out of the chaos and to reunify what they viewed as a dangerously fragmented urban populace.

Despite a recent outpouring of scholarly studies of American holidays and rituals, late nineteenth and early twentieth century holidays have gone largely unexamined. Several studies have explored celebrations in the early republic as sources of nation building and national identity, and a number of others have probed African American celebrations from the colonial period to the Civil War.[2] Two other recent works have examined holidays and commemorations in the twentieth century and in the Cold War era.[3] Less attention has been paid to the period between the Civil War and World War I, although recent studies have focused on German and Norwegian holidays, emancipation commemorations, and Labor Day. But aside from Leigh Eric Schmidt, who has scrutinized the interaction of consumer culture and religion in several holidays, no general study has been made of the tremendous rush of holiday invention in this period.[4]

In this book I examine the holidays invented or revived between the Civil War and World War I. My focus is on secular holidays that were commonly celebrated in public or semipublic spaces such as city streets, parks, squares, and halls, that were planned and organized rather than spontaneous, and that were generally open to and encouraged public attendance. My analysis begins with Victor Turner's premise that collective ritual does not simply mirror culture but generates it and is informed as well by Jürgen Habermas's conception of the public sphere as a bourgeois creation. Public holidays are, to use Eric Hobsbawm's much-quoted term, "invented traditions" whose primary purpose is the creation of unity or what Benedict Anderson has called "imagined communities."[5] In the public celebrations of the many and diverse holidays that spanned these fifty-five years, various American constituencies imagined their nation.

The holidays and their public celebrations were primarily products of the middle classes, although civic-minded elites got involved in the process in the late nineteenth century, and organized labor invented and sponsored labor holidays. Class remains a notoriously slippery concept for historians of the

United States, and scholars have a tendency to define the middle class so broadly as to defy meaning. I define the middle class both occupationally and ideologically. It encompassed professionals, ministers and rabbis, journalists, educators, reformers, entrepreneurs, shopkeepers, clerks, and managers. Members generally subscribed to an ideology of upward mobility, believed in the efficacy of education and capitalism, and cultivated values of order, industry, progress, sobriety, and self-discipline leading to proper (sedate) public behavior. Although the middle class was dominated by native-born whites, ethnic and black communities had their own middle classes as well. Believers in the transformative powers of education, the middle classes saw holidays, like other emergent middle-class institutions such as museums, as opportunities for mass edification and alternatives to popular amusements.[6] Despite differences in occupation and outlook, skilled workers and the upper class did assent to many aspects of middle-class ideology, and these beliefs also informed the celebrations they sponsored.

As Alexis de Tocqueville noted and Mary Ryan has documented extensively, voluntary association had become the emblematic form of organization in democratic America, particularly for the middle class. Given the chronic lack of governmental funding and support for annual festivities, these associations of volunteers assumed the responsibility for financing and sponsoring holiday celebrations. Men and women in association created and scripted the majority of these events. Some associations were created specifically for this purpose, including the *juntas patrióticas* that planned Mexican Independence Day celebrations and the committees that conceived of and organized the George Washington inaugural centennial. In other cases, established organizations, such as labor unions and veterans' societies, found holiday celebrations conducive to their goals. Lending enthusiastic support to this endeavor was the press, another characteristic middle-class institution. Journalists, editors, and publishers not only participated as organizers but also provided publicity and propagandized on behalf of the holiday celebrations organized by these associations.[7]

Although associations sponsored holiday celebrations in part to fulfill group goals, whether proper recognition of veterans or citizenship rights for African Americans, the most important function of holidays was to reconstruct America, to imagine the nation through the eyes of group members.

Thus, organizations of veterans, African and ethnic Americans, and skilled workers all sought, through public celebrations, to sustain their own claims to be exemplars of Americanism. The groups that organized such celebrations sought to foster a broader unity, whether of all workers, all Polish or African Americans, or even all Americans. The rituals they scripted insisted that those who participated shared a common and immutable history and traditions. John Gillis has suggested that "[t]he core meaning of any individual or group identity, namely, a sense of sameness over time and space, is sustained by remembering." Public celebrations presented annual occasions for the ritualized remembering that developed that sense of identity.[8]

The public that the sponsors sought to convince, however, often had other ideas. True to Ryan's definition of the public as a "space where a society's members . . . mounted debates rather than established consensus," public holiday celebrations proved to be contested ground.[9] Socialists attended the Labor Day celebrations of Chicago trade unions, for instance, not to affirm the unions' vision of America but to proselytize their members. African Americans rejected efforts to cast them as second-class citizens, and immigrants insisted on Americanizing on their own terms. Celebrations often revealed what divided Americans and did so most starkly when those conflicts resulted in separate commemorations, such as socialist and trade unions' Labor Day exercises or Norwegian American religionists and nationalists' festivities for Norwegian Independence Day. In other cases individuals dissented by eschewing the public celebrations entirely in favor of private or family rituals or more attractive alternatives in the form of popular amusements and commercial recreation.

The variety of responses to public holiday celebrations suggests that their organizers never had complete power to shape American identity. Indeed, holiday sponsors often disagreed vehemently among themselves. The open conflicts and the more subtle subversions that pervaded holiday celebrations reveal that the imagined nation has always been contested, in substance and in meaning, by racial and ethnic minorities and by those of divergent religious beliefs or ideological persuasions. Centrifugal forces, which have consistently proven themselves as powerful as centripetal ones, continually undermined attempts at creating a homogeneous Americanism. The investigation of American public holiday celebrations thus reveals a process of collaboration, negotiation, and contestation, which produced competing images of America.

The best window on public holidays in the late nineteenth and early twentieth centuries is the popular press. Because journalists generally supported the goals of such events, they promoted holiday rituals heavily in their pages, editorialized on the significance of commemorations, and published extensive descriptive accounts of the rituals and oratory. Programs and souvenir books, although they exist only for the largest celebrations, also furnish descriptions as well as information on the process of organizing these events. In addition, education journals and patriotic manuals, which proliferated at the turn of the century, provide a fertile source of information on prescribed exercises and attempts at institutionalizing holiday celebrations.

Jack Santino points out that "[a]lthough our holidays are nationally celebrated, they are always personally interpreted."[10] The most difficult element to uncover, as always, is this interpretation. The extent of participation in such events and the degree to which participants assented to the sponsors' visions of America remain maddeningly elusive. In addition to published attendance figures and the occasional report of public opinion, I have relied upon foreign-language, African American, labor, and socialist newspapers to provide some insight into their respective audiences. Beyond this evidence, I have had to rely upon the historian's arts of inference and informed speculation.

Americans in 1865 already had a long tradition of group celebrations of public holidays. The Fourth of July and, to a lesser extent, Washington's Birthday, had regularly occasioned separate celebrations by African Americans, abolitionists, temperance advocates, Sunday schoolers, ethnic associations, artisans, and political parties, in which each group constructed American identities that served its interests. The antebellum surge in immigration had added another element to the centrifuge, as immigrants contributed holidays such as St. George's, St. Andrew's, and St. Patrick's Days to the American calendar. At the same time, the progress of emancipation in various states and foreign countries had led African Americans to create new emancipation holidays. The rise of commercial recreation, which offered alternative ways to spend one's holiday free time, contributed the final element to the fragmentation of the antebellum holiday calendar.

Although the Civil War provided some temporary impetus toward greater national unity, the postbellum era witnessed such an intensification of the centrifugal forces that had fragmented Americans before the war that some Americans feared unity had become a chimera. The rift between the North and the South continued after the war, as did the nation's race problem, which had been complicated rather than resolved by emancipation. The increasing pace of industrialization produced disaffected workers at odds with their employers, while the immigration that industrialization engendered introduced millions of newcomers with a dizzying array of languages and cultures.

Each of these forces contributed to the remaking of the American holiday calendar in the late nineteenth century. Chapter 1 examines the separate Memorial Days created by southern women and northern men out of the great losses of the Civil War and the new middle-class rituals of mourning. The veterans' organizations and ladies' memorial associations who sponsored these holidays envisioned America in sectional terms. Even in the periods of greatest animosity, however, the stories that Union and Confederate veterans told were strikingly similar. Both sides relied on bourgeois conceptions of gender that placed women in the roles of caretakers and mourners and men in the roles of warriors, protectors, and public leaders. Most importantly, despite biracial beginnings in the North, even the federal Memorial Day constructed America as a white nation, which protected black victims but did not extend them full citizenship. This shared vision made it relatively easy for white Northerners and Southerners to reconcile after the end of Reconstruction. Sacrificed on the altar of this reconciliation, African American veterans held their own Memorial Day exercises, wherein they stubbornly persisted in constructing a biracial America by telling their own story of courageous black soldiers fighting for the freedom of their brethren and for American principles.

African Americans and their white Republican allies also created a new Emancipation Day holiday to celebrate what they saw as the fulfillment of the promise of the Declaration of Independence. At the Emancipation Day exercises investigated in chapter 2, they envisioned an America that was not "a white man's country" but one to which African Americans had contributed materially and would continue to do so. In addition, many freedpeople celebrated local Emancipation Days, such as the anniversary of the fall of Richmond, which had constituted the practical grant of freedom to Richmond's slaves. Although African American leaders sought to make Emancipation Day a legal and national holiday, by the turn of the century it had become an overwhelmingly black holiday. Moreover, African Americans found that they had to continue to fight on Emancipation Day, as they had before the war, for acceptance as equal citizens in the American republic.

Organized labor, too, had been profoundly influenced by abolition and sought to spread emancipation to the nation's wage slaves. Chapter 3 explores the origins of Labor and May Days, both of which grew out of the eight-hour movement and organizing efforts in the postwar era. The pragmatic trade unions that controlled Labor Day and the socialists who quickly came to dominate May Day, however, presented differing visions of America. Although both agreed on the centrality of labor, they conflicted on its relation to capital. If the pragmatists accepted capitalism, in their celebrations they also posited skilled workers as the equal partners of capitalists. Labor Day discourse blended the upwardly striving philosophies of artisans and the middle class to create a peculiarly classless Americanism. Radicals, on the other hand, rejected out of hand any partnership with capital and presented an alternative vision of America that defined the working class and its contributions in more clear, more inclusive, and more oppositional terms.

In their efforts to attract workers to their celebrations and their organizations, labor unions faced competition from ethnic associations, which created or transferred to the United States a multitude of holidays in the late nineteenth century. Chapter 4 focuses on these celebrations, which served not only to cultivate ethnic identity and patriotism but also to construct ethnic Americanism. Like veterans, African Americans, and organized labor, ethnic associations lectured their audiences on ethnic contributions to America. They insisted that Americanism did not preclude ethnicity and that one could be a good American while maintaining one's ethnic loyalties.

They continued to assert this principle, even as they faced increasingly coercive Americanization efforts. In the late 1880s many middle- and upper-class Americans feared that the nation was about to succumb to anarchy. Rapid industrialization had created a new industrial and financial elite, broadened and redefined the middle class, and accelerated the process of proletarianization of the working class. The struggle between capitalists and their employees for control of the workplace and the fruits of capitalism had led to a series of increasingly violent confrontations, culminating in the Haymarket Square bombing in 1886. At the same time, the immigration that industrialists encouraged to provide an ample, cheap, and divided workforce was bringing together an unprecedented variety of cultures. The growing militance and ethnic diversity of the working class propelled civic-minded members of the emergent business elite into the public arena.[11] They discovered that public holiday celebrations provided ideal forums for instructing the working and lower classes, including immigrants, in patriotism and citizenship. They found the solution to the crisis of public order in their vision of a homogeneous America marked by respect for the law and loyalty to only one flag. Chapter 5 examines three massive anniversary celebrations at the turn of the century, in which civic elites promulgated their law-and-order patriotism. To institutionalize their vision of America they turned to the public schools. In this effort they allied themselves with veterans' organizations, patriotic societies, and educators to produce a sustained campaign of civic education in the nation's schools.

Although this crusade continued into the early twentieth century, progressive reformers and educators began to alter its terms. They agreed that urban life had become dangerously disordered, but they perceived the problem as systemic rather than personal and individual.[12] By changing the urban environment, they hoped to create patriotic citizens. At the heart of their vision of America, however, stood not law and order but the community, wherein members sacrificed themselves for the common good. Progressives developed community-based celebrations for a variety of holidays, including Arbor Day and the Fourth of July, and these celebrations form the subject of chapter 6. On these occasions Progressives articulated a more pluralistic vision of America, albeit one that still privileged whiteness and the middle class. The advent of World War I, however, put even this limited pluralism to the test, and Progressives succumbed to Americanization pressures in their wartime celebrations. The war also led to the creation of the era's final holiday, Armistice Day, the purpose of which was to commemorate the Allied victory in World War I and the soldiers who had made it possible. As with Memorial Day, the vision of America promulgated on Armistice Day was one wherein veterans constituted the truest Americans. Public holidays had come full circle, ending where they had begun in an America epitomized by its citizen soldiers.

I

MEMORIAL DAYS

T 1879 MEMORIAL DAY exercises at New York's Academy of Music, railroad magnate Chauncey M. Depew began his address with an appropriately flowery history of the newest of the nation's holidays. "When the War was over," he began, "in the South, where, under warmer skies and with more poetic temperaments, symbols and emblems are better understood than in the practical North, the widows, mothers, and children of the Confederate dead went out and strewed their graves with flowers." That had been, Depew asserted, a nonpartisan gesture of love and grief. He told the audience that "at many places the women scattered them [the flowers] impartially also over the unknown and unmarked resting places of the Union soldiers." This action by Confederate women had served to bridge the sectional gap and to stimulate healing. "As the news of this touching tribute flashed over the North," Depew proclaimed, "it roused, as nothing else could have done, national amity and love, and allayed sectional animosity and passion."[1]

As Depew suggested, the terrible destruction of the Civil War had inspired the creation of a new national holiday that held out the promise of reunifying the war-torn country. Despite their differences, Northerners and Southerners shared their grief over the brothers and husbands, fathers and sons, who had died defending causes they believed noble and righteous. The white middle class also shared rituals of grief that centered on rural cemeteries and grave decoration and out of which Memorial Day grew. Within a few years after the war, the holiday had become an institution in both the North and the South. In contrast to Depew's sentimentalized history, however, the holiday had done little to foster reconciliation by 1879; instead, it had contributed to the perpetuation of sectional animosities.

Rather than a single holiday, in fact, two related but distinct Memorial Days emerged—the federal one and the Confederate one. On these days Northerners and Southerners not only honored their war dead but also instructed the populace on the significance of those deaths for American society. Despite the essential differences in the North and the South's heroes and causes, the stories of the war perpetuated on the federal and Confederate holidays bore striking similarities. Both sides had fought for causes they believed to be just—the preservation of the Union in one case and the preservation of the principles of the American republic in the other. On each holiday participants proclaimed their vision of America to be the true one.

The values and racial blinders of the predominantly white and middle-class organizers of the holidays shaped the stories of the war. In the rhetoric and ritual of Memorial Days, the dead and surviving white veterans on both sides epitomized the nineteenth-century masculine virtues of courage, leadership, and the willingness to sacrifice one's life for principle and country. The holiday defined a peculiarly middle-class and American view of class, in which private soldiers and sailors were as worthy of respect as their officers, and no class lines divided them (although it was the former officers, not privates, who took the leading role at Memorial Day exercises). The white women the soldiers had left behind were celebrated on Memorial Day as embodiments of the feminine ideals of patient love, benevolence, and loyalty to their men and country.

Largely missing from the official stories of the war, although they participated in federal exercises, were African Americans, who had arguably the strongest claim to have fought for the fulfillment of American principles. The essential racism that prevented most white Americans from seeing African Americans as anything other than subordinates or victims, along with the similarity of the white northern and southern stories of the war, enabled reconciliation to proceed rather rapidly once Reconstruction ended, but it was reconciliation for whites only. African Americans, shut out of white Memorial Day celebrations, held their own exercises, in which they continued to remind Americans that the central story of the Civil War had been the abolition of slavery and the realization of the American ideals of liberty and equality.

ROOTS

No holiday had been established to mourn the dead soldiers of the American Revolution, although tribute was paid to the heroes of that war on the Fourth of July. The idea of a holiday specifically to mourn the dead was a product of the nineteenth-century convergence of sentimental, evangelical, and romantic attitudes toward death, mourning, and the hereafter, which coalesced in the rural cemetery movement in the 1830s.[2] The rural cemetery movement transformed graveyards from mere bone repositories to scenic retreats wherein the living might visit and communicate with the dead, whose spirits, according to contemporary consolation literature, hovered nearby. Drawing on romantic aesthetics of beauty and the spiritual in nature, promoters of the rural cemetery designed their "cities of the dead" to facilitate this communication between the living and the dead, situating the cemeteries in areas of natural beauty—in wooded areas or on bluffs overlooking rivers and streams—and encouraging the living to contribute to the improvement of that beauty. One of the most popular ways of doing the latter by the mid-nineteenth century was to strew flowers on the graves, a custom possibly brought over by German immigrants. At least two accounts of Memorial Day origins specify that the originators were inspired by the German custom of grave decoration on All Saints' Day.[3]

By their visits and the beautification of their relatives' resting spots, the living preserved and venerated the memory of the dead and also imbibed the lessons that the lives of the dead held for the survivors. And who was better suited to pass on such lessons than the valiant heroes of the late war? Rather than spawning a radically new holiday, the carnage of the Civil War simply intensified and lent urgency to an emerging custom. The sheer magnitude of the loss of the nation's young manhood, the sacrificed youth of the dead soldiers, and the pathos of the widows and orphans left alone furnished the perfect materials for lessons to the nation's survivors.

If Memorial Day became an occasion to commemorate the fallen soldier as the epitome of masculinity, its origins tell us as much about the nineteenth-century construction of femininity, as Depew's tale suggests. One of the most popular Confederate stories about the origins of the holiday fused Victorian sentimentalization of children, the maternal role of women, and gendered mourning practices. This story, reprinted often in the *Confederate Veteran* at the turn of the century, credited Mrs. Charles J. Williams of Columbus, Georgia, with instituting Memorial Day. After her soldier husband died (of disease) in 1862, the story went, she and her young daughter made daily pilgrimages to his grave, where they "often comforted themselves by wreathing it with flowers. While the mother sat abstractly thinking of the loved and lost one, the little one would pluck the weeds from the unmarked soldiers' graves near her father's and cover them with flowers, calling them her soldiers' graves." The child died soon after, so the story went, and "[t]he sorely bereaved mother then took charge of these unknown graves for the child's sake." Tending the graves made Mrs. Williams think "of the thousands of patriot graves throughout the South, far away from home and kindred, and in this way the plan was suggested to her of setting apart one day in each year, that love might pay tribute to valor throughout the Southern states."[4]

Despite the apocryphal nature of this tale, the Columbus Ladies' Memorial Association, of which Mrs. Williams was secretary, most often received credit for originating Memorial Day, on 26 April 1866. The association's official history claimed that the idea for the holiday came from Lizzie Rutherford, whose reading about the German custom of grave decoration on All Saints' Day had suggested to her the possibility of similarly setting aside a day to decorate soldiers' graves. According to this history, Williams's significance was as a publicist who helped to spread the holiday throughout the South.[5]

The truth of the origins of Memorial Day is doubtlessly lost forever in the morass of romanticized histories, but we do know that women who had been active in wartime aid societies redirected their benevolent energies after the war to organizing memorial associations in cities and hamlets across the former Confederacy. The Columbus Ladies' Memorial Association, for example, was the postbellum descendant of the town's Soldiers' Aid Society. The first task of those associations in many instances was to create a Confederate cemetery or, more commonly, a Confederate section in existing cemeteries. In addition to seeing to the proper burial of the Confederate dead, the women instituted a ritualized remembrance of them. In the spring of 1866 a number of memorial associations, including the one in Columbus, sponsored their first official Memorial Days.[6]

In an open letter to southern women and editors in March 1866, Mrs. Williams elucidated the purpose of this new holiday: "[W]e can keep alive the memory of the debt we owe [the Confederate dead] by dedicating, at least one day in each year, to embellishing their humble graves with flowers." It was the least, she suggested, that the grieving women could do for the soldiers who had died in their defense. If man's task was to fight to defend principle and home, then woman's task was to memorialize those who had died doing so. "The veriest radical that ever traced his genealogy back to the deck of the *Mayflower*," Williams concluded, "could not refuse us the simple privilege of paying honor to those who died defending the life, honor and happiness of the Southern women."[7]

The holiday spread quickly in the South, although former Confederates never did celebrate one universal Memorial Day. Richmond alone commemorated three Confederate Memorial Days, sponsored by the ladies' memorial associations of the Hollywood, Oakwood, and Hebrew Cemeteries. The date of the holiday varied across the South, based on local history and the blossoming of spring flowers. In the lower South, 26 April, the anniversary of General Joseph Johnston's surrender, was common. Other popular dates were 10 May, the date of Stonewall Jackson's death, and 3 June, Jefferson Davis's birthday. The date chosen was, in some cases, quite localized. Petersburg, Virginia, for example, decorated graves on 9 June, which was the anniversary of the 1864 repulse of a Union attack by a small band of old men and boys. One early twentieth-century compiler noted the existence of at least eight different Memorial Days in the South, ranging from 26 April to 13 June.[8]

Several northern towns also claimed to have originated Memorial Day, and their stories, like those of their southern counterparts, centered on mourning women. Boalsburg, Pennsylvania, for instance, called itself the "birthplace of Memorial Day" and traced the holiday to 1864 when the grieving mother of Amos Meyers, who was killed at Gettysburg, decorated his grave. The *Chicago Tribune* claimed an even earlier origin. In 1895 the paper declared that on 13 April 1862 four women had strewn flowers on the graves of soldiers buried in Arlington Heights. "These tender and devoted floral obsequies to our dead heroes," the paper continued, "became contagious and other women in various parts of the country, inspired by their patriotic example, soon followed in their footsteps." Waterloo, New York, holds the distinction of congressional recognition of its claim to have celebrated the first Memorial Day on 5 May 1866.[9]

Despite these claims, the catalyst for the federal holiday was apparently a northern woman influenced by the Confederate Memorial Day. In the spring of 1868, Mrs. John Logan of Chicago accompanied some friends on a tour of the battlefields around Richmond and Petersburg, Virginia. While there, according to her later reminiscences, she was touched by the care lavished on the Confederate soldiers' graves and learned of the Memorial Day custom. Rather than organize a similar women's group to inaugurate the custom in the North, however, she told her husband that she "wished there could be concerted action of this kind all over the North for the decoration of our own soldiers' graves." Her husband, a Republican congressman and Civil War general who had recently been elected commander in chief of the Grand Army of the Republic (GAR), an organization of Union veterans, thought it a splendid way to honor the fallen Union soldiers. On 5 May 1868 he issued a general order to all GAR posts designating 30 May "for the purpose of strewing with flowers or otherwise decorating the graves of comrades who died in defense of their country during the late rebellion."[10] Although the veterans of the GAR took control of the federal exercises, women nevertheless played a significant role, particularly in securing flowers and decorating the graves.

"MINISTERING ANGELS": WOMEN'S ROLES ON MEMORIAL DAY

That women, who were then restricted primarily to decorative and allegorical functions at public demonstrations, should assume such a major role in the new holiday followed logically from the dictates of mid-nineteenth-century conceptions of gender. Evangelical Christianity and the construction of "women's sphere," as historians of women have demonstrated, provided opportunities for middle-class women to forge a broader role for themselves in the "moral" sphere of the public realm by building orphanages, caring for wounded soldiers, or feeding the poor. Memorial work similarly dramatized the gender roles of beneficence and maternalism dictated by evangelicalism and domestic ideology. What better illustration of these roles than to tend the graves of the tens of thousands of Confederate soldiers who had neither local families nor a federal government to perform this labor of love? The *Augusta (Georgia) Chronicle* described the women who decorated Confederate graves on that town's first Memorial Day as "ministering angels who with garlands and crosses and anchors and chaplets of roses, vied with the other in adorning the graves of their dead defenders." The article noted that many of the dead soldiers had been cared for before their deaths by the same women who continued to tend to them in death.[11]

As the lack of government care suggests, the role of women in the Confederate Memorial Days had practical as well as cultural roots. The federal government established a system of national cemeteries for the Union dead after the war, but the Confederate dead had no access to this service and were buried in local cemeteries. The ladies' memorial associations took as their primary purpose the maintenance of Confederate graves. In their initial appeal for support from southern women, the founders of Richmond's Hollywood Memorial Association pledged "to rescue from the oblivion to which they are passing the graves of the great host which perished in the war and sleep undistinguished in our cemetery." This female labor of love relieved cemeteries of the financial burden of tending the graves of the tens of thousands of Confederate soldiers who no longer had a central government to provide even minimal care for them.[12]

In addition, although Union veterans organized to pay public homage to their comrades-in-arms, it was virtually unthinkable in the immediate postwar era that Confederate veterans should do the same. It was one thing for the wives and mothers of dead soldiers to mourn them and to pay homage to their memory; had the surviving rebels done the same, it would have seemed tantamount to treason. James H. Gardner, an officer of the Hollywood Cemetery Company in Richmond, recognized this in a letter to his daughter about 1867 Memorial Day exercises at the cemetery: "I have heard of no unpleasant occurance [sic], but if the management had not been under the control of the ladies, [a] thousand bayonets would have bristled to prevent the celebration."[13]

Not only were women viewed as the natural caretakers of the dead soldiers, but also they (and their children) composed the bulk of the bereaved and thus were the primary group of mourners. Nineteenth-century gender ideology stereotyped women as being more religious than men and led by their hearts, which suggested that they grieved more deeply than men. Sentimental fiction, prescriptive literature, and mourning customs all affirmed this gendered mourning.[14]

Memorial Day exercises in both the North and the South strikingly affirmed the identification of women with mourning and caretaking roles. A Richmond newspaper's account of the first grave decoration ceremonies in Memphis in 1866 highlighted women as the chief mourners, describing "the grey-haired matron, with tottering steps, placing chaplets and wreaths upon the roofs of the darkened houses containing her sons and grandsons; the widow, scattering buds above the stiffened form of her heart's pride; the sister, festooning the humble head-board of a lost brother." As they scattered flowers, a symbolically charged tableau unfolded. More than one hundred young women from the State Female College processed through the cemetery in twos, "each couple bearing a chaste wreath between them," which "they silently placed down as an offering of the heart teeming with love and reverence to the gallant dead." Although the veterans of the GAR took a greater role in grave decoration on the federal holiday, women played the chief mourning role on those occasions as well. A report about Decoration Day in Chicago's Graceland Cemetery in 1890 noted that "[a]lmost every grave . . . was surrounded by groups of women who were setting out plants in the rich black loam." Chapters of the Women's Relief Corps (WRC), an organization formed during the war and recognized by the GAR as its women's auxiliary in 1881, and the Ladies of the GAR, another auxiliary, assisted the veterans in decorating graves.[15]

The national iconography of Memorial Day reinforced the mourning role of women. Holiday pictures featured women, many in mourning wear, dec-

Memorial Day in Hollywood Cemetery, Richmond, 1867. The illustration indicates the predominance of women in the Confederate commemoration. (From *Harper's Weekly*, 1867; courtesy of the Library of Virginia)

orating soldiers' graves or otherwise remembering the dead. The traditional allegorical female figure remained common as well. An 1884 *Harper's Weekly* illustration, for instance, featured a woman in classical garb in the depths of grief, prostrate on a soldier's grave. Holiday music and poetry amplified the theme. Holiday exercises included songs such as "Who Will Care for Mother Now?" A poem in the *Confederate Veteran* in 1896 told of a female "mourner clad in sombre black" who, with her granddaughter, "strewed white blossoms o'er the mounds" in Richmond's Hollywood Cemetery.[16]

Like the granddaughter in the poem, children, especially young girls, were also cast as mourners, in actuality and as symbols, on Memorial Day. The first Memorial Day in Lynchburg, Virginia, featured "seven or eight hundred children, all in their Sunday attire, and, decked with wreaths and boquets [sic]." Girls in Chicago's Oak Woods Cemetery in 1900 took on allegorical roles to symbolize the nation's mourning of a new group of war dead. Forty-five girls in white, representing the states, scattered flowers in the lagoon as a tribute to the naval heroes who had died at sea in the Spanish-American

War. A special role was reserved for the orphans of the soldier dead, who paid ritualized tribute to their departed fathers on Memorial Day. Children from a Washington area orphanage received baskets of flowers to strew on the graves in Arlington National Cemetery on the first federal Memorial Day in 1868. Participants in exercises at Chicago's Bohemian Cemetery in 1890 witnessed a particularly poignant scene, as two orphaned Czech girls recited poems at the graves of their dead fathers.[17]

Bereft orphans were also the subject of Memorial Day literary efforts. In Tucson in 1890, little Mamie Hoff reportedly moved the audience to tears with her recitation of "You Put No Flowers on My Papa's Grave." A fictional story that appeared the same year in the *Youth's Companion* told of a poor girl whose veteran father has recently died. She and her brother have to move to the West, but the girl worries that no one will care for her father's grave. Therefore, on Memorial Day, she returns to the cemetery where her father is buried and waits eagerly for the holiday crowd to decorate her father's grave. When they pass by without stopping, she throws herself on the grave, weeping. Moved by her grief, they return, and "each one cast a flower beside the head-stone of her father's grave." The children bring flowers and sympathy for the plight of the orphaned girl. "The little girls, all in white," enact the proper role of their gender by "[throwing] kisses as they passed to the forlorn and fatherless girl beyond." Afterward, representatives from the local GAR post assure her that her father's grave will never be neglected again.[18]

Such stories reinforced the gender roles girls learned from observing their mothers and other women on Memorial Day. Holiday iconography and fiction supplemented this instruction. It is the girl, not her brother, who worries that her father will not be remembered on the holiday and who makes the trip back to see that he is. Allegorical holiday pictures often featured girls dressed in virginal white bearing flowers and helping their mothers to decorate graves. In one such sketch in *Harper's Weekly*, a host of girls with flowers wait outside a cemetery gate, where a woman in black stands and points to the graves inside. Even in play fictional children replicated the roles of their elders. In a story published in 1882, Posie makes a soldier doll for her brother Popsie's birthday, which is on Memorial Day. The children then hold their own Memorial Day exercises. Popsie buries his soldier, and Posie decorates the grave with the first rosebud from her "pet" rose bush. Another short tale warned what happened to girls who did not fulfill their proper roles. In it a little girl forgets to water the flowers that her mother had cut for Memorial Day. The flowers wilt and cannot be used, and the girl is sent to her room. Her punishment for neglecting the duty of her gender is to be deprived of the Memorial Day experience.[19]

As these stories and the history of the holiday itself suggest, caretaking was another aspect of feminine identity embedded in Memorial Day activities. Holiday orators, invariably male, offered accolades to the women who had cared for the soldiers, in life and now in death. A Grand Army man in Tucson in 1885 praised the "devoted mother, the heroic wife, the courageous sweetheart, . . . [who] like ministering angels, cared for and nursed [the soldiers] when sick and wounded, or . . . gently closed their eyes when dead," and who on Memorial Day "testified their undying devotion to the soldier's cause by contributing beautiful flowers to adorn our heroes' graves." Confederate veterans used similar language to laud the southern women who had supported the cause, nursed the wounded, provided solace to the dying, and tended the Confederate soldiers even in death by caring for their graves. One speaker asserted that the women who organized the ladies' memorial associations had "done more, than all besides, to fix the standard of virture [sic] and patriotism by which the cause of the Confederacy and its adherents must be judged."[20]

In the ladies' memorial associations of the South, this caretaking role was institutionalized and greatly expanded. The women of the memorial associations used the skills that they had honed in tract and temperance societies to publicize and to fund Memorial Day exercises, to maintain Confederate graves, to pay for the removal and reburial of Confederate dead from northern battlefields, and to build permanent monuments to their memory. These tasks necessitated tremendous organizing, motivational, and fund-raising skills, as well as extraordinary commitments of time, effort, and money. The activities of one of the most prominent of the ladies' memorial associations, Richmond's Hollywood Memorial Association, illustrate the extent of the caretaking activities of southern women. Less than a year after its founding in 1866, the association began to raise funds to erect a memorial in Hollywood Cemetery. Through benefits, sponsorship of lectures, and a bazaar, which alone raised over $18,000, the women quickly obtained sufficient money. The monument, a ninety-foot pyramid of James River granite blocks, was dedicated on 6 November 1869. The capstone was guided by a convict laborer who scaled the pyramid, a feat repeated on subsequent Memorial Days by young men who annually hung a wreath from its top. This pattern was repeated in cemeteries throughout the South, as ladies' memorial associations raised funds, selected monumental designs, and oversaw their construction.[21]

The Hollywood Memorial Association also solicited funds to remove and to rebury in Hollywood the bodies of Confederate soldiers buried on northern battlefields. Its largest project was the transfer of the remains of five thousand southern soldiers buried at Gettysburg, for which it successfully raised funds from the other states of the former Confederacy and from Memorial Day collections. Beyond such special causes, the women of the Hollywood and other associations held ice cream socials and bazaars and sponsored excursions and lectures on the war to raise the money necessary to mark and to maintain the Confederate graves and to buy Memorial Day flowers. Most significantly, the women of the ladies' memorial associations sponsored and organized the annual Confederate Memorial Day exercises that kept alive the memory of the war and its soldiers. Several weeks before the holiday the association's members met to plan the exercises and to invite orators. They recruited male volunteers to clean up the soldiers' sections of the cemeteries and clergymen and prominent veterans to conduct and to speak at the exercises. They arranged to have sufficient flowers, supplementing those purchased by the association with flowers donated by individuals and businesses. A day or so before the holiday the members met to weave flowers into wreaths and crosses.[22]

Women played a less active role in organizing the federal holiday, which male veterans effectively controlled. Local GAR posts had standing committees that planned the annual memorial exercises. Nevertheless, the women of the Women's Relief Corps, like their counterparts in the ladies' memorial associations, raised money for Memorial Day flowers and arranged them for grave decoration. After his oration at Richmond's Seven Pines National Cemetery in 1888, Theodore Bean wrote to the sponsoring GAR post to praise the "noble women" of the corps, to whom he dedicated "the words I spoke amid the flowers they furnished."[23]

Although southern women took a much greater role in the planning of Memorial Day than in other public holidays, when it came to the holiday itself, they, like northern women, returned to a more traditional role at the ac-

Daisies gathered for Decoration Day, 30 May 1899. Young women typically wove flowers into wreaths to lay on soldiers' graves on Memorial Day. (Photograph by Frances Johnston; courtesy of the Library of Congress)

tual ceremonies. Circumstances in the South might dictate that women play a leading part in memorializing the dead, but gender conventions dictated that the public roles of oratory and parading be reserved for men. Women thus expanded their public activities while conforming them to the expectations of their gender, as they did with other benevolent work.[24]

FROM RITES OF MOURNING TO RITES OF TRIUMPH

The Memorial Days organized by the ladies' memorial associations, the GAR, and the Women's Relief Corps featured similar rituals and exercises.

The holiday often began with a Protestant church service, the highlight of which was a special sermon eulogizing the dead warriors. The women of the memorial associations and the relief corps attended en masse, as did members of the GAR and other organized and unorganized veterans, generally in uniform. The act of beginning the exercises in churches reveals the sacred nature of the holiday for its organizers. The former foes agreed that Memorial Day, as one of the main venues for instructing Americans in the meaning of the war and of their own sacrifices, was the most sacred of American holidays. In Tucson in 1885, Colonel Z. L. Tidball explained that "to every member of the Grand Army of the Republic; to every American, soldier and civilian alike, Memorial Day is as sacred as Independence day of our forefathers, and as much to be revered." Richmond's Rev. H. D. MacLachlan seconded that idea in a holiday sermon titled "The Religious Aspect of Patriotism," in which he proclaimed that "Decoration Day is a sacrament."[25]

After the religious services, mourners made their way in somber but informal procession to the cemeteries. The ceremonies opened in the soldiers' section with a prayer by a local clergyman, often a veteran himself, followed by patriotic oratory and ruminations on the meaning of the war and the lessons taught by the soldiers' sacrifice. Memorial Day addresses were invariably pronounced by distinguished veterans at both the federal and Confederate exercises; only veterans qualified as experts at decoding the war. Richmond's Hollywood Memorial Association declared that its custom was to "confine its invitations only to those who were actively engaged in the service of the Confederacy." The GAR restricted oratorical duties to its own members at its federal exercises. On some occasions the exercises included the dedication of a monument to the fallen. Grave decoration either preceded or followed the rhetorical exercises, and the ceremonies closed with a benediction, the playing of "Taps," and a twenty-one gun salute.[26]

Women's participation in the exercises of the day largely conformed to nineteenth-century expectations. They never served as official orators, although they gave brief addresses at times. At Chicago's Rosehill Cemetery in 1893 the visiting national president of the Women's Relief Corps pronounced "a tribute to the unknown dead," and a representative of the United Daughters of the Confederacy addressed the United Confederate Veterans of New York in Mount Hope on Memorial Day 1914. Maintaining the proper feminine role, however, the latter asserted that "service to a Confederate Veteran is the highest privilege of a Daughter of the Confederacy." In between the male-dominated main events of oratory and prayers, women and children recited poetry and played and sang mournful airs. At Richmond's Seven Pines National Cemetery in 1895, for example, the choir of the Women's Relief Corps opened the exercises by singing the "Star-Spangled Banner," Mayme Leahy recited "Converse with the Slain," and Emma Lawton sang "Heroes Sleeping," accompanied by Bessie Pattee on a portable organ. In Tucson in 1890 a chorus of little girls sang the "Soldiers' Memorial Hymn," and young Charlie Rouse recited "The Sleeping Sentinel."[27] This division of labor reinforced the supporting role played by women and children, in contrast to the male heroes, who were both the honorees and the main actors in the exercises.

The central ritual of the day's exercises, however, belonged predominantly to women, assisted by children. Either before or after the literary and rhetorical exercises came the grave decorating. A sober, quasi-religious procession of women, children, and veterans moved from grave to grave, dispensing their flowers. Women's roles of mourning and adorning now took center stage. Like the music and poetry, grave decorating fit nicely within the sphere of acceptable public activities for women. In the years immediately after the war, when private and public grief peaked, the "feminine" touch of grieving seemed more appropriate than the martial spirit common to American public holidays. "It is the more impressive," the *Richmond Dispatch* editorialized in 1870, "when the day is not observed by any noisy demonstration or pompous ceremonies, such as men are wont to use in making known their respect for the heroic dead, but when woman's warm heart impels the observance, and the tribute paid to departed valor is only the placing of Spring's brightest flowers upon the graves in which the soldiers' bones repose."[28]

The "noisy demonstration" and "pompous ceremonies" of men did not long remain absent, however. As the southern states "redeemed" themselves from Reconstruction in the 1870s, ex-Confederates were able to play a more prominent role in Memorial Day exercises. The military parade and drill, typical of American holidays between the Revolution and the Civil War, also returned as the distance of time diminished grief. As early as 1875 Richmond's Hollywood Memorial Day featured a procession of veterans. After helping to decorate the graves of their comrades, the former Confederates re-

GAR Memorial Day parade in Chicago, 1912. By the late nineteenth century, the Grand Army of the Republic had incorporated public processions into its holiday in an effort to draw more Chicagoans. Here spectators line South Michigan Avenue to watch the veterans march. (Courtesy of the Chicago Historical Society, negative number DN-58756)

formed their ranks and held a dress parade at the cemetery. The martial procession entered federal celebrations at about the same time. In an attempt to broaden the appeal of and more widely diffuse the lessons of Memorial Day, Chicago's GAR posts began in 1878 to stage the traditional crowd pleaser, a military parade through the business district, on the afternoon of Memorial Day. By the mid-1880s the procession had expanded to include most of the city's Grand Army men, as well as platoons of police and firemen, regiments of the state National Guard, and fraternal organizations.[29]

The emergence of the procession demarcated an increasingly male-dominated holiday as well as a move away from mourning to celebrating the virtues and the causes of the dead and living veterans. As time distanced the veterans from the suffering of the war and they focused nostalgically on its camaraderie, they even began to celebrate war itself on Memorial Day. In describing Chicago's 1893 parade, the *Chicago Tribune* noted that "it was magnificent because of . . . the inbred delight the American citizen has for the pomp and circumstance of war." This celebration was a far cry from the funereal aspect of early commemorations. Women participated in the Memorial Day parades, as in other nineteenth-century parades, primarily as spectators or allegorical figures. The women of the ladies' memorial associations did ride in carriages in the Confederate Memorial Day processions, and in Chicago in 1893 a group of female cadets dressed in red, white, and blue marched in a cross formation in the procession. More typical, however, was the young woman representing America who, draped in the national colors, rode on the decorated carriage of the Pioneer Hose Company in Tucson in 1885. Although the holiday processions remained largely male preserves, in the late nineteenth century their sponsors encouraged cadet corps and other children to take a larger part, as the Civil War generation aged and worried about who would carry on its work. The *Chicago Tribune* editorialized in 1890 that it was "more than ever necessary . . . before [the veterans] pass away that they should impress the patriotic associations of the day upon the young and acquaint them with its historic significance, so that they may continue the observance of this beautiful anniversary." In 1895 the highlight of Richmond's Hollywood Memorial Day parade was a children's brigade composed of some eight hundred boys and girls between the ages of seven and thirteen. They were escorted by veterans; parents were informed that they could not march with their children because "they [would] destroy the symmetry and beauty of the column."[30]

Even in the more martial and triumphal Memorial Day of the turn of the century, women and children thus continued to play a vital role. Although women's roles on Memorial Day stretched the boundaries of appropriate feminine behavior under contemporary gender constraints, they did not break through them. They did not give speeches, and they rarely marched in procession. They could not, by virtue of their gender, be the "heroes" of Memorial Day; indeed, their gender cast them inevitably into a supporting role. Nevertheless, the women who participated in Memorial Day exercises, particularly in the South, exercised a great deal of power. They raised and distributed large sums of money. They organized, scripted, and directed holiday exercises. They paid for and chose designs for monuments to the dead. In contrast to the other main American patriotic holidays of the time, the Fourth of July and Washington's Birthday, women were essential to the new Memorial Day. Without them, there could have been no holiday.

"REVIVING THE BITTER MEMORIES OF CONFLICT"

For observers such as Chauncey Depew, the dominant role of women in Memorial Day exercises had seemed to offer a way to heal sectional animosities. He and other speakers made much of the fabled acts of women decorating both Union and Confederate graves, suggesting that it was women who paved the way for reconciliation. A northern professor suggested in 1894, for example, that the gendered nature of the holiday contributed to its healing potential: "When the Southern women, after sorrowfully decorating the graves of their own soldiers, passed to those of the Union dead and placed flowers upon their graves, they exemplified that maternal affection which is grander and more lasting than patriotism."[31]

In reality rather than in nostalgic retrospect, neither women nor men felt particularly conciliatory after the war and during Reconstruction. Occupying Union soldiers only reluctantly allowed local women to decorate Confederate graves during and immediately after the war; one commander referred to the practice as "maudlin sentimentality." Women in Catholic-dominated New Orleans had begun decorating Confederate graves on All Saints' Day during the war and continued to do so secretly even after Gen. Benjamin Butler's outright prohibition of this activity.[32] Butler's action presaged future discord over Memorial Day.

The former foes even argued about the name of the holiday and who had the best claim to it. It was known from the start as Memorial Day in both the North and the South, but the federal holiday became more popularly known as Decoration Day, which the *Richmond Dispatch* speculated was "to distinguish it from the Southern 'Memorial Day.'" The GAR, however, campaigned against the use of the new name as insufficiently descriptive of the day's purpose, declaring in an 1882 resolution that the proper name of the day was Memorial Day. Former Confederates, for their part, asserted their claim to the name and fiercely denounced those who called the Confederate holiday Decoration Day or who called for a merger of the southern holiday into the federal one. For example, in an article published in the *Confederate Veteran* in 1902, Maj. T. O. Chestney reprimanded the United Daughters of the Confederacy for using the term and pleaded, "Won't you explain that the word 'Decoration' has no application to Memorial Day at the South? Memorial Day is exclusively Southern by legislative acts and historical use." He asserted that the two names "fitly demonstrate[d] the difference between the hallowed Memorial and the triumphant Decoration." Despite the efforts of Union and Confederate veterans, popular usage of the appellation "Decoration Day" continued to grow across the nation.[33]

As Chestney suggested, the federal holiday did indeed focus not just on mourning the dead but on celebrating the Union triumph over the forces of rebellion. The Grand Army controlled the exercises and made them emphatically sectional, particularly during Reconstruction, when the organization was closely connected to the Radical Republicans. John Logan made clear that the purpose of the federal Memorial Day, despite its southern origins, was to remember the sacrifices only of the Union dead. "Let us," he proclaimed in his first holiday address in 1868, "gather around their sacred remains and . . . raise above them the dear old flag they saved from dishonor." The national leadership of the GAR made observance of Memorial Day obligatory for every post and individual member, and local posts generally sponsored the holiday exercises.[34]

The GAR did not hesitate to move beyond words when its vision of Memorial Day as a Union holiday was threatened. In 1869 the Grand Army, taking General Butler as its model, resolved that "to throw flowers on Confederate graves would be a desecration of the graves of loyal Union soldiers." At Arlington National Cemetery, on the borderland between the Union and the Confederacy, the local Grand Army post sent armed guards to prevent ex-Confederates from decorating the graves of their comrades. The *New York Times* sadly concluded, after this event and other such displays of Union sectionalism, that "Decoration Day, as it has been inaugurated, is a day that can never become national." The problem, the *Times* argued, was that the holiday was patently sectional. "It is an appeal to the patriotism of one section at the expense of the pride and feeling due the other section. . . . It is a method of reminding the North that it is a conqueror, and the South that it is conquered." The paper condemned the GAR's management of the day, claiming that "it is an occasion for heaping epithets of infamy upon one set of graves while piling flowers upon another set—for reviving the bitter memories of conflict, scattering afresh the seeds of hate, and, under the pretense of glorifying Union heroes, invoking curses upon the misguided but scarcely less heroic Confederate dead."[35]

Such criticism had little effect in the early years of the holiday. In Frederick, Maryland, diarist Jacob Engelbrecht pointedly noted in 1871 that on Decoration Day "the Singing was done by the Lutheran Choir except such part of the choir who belong to the Rebel party." Gen. William T. Sherman bluntly asserted before an 1886 Memorial Day audience in Chicago that the Confederate cause was but "treason." Confederate veterans vociferously disagreed. The southern states, they declared, had fought for their sovereignty just as the colonies had fought to be free and independent states. Responding to the epithet of "rebel," a speaker at a cemetery near Baltimore in 1879 told his audience that "rebel" was a name for Americans to be proud of: "We are children of a common country whose cradle was Rebellion" and whose father was "the arch-rebel of the eighteenth century—George Washington!"[36]

Keeping sectional passions alive on Memorial Day was in part a calculated means to a larger end for the GAR. The organization used the holiday to keep fresh in the public mind the memory of the sacrifices of the Union dead and, more to the point, the surviving veterans who guarded their graves and paid them homage. The United States was notorious for its public and governmental indifference to the plight of its war veterans, and Civil War veterans sought to change this situation by keeping themselves in the public eye and conscience. Every Memorial Day Union veterans reminded Americans that they had been the saviors of the republic and thus had earned the public's everlasting gratitude. On the other side, Confederate veterans assured their Memorial Day audiences that they had fought to defend the nation's dearest principles of freedom, self-government, and the right of rebellion.

A GAR orator in 1885 declared that "for everything that they enjoy, the people of the United States should forever remember the Grand Army of the Republic, whose sacrifices were the price of the country's prosperity and happiness; and in the complete enjoyment of peace and plenty, the Nation should not be unmindful of its obligations to its patriotic defenders." Those obligations included more than simple homage to the dead. The GAR wasted no time in showing the government precisely how it might repay Union veterans. In 1868 the organization called upon Congress to enact legislation making "honorable service" as a soldier or sailor a qualification to civil office and to appoint an "equitable" number of veterans. In addition to demanding hiring preferences, the GAR lobbied for pension legislation and support for the construction of homes for aged and disabled soldiers. At Memorial Day exercises in 1885, for example, Chicago's Grand Army men adopted a resolution calling upon the Illinois House of Representatives to pass "the Senate bill appropriating $200,000 for the purpose of erecting a home in the State of Illinois for the use of our disabled soldiers." In 1893 Memorial Day speakers spent the bulk of their time defending pensions for veterans.[37]

Confederate veterans, like their Union counterparts, also sought benefits, but lacking a federal government favorable to this request, they had to raise their own funds, with the assistance of the ladies' memorial associations. For example, Richmond's Lee Camp, a Confederate veterans organization, raised money for a home for Confederate veterans, which it dedicated on Hollywood Memorial Day in 1885. Although they had no claim to federal pensions for the Civil War, those Confederates who had fought in the Mexican War sought pensions for that service. Veterans and the ladies' memorial associations also lobbied state governments for funds for maintenance of Confederate graves. After extensive lobbying by the Hollywood Memorial Association, for example, Virginia's General Assembly in 1914 appropriated enough money to place the Confederate section of that cemetery in perpetual care.[38]

The aim of securing both respect and material benefits for veterans was not the only thing Union and Confederate veterans had in common. Although northern and southern veterans saw the war through sectional lenses, the basic outlines of the stories they told on Memorial Day, like the exercises themselves, were similar. In his path-breaking work on Memorial Day, sociologist W. Lloyd Warner observed that the holiday's "principal themes are those of the sacrifice of the soldier dead for the living and the obligation of the living to sacrifice their individual purposes for the good of the group." At special Memorial Day exercises in 1885, the year of Ulysses S. Grant's death, Gen. John Logan confirmed this theme by proclaiming that "[n]o more lofty acts are to be found in the records of authentic history than the noble sacrifices of the American soldier upon the field of battle, and the votive offerings of his countrymen upon the holy altar of his memory." Union and Confederate veterans alike depicted the soldier dead, and by extension themselves, as representatives of the pinnacle of American manhood. To hear Memorial Day speakers tell it, the living veterans as well as the dead were to a man courageous, noble, honorable, and virile. At Richmond's first Oakwood Memorial Day, for example, the orator averred that "right or wrong, no braver men ever lived than the Confederate soldiers."[39]

As they had during the war, both Union and Confederate veterans drew on the founders of the American republic to explain and to justify the causes for which the Civil War had been fought. General Sherman asserted that the "patriotic masses" who rushed to join the Union army in 1861 had "demanded that the glorious Union of our fathers 'must and shall be preserved,' cost what it might." The former Confederates, for their part, defended secession as being in keeping with the American Revolution and the principles of the U.S. Constitution. As a North Carolina orator put it in 1901, "What was right and meritorious in the Continental statesman and soldier cannot have been wrong and blameworthy in the Confederate."[40]

Memorial Day exercises in both the North and the South also depicted an America without class barriers or boundaries. Memorial Day speakers extolled the virtues of the private soldier and sailor. In 1909 an orator in Richmond proclaimed that "the Confederate Army was the most democratic army the world ever saw; the most truly representative of all classes and conditions of the people." Union veterans described their army in similar terms. In the children's story about the orphaned girl who returns to decorate her father's grave, the local GAR men tell her that they "think the daughter of Sylvester Wright is as true and noble and as worthy of our deepest respect as the grandest woman in the land." Veterans, ladies' memorial associations, and their allies on both sides of the divide raised funds to erect monuments to honor the common soldier, the unknowns, and specific batteries and brigades. Many memorials, such as one dedicated in a Chicago cemetery in 1870 to Bridges's Battery, listed the names of the dead, giving each a permanent bit of fame. With great fanfare, Richmond's veterans unveiled in 1894 a monument specifically dedicated to the private soldier and sailor, and other cities followed suit.[41]

All the emphasis on the private soldier did not cover a deep-seated ambivalence toward the lower classes on the part of the orators and organizers of Memorial Day. Privates might be praiseworthy in the aggregate, but it was the former officers who spoke at holiday exercises. Memorial Day oratory reminded ordinary veterans that they had been but cogs in the war machine run by great military leaders such as William T. Sherman, Ulysses S. Grant, Stonewall Jackson, and Robert E. Lee. In his speech dedicating a monument to Gen. Thomas Ransom, Sherman declared that in 1861 "the farmer left his plow in the furrow, the carpenter the nail half driven, . . . and the boys at school closed their books, all asking to be led" against the Confederate enemy; fortunately, Ransom had been available. The leadership of both the GAR and the United Confederate Veterans (UCV) was dominated by former officers, and the membership was primarily middle class in both origin and outlook. Grand Army man Theodore Bean even expressed the middle-class belief in upward mobility in his exaggerated claim in 1888 that "the poor privates in war, became the prince [*sic*] of wealth in peace."[42]

COMRADES (ALMOST) ALL

As a result of pressure from the GAR, most states outside the former Confederacy had made Memorial Day a legal holiday by the 1880s, and the federal government recognized it in 1876. Southern states, at the instigation of the ladies' memorial associations and Confederate veterans, followed suit by legalizing Confederate Memorial Day after Reconstruction. Americans who failed to attend Memorial Day exercises or to show proper respect for the dead soldiers and the living veterans drew the veterans' greatest scorn. Union and Confederate veterans alike bemoaned the public indifference to and the desecration of their sacred holiday. In 1870, for example, just five years after the end of the war, a mere 5,000 Chicagoans (out of a population of 298,000) attended Memorial Day exercises. In the South, where most of the war was fought and a much higher percentage of the population had died, Confederate Memorial Day exercises drew larger crowds, but attendance also suffered a decline. In 1885 an editor for the *Richmond Dispatch* recalled wistfully the early days when "volunteers were numerous, and the scene on decoration-day was a solemn and impressive one at Hollywood"; this participation, he asserted, stood in shameful contrast to the few hands that now turned out to perform that labor of love.[43]

There were practical reasons for the small crowds. Most of those who attended Memorial Day ceremonies were probably either veterans or civilians with direct connections to veterans or dead soldiers. Moreover, making Memorial Day a legal holiday did not mean that all workers had the day off. Some employers did not close their businesses, and self-employed workers often could not afford to take the day off. Charles E. Adams, a Boston woodcarver, noted in his diary on Memorial Day 1886 that he "went to work today although there were several places of business closed." In 1888 and 1889 he also worked all day. In 1887, the one year he did not work, his diary reveals the variety of activities that might fill an individual's Memorial Day. In the morning Adams mowed the lawn, went to the cemetery with his aunts, then played ball, and ate dinner at his uncle's home. In the afternoon he and two female friends took the boat to Portsmouth, where they watched the parade to the cemetery and went out for ice cream. Afterward they accompanied his aunt and her guests to the marines' drill. After supper at his aunt's home, Adams returned to Boston.[44]

By the late nineteenth century a growing number of Americans, like Adams, took the opportunity of a rare holiday to indulge in various forms of amusement. GAR protests against the desecration of the day had shifted by the 1880s from Southerners who dared to decorate Confederate graves to Americans who passed the day at picnics, on excursions, and in other recreational pursuits. The national orders for the holiday in 1885 directed Grand Army posts to "let no idle merry-making mar its consecrated hours." Confederate veterans were no less vehement in their denunciation of the intrusion of recreation into their sacred holiday. In 1904 a UCV commander in Georgia had words with officials at Georgia University and the Georgia School of Technology over sporting events scheduled for Memorial Day. He reported to the *Confederate Veteran* that he had secured their vow that such activities would not happen again, concluding, "We know that these boys will be true to this sacred promise for the sacred day, because they are of that same stock of Southern soldiers." In the eyes of veterans, Memorial Day dances, ball games, and races clearly did not convey the proper respect for the dead. The complaints of veterans and their partisans, however, had little effect on the transformation of Memorial Day into another day of recreation for many, perhaps most, Americans. In Chicago the Memorial Day Bicycle Road Race all but eclipsed the cemetery exercises in the 1890s. On the day after Memorial Day in 1895, for example, the lead story in the *Chicago Tribune* was on the winner of the race. Accounts of the ceremonies at the cemeteries began on page nine.[45] The parades instituted in the 1880s may be interpreted in part as an effort to lure larger crowds on Memorial Day by appealing to the popular taste for spectacle and entertainment.

The push to keep Memorial Day holy was one of the forces pulling Union and Confederate veterans together in the 1880s. In an ironic twist, given the nineteenth-century gender ideology that depicted women as more sentimental and conciliatory, Memorial Day became an occasion for reconciliation only after it became more martial and masculine. Despite the lingering sectional animosities that colored early Memorial Days, the similar outlines and emphases of the stories told on the federal and Confederate Memorial Days, combined with the shared war experiences and national heritage of the veterans, paved the way for reconciliation. The racial ideology of white superiority that pervaded both the North and the South ensured that reconciliation would be for white veterans only. African Americans who had fought for the Union found themselves and their contributions rendered nearly invisible on Memorial Day by the end of the nineteenth century.

The war weariness that had spurred the end of Reconstruction ushered in a more conciliatory Memorial Day beginning as early as the late 1870s. On Memorial Day in 1877 signs of reunion abounded, as the recently inaugurated Republican president, Rutherford B. Hayes, was invited to combined exercises for the blue and the gray in Tennessee, and the ex-Confederate postmaster was invited to participate in exercises in Ohio. A former Confederate addressed GAR men in Brooklyn that year as well, taking pains to assure them that Southerners had accepted the supremacy of the Union and had nary a thought of disunion. In a further show of conciliation, a Baltimore GAR post decreed that although "it can not as a body decorate the graves of any but Union soldiers," it would nevertheless "respect the action of any member who may individually decorate the graves of the Confederate dead."[46]

This initial rhetoric of reconciliation reflected revulsion at partisan politics and the politics of Reconstruction by blaming the divisiveness of the holiday not on veterans but on politicians, particularly the Radical Republican architects of Reconstruction. The Confederate general who spoke in Brooklyn in 1877 blamed secession, wartime atrocities, and Reconstruction on politicians, as did Maj. Baker Lee at Norfolk's Confederate Memorial Day exercises ten years later. No sooner had the "scarred veteran . . . laid his arms aside," asserted Major Lee, than "the wily politician . . . stalked upon the scene and struck down the hands about to be clasped in fraternal fellowship again between the gallant men of both sides." Orators at federal exercises agreed. In his 1879 address, for example, Chauncey Depew described Reconstruction as "bad men, imported and native-born, taking advantage of the newly enfranchised and uneducated vote, [who] seized upon the governments of those States to plunder and steal."[47]

A common theme of such oratory was that the veterans themselves harbored no lasting enmity. A Northerner speaking in 1888 before Richmond's GAR recited incidents illustrating the friendship and mutual respect between Confederate and Union soldiers, both during and after the war. Gen. William Ruffin Cox averred in his Confederate Memorial Day oration in 1911 that "between the brave soldiers of the North and the South there was never any personal antagonism during this long and bloody struggle." Reconciliation, in the eyes of such speakers, was a sign that the veterans' spirit had triumphed over that of the politicians.[48]

Although such reports exaggerated the lack of hatred between the former foes, they did provide a direction for reconciliation. With Reconstruction over, white Americans seemed eager to put the political issues of the war, particularly secession and slavery, behind them. Indeed, many Americans without direct ties to the dead or veterans wanted to put the war itself behind them, which was anathema to veterans of both sides. It was perhaps natural that veterans who thus found themselves in danger of becoming irrelevant to their changing society might see themselves as having more in common with their former enemies than with "civilians." The depoliticization of the war enabled veterans to refocus the nation's view of the war by recasting it as a story of soldierly valor, heroics, and camaraderie.[49]

Stuart McConnell has argued that the GAR, which had been hurt by its association with Reconstruction politics and by the depression of the 1870s, was reborn in the 1880s as more of a fraternal organization. Although the organization still centered its activities on recognition of and benefits for veterans, its members grew more interested in reviving the camaraderie of camp life than in reviving the conflicts of the war. A similar spirit moved Confederate veterans to organize the United Confederate Veterans in 1889. Like the GAR, the UCV focused on perpetuating the image of the Confederate soldier, dead or living, as the quintessential American hero. Also like the GAR, it recognized the importance of Memorial Day to this outcome. Although the ladies' memorial associations continued to sponsor Confederate Memorial Days, local UCV camps took an active interest in the exercises, organizing the parades, supplying speakers, providing a military presence, and even selecting the date of the holiday. The organization's constitution avowed that "this Federation shall religiously observe the celebration of Memorial Day. Each camp, brigade and division shall have full authority to designate its own."[50]

Union and Confederate veterans alike sought in the 1880s and 1890s to recreate wartime fellowship. In its 1883 constitution, Richmond's Lee Camp of Confederate Veterans, which later became Camp 1 of the UCV, noted that the purpose of the group was neither sectional nor political. Beyond "perpetuat[ing] the memories of our fallen comrades" and caring for the disabled, the organization's main purpose was "to preserve and maintain that sentiment of fraternity born of the hardships and dangers shared in the march, the bivouac and the battlefield." The focus on battlefield camaraderie led to a recognition of the commonality of such experiences and fed an impulse toward reconciliation with former foes. The veterans of Lee Camp "proposed not to prolong the animosities engendered by the War, but to extend to our late adversaries on every fitting occasion courtesies which are always proper between soldiers." They lost no time following through on this proposition; the camp hosted members of a Philadelphia GAR post in May 1883.[51]

Lee Camp was not alone in such conciliatory gestures. The 1880s, in fact, saw something of a golden age of reconciliation for Civil War veterans, marked by a series of blue-gray reunions kicked off by centennial celebrations of the American Revolution. In one of the earliest reunions, Boston veterans welcomed a regiment from South Carolina to the 1875 centennial of the Battle of Bunker Hill. It was in the 1880s, however, that these reunions really flourished. In 1881, for example, members of the GAR's Aaron Wilkes

Post of Trenton, New Jersey, stopped for a visit with Confederate veterans in Richmond on the way home from the Yorktown centennial celebration, and the Richmonders returned the courtesy in 1882 and 1883. Lee Camp's minute books reveal additional trips in the 1880s to GAR posts in Boston, Newark, Washington, Baltimore, Auburn, New York, and Gettysburg. In the same decade the camp hosted visitors from Philadelphia, New York, Trenton, and Newark.[52]

Memorial Day exercises also demonstrated the pervasiveness of reconciliation. In 1880 the *Richmond Dispatch* noted approvingly that some ex-Confederates had joined their former enemies in federal Memorial Day ceremonies. The city's Confederate Veterans Home had been built in part with contributions from the GAR, and the Wilkes Post returned in 1885 for its dedication. While there, post members, along with Richmond GAR men, joined Lee Camp in commemorating Hollywood Memorial Day. The farther away from the center of Civil War fighting a town was, the more painless reconciliation proved to be. For example, the *Tucson Arizona Daily Star* in 1880 urged that Memorial Day be a day of national reconciliation:"The wounds of the fraternal strife are healed by mutual sympathy for the departed heroes. On this day let the clouds of sectionalism be dispersed, forgetting the past and looking forward to the bright and undimmed future." Although the GAR still sponsored and planned the Memorial Day exercises in Tucson, Confederate veterans marched with their former foes and local fraternal organizations in the annual processions. In 1885 the ex-Confederates even preceded the local GAR in the parade order.[53]

In Chicago as well, reconciliation sentiment emerged in the 1880s despite some GAR recalcitrance. Although the GAR rebuffed a proposal from ex-Confederates to hold a grand reunion of the blue and the gray in Chicago in the summer of 1886, the city's Ex-Confederate Association clung to conciliatory sentiment. That Memorial Day its members decorated Union as well as Confederate graves at Oak Woods Cemetery, which held the remains of Confederates who had died at a nearby prison camp. The *Chicago Tribune* reported that even before they decorated the graves of their comrades, the former Confederates paused to lay a floral cross at the site of the Union graves. Four years later eight GAR posts, including the black John Brown Post, saluted the Confederate dead of Oak Woods after their regular exercises over the graves of their own comrades. After the band played a dirge for the dead, orator W. B. Phipps delivered an address of reconciliation, in which he conceded that the Confederates had fought for a cause they considered just. Now, he concluded, "the North and the South would go hand in hand in their efforts to leave to posterity the grandest country on which the sun ever shone."[54]

Richmond's Lee Camp provides perhaps the clearest example of the conciliatory spirit animating veterans in the 1880s. It arranged annually with area GAR posts to have reciprocal representation at each group's Memorial Day exercises. In 1883, for instance, the camp adopted a resolution to "invite Phil Kearney [*sic*] Post No. 10 GAR to unite with us in the Memorial services at Hollywood" and accepted that post's invitation to "accompany us to the National Cemetery on the 30th." In 1886, following the death of Ulysses S. Grant, Lee Camp even sent a delegation to Brooklyn as Memorial Day guests of the Grant Post to honor Grant as a soldier and general and to present an evergreen and a floral arrangement for his tomb. The delegation thanked the Grand Army men for "the ovation we received at the hands of your people," while the Grant Post praised Lee Camp's presence as the fulfillment of the "new era" Grant had prophesied on his deathbed, "when there is to be great harmony between the Federal and Confederate."[55]

In a further gesture of reconciliation, the Hollywood Memorial Association in 1888 changed its Memorial Day to the same date as the federal holiday. That Memorial Day was the climax of reunion for Richmonders. Union and Confederate veterans were inordinately busy. First they attended exercises at Seven Pines National Cemetery. Then they saw Confederate remains from that cemetery placed on a train and accompanied them to Hollywood Cemetery, where the Union veterans assisted their Confederate counterparts in reburying the remains. The GAR's Kearny Post had earlier requested and received permission for "the privilege of planting . . . 100 living roses on the graves of Confederate soldiers in Hollywood." The reburial and the grave decoration were followed by the rhetorical exercises under the united flags of the United States and the Confederacy.[56]

Lee Camp was unusual among Confederate organizations only in the scope and enthusiasm of its reconciliation activities. It was the only Confederate group to send representatives to Grant's funeral, for example. There were those who dissented from this sentiment, however. Some Confederate veterans refused to join the UCV because they abhorred its reconciliationist bent. One Maryland veteran boasted to the *Confederate Veteran*, "We have no ex-Confederate societies, but several large, strong, and active Confederate societies." As to reconciliation, he declared, "We have never mixed in any manner with the other side—have no joint reunions, no joint banquets, no decoration or memorial days in common. In fact, we do not mix, we go our way and they go theirs, and we find we gain more respect by so doing." He hinted that those who socialized with their former enemies lacked the courage of their Confederate convictions. "We do not belong to that class of Confederates that believed they were right," the Marylander explained. "We *knew* we were right in 1861, we *knew* we were right when the war closed, and we *know* today that we were right."[57]

Even for Lee Camp the reunion activities of the 1880s proved short lived. Its Memorial Day blue-gray reunions and visits to northern cities ended in the 1890s as precipitously as they had begun. Perhaps the joint exercises of 1888 provided some sort of closure for the veterans, making such gestures less necessary in the future. Or perhaps the veterans were simply exhausted. In the 1880s Lee Camp attended or sent delegates annually to federal exercises at the two local national cemeteries in addition to the three local Confederate Memorial Day exercises. A new element entered the mix in the mid-1880s when Norfolk's Pickett-Buchanan Camp of Confederate Veterans began to invite Lee Camp to its memorial exercises. These invitations (and reciprocal ones from Lee Camp) exploded in the 1890s with the expansion of the UCV, and Lee Camp dropped its attendance at federal exercises in favor of sending delegations to the memorial exercises of its former comrades in Norfolk and Petersburg.[58]

The camp demonstrated its newfound lack of interest in federal exercises when its secretary noted cryptically in 1894 that a "[c]ommunication was received from Grand Army of the Republic in reference to the proper observence [sic] of Decoration Day May 30th. Laid on table." When the Young Men's Business Association sought to bring the GAR's annual encampment to Richmond in 1899, the veterans of Lee Camp responded in a decidedly less welcoming manner than they might have in the 1880s. They asserted that while they would welcome individual Union veterans, it was "out of the question for us as a Confederate Camp to extend an invitation to the GAR to be our guests in '99." Their objections suggest conflict with Grand Army policy. They complained that the GAR had objected to the UCV's proposal of a reunion in New York a year earlier. In addition, they noted that "we could not as a Confederate Survivors' Association consent to parade with any organization to whom our flag would be objectionable and who recognize negroes on equality with us."[59]

This statement revealed the limits of reconciliation. For Confederate veterans in the 1880s, reconciliation was possible when Union veterans clearly respected their courage and their fighting. But by the 1890s they wanted more. As they formulated the ideology of the Lost Cause, Confederate veterans sought some acknowledgment from their former foes that their cause had been noble. An orator at Memorial Day exercises at Richmond's Oakwood Cemetery in 1890 proclaimed that "[i]n all the galaxy of fame there is no brighter constellation than that of the heroes of the Lost Cause" and asked, "Who is so mean as to deny them the honor which they have so justly won?" The Confederate soldiers, he asserted, "were moved by the very same spirit that actuated Washington and Jefferson, Adams, and all the other founders of this republic, when they threw off the yoke of British oppression."[60]

The GAR had a harder time swallowing this view. The former Confederates might be recognized for their bravery, welcomed into the fraternity of soldiers, and entertained when they came to visit, but so long as the GAR controlled Memorial Day, it remained clear that America's debt was to the Union veterans. To honor the Confederate cause would diminish the purity of the Union cause. Most Grand Army men probably agreed with an orator in Chicago in 1886 who announced contemptuously, and to great applause, in reference to Jefferson Davis's recent speaking tour, "It is not a suitable time to hear an impotent voice, one, as it were, rising from the grave, with words of praise and words of excuse and words of defense of the Lost Cause. The Lost Cause was lost none too soon." About as far as GAR men would go was to describe the Confederates, as President Theodore Roosevelt did before them in 1902, as "the men in gray, who with such courage, and such devotion for what they deemed the right, fought against you."[61]

Facing this impasse, the reconciliation fervor of the 1880s cooled, although blue-gray reunions continued to occur sporadically over the years. Whatever the GAR's reservations, however, it was clear that much of the rest of the nation was passionate about reconciliation by the turn of the century. President McKinley spoke at the 1900 unveiling of a monument to the Maryland soldiers of both sides who had fallen at Antietam, and Arlington National Cemetery permitted its first Confederate Memorial Day exercises in 1903. Reconciliation became a popular theme of Memorial Day poetry and literature as well. As Nina Silber and Gaines Foster have shown in their examinations of the triumph of the Lost Cause in the North and the South, respectively, white Northerners and Southerners alike fell in love with the myth of the Lost Cause and the antebellum South, as illustrated in the popularity of plantation stories, plays, and songs.[62] Industrialists and financiers seeking to realize the gains of the South's economic potential also found the myth expedient.

THE APOTHEOSIS OF THE CONFEDERACY

Although Grand Army men found it impossible to accept crucial elements of the celebration of the Lost Cause, they could tolerate it, as long as it did not directly challenge their story of the war. In the 1890s veterans moved from the more spontaneous and idiosyncratic acts of reconciliation of the 1880s to well-planned and massive spectacles of reunion. In these efforts they received aid from northern and southern business and financial leaders who trumpeted the New South creed and saw reunion as a source of profit and social stability. In these spectacles white Northerners and Southerners forged a compromise that enabled ex-Confederates ceremonially to reenter the Union. The grandest of the spectacles centered on the Memorial Day dedications of two Confederate monuments, one to Robert E. Lee in Richmond, the former capital of the Confederacy, in 1890, and the other five years later in Chicago, dubbed "the greatest South-hating city in all the country" by one Richmond paper.[63]

The Lee monument exercises represented the epitome of Confederate veterans' efforts to conflate the South's rebellion with the American Revolution, but those efforts were ultimately successful, according to Kirk Savage, because of the backing of Richmond's business community and other New South advocates. The equestrian statue, the ceremonies, and the oratory conspicuously evoked the Washington monument unveiled in Richmond shortly before the war, revealing a deliberate effort to elevate the Confederate commander to the national status enjoyed by his fellow Virginian and commander. At the unveiling ceremonies on 29 May 1890, Col. Archer Anderson, orator of the day, strained to show that Lee had modeled his character after his fellow Virginian: "It may well be believed that Lee made Washington his model of public duty, and in every important conjuncture of his life unconsciously, no doubt, but effectively asked himself the question: 'How would Washington have acted in this case?'"[64]

The celebration engendered negative commentary in some, generally Republican, quarters outside the former Confederacy. President Benjamin Harrison's secretary of war prohibited the U.S. Marine Band from participating in the dedication exercises, for example, and the *Chicago Tribune* expressed outrage that a Confederate flag had been placed in Washington's hand. The most trenchant criticism of the occasion, not surprisingly, came from Richmond's African American community. John Mitchell Jr., editor of the *Richmond Planet*, had no argument with Confederate veterans honoring the memory of their leaders; however, he complained, "[t]he South in its efforts to be true to its leaders goes too far in its adulation." This adulation of the Confederacy, he argued, could not possibly promote loyalty to the Union: "Rebel flags were everywhere displayed and the long lines of Confederate veterans who ... attended the reunion to join again in the 'rebel yell' told in no uncertain tones that they still clung to theories which were presumed to be buried for all eternity."[65]

Most white Americans, however, appeared not to see any threat to the Union in the unabashed celebration of the Confederacy, which stirred little outrage outside of the African American population. The proceedings drew an estimated seventy-five to one hundred thousand viewers, including Confederate veterans from across the country. The appeal of the monument ceremonies and the Confederate Memorial Day, although muted outside the realm of the former Confederacy and its sympathizers, was not lost on the rest of the nation. The *Richmond Dispatch* noted that the *New York Herald* had defended the monument and the South's loyalty to the Union and had suggested that those who sought to use the former to discredit the latter were politically motivated. *Harper's Weekly* rather disingenuously explained that the Confederate flag "no longer meant disunion" and asserted that the celebration demonstrated "how completely the wounds of the conflict have been healed."[66]

The 1895 dedication of a monument by the Ex-Confederate Association in Chicago's Oak Woods Cemetery on the federal Memorial Day showed even more clearly the extent of this healing. Although a Massachusetts GAR commander condemned the occasion as a "blasphemy" of "our Grand Army Sabbath," it aroused little opposition even from Grand Army men in Chicago. Some fifty thousand Chicagoans, far more than had ever attended a local Memorial Day celebration, turned out to catch a glimpse of such Confederate notables as generals James Longstreet, Fitzhugh Lee, and Wade Hampton. According to Hampton, the monument to the Confederate prisoners who had died at nearby Fort Douglas dramatized, as no prior gesture had, the hand of fellowship and reconciliation extended from the North to the South. The support of Chicagoans for the Confederate monument, through financial contributions and their participation in the dedication, provided proof that they did esteem the courage and sacrifices made by the six thousand Southerners who lay at Oak Woods, if not their cause. It also testified to the success of the myth of the Lost Cause. The *Chicago Tribune* reported that at the close of the exercises the crowd fell upon the flowers, wreaths, and palmetto trees with which the ex-Confederates had adorned the monument and graves, tearing them to bits and carrying away the pieces as souvenirs of their brush with the Old South.[67]

In addition to the romance of the Lost Cause, Chicago businessmen and financiers were attracted by the more practical economic possibilities of reconciliation. Commercial intercourse, the backbone of the New South, formed the invisible spine of the Oak Woods reunion. The welcoming committee that received the ex-Confederate officers was composed of a cross section of Chicago's business and commercial scene. The banquet given for the visitors on the eve of the Oak Woods dedication made the connection between business and reconciliation crystal clear. After welcoming the city's guests and declaiming on the noble sentiment of reconciliation that had brought them there, Ferdinand Peck, president of the citizens' committee in charge of the banquet, got down to the real point of sectional reunion: "Outside of sentiment and patriotism there will come from this assemblage and the fraternal feeling thereby established closer commercial union and business relations between the citizens of our country, thus enlisting in a larger degree the investment of the capital of this section in developing the vast resources of the Southern States." The ex-Confederates responded in kind. Lt. Gen. Stephen D. Lee of Mississippi expressed the Southerners' appreciation of both the warm welcome and the commercial penetration of the South by Northerners: "We invite you to invade us again, not this time with your bayonets, but with your business."[68]

With the support of the business community, the populace, and even the GAR, the monument dedication drew few protests. Once the business community had come down on the side of reconciliation, even the *Chicago Tribune* could support it, concluding that the dedication ceremonies had "constituted . . . the formal close of the period of ill-will engendered by the War of the Rebellion." The president of the dedicatory exercises was even a GAR man and the former commander of the U. S. Grant Post. At least one speaker at the GAR's own exercises that day, however, offered evidence of discomfort with the Oak Woods spectacle. Chicago's South Side was already home to the majority of its black population, which meant that the black John Brown Post was one of those that hosted the GAR exercises at Oak Woods. The orator at those ceremonies in 1895 criticized the reconciliation taking place across the cemetery, contending that the federal soldiers had fought not solely for political union but for the "sublime" moral principle of freedom for African Americans. He expressed his willingness "to clasp hands with my Southern friend and forget that his father and my father fought in bitter and deadly contest," but he admonished his audience never to forget "the imperial fact that the men in blue fought for the right and the men in gray fought for the wrong." Such voices, however, tended to be drowned in the general good fellowship of reconciliation and acceptance of the Lost Cause that pervaded Chicago. In stark contrast to the fifty thousand Chicagoans who crowded the Confederate plot at Oak Woods, only five thousand attended the GAR exercises.[69]

If the Lee monument exercises demonstrated the lengths to which Southerners could go by 1890 in apotheosizing the Confederacy without incurring significant disapproval from northern whites, the Chicago monument gave evidence of the near total capitulation of the white North to the myth of the Lost Cause and the benefits the myth held for business. The tributes to the

Confederacy, which a few years earlier might have been viewed as a call to renewed hostilities, now evoked few fears of division. The Lost Cause celebrated the Confederacy and justified secession in 1861 but promoted no disloyalty in 1890. Memorial Day orators performed intricate rhetorical
maneuvers to prove that loyalty to the cause of the Confederacy was not at
all inconsistent with loyalty to the United States. In one particularly tortured
passage, the Reverend Peyton Hoge proclaimed that, although the Confederacy had been vanquished, and rightly so, its principles were still the foundation of America. "[F]idelity to the memory of the Lost Cause," he declared
without apparent irony, "is perfectly consistent with loyalty to the Union in
which we have again taken our place among our peers. But as principles, that
for which these men fought can never perish, and the cause for which they
died can never be lost; for these principles are still the bulwarks of our
freedom." The boldest of the Confederate celebrators even asserted, as
Gen. Fitzhugh Lee did in 1890, that the southern soldiers had not even been
defeated militarily: "At last the Southern soldiers, broken down from whip-
ping the North, surrendered."[70]

Thus was total defeat transformed into Confederate triumph, with hardly
a whimper from the white North, which accepted the myth of the Lost Cause
as the price of sectional reconciliation. Indeed, the apotheosis of the Confederacy paradoxically served the cause of reconciliation, as the white South's
snatching of ideological victory from the jaws of military defeat enabled it to
rejoin the Union as an equal partner, not a vanquished foe. If the North had
saved the Union, the Confederacy had preserved its principles. In the quest
for reconciliation, most white Northerners could overlook the inconsistencies
between the Lost Cause and the Union veterans' story of the war.

AFRICAN AMERICANS AND MEMORIAL DAY

For black Americans it was a different story. They were sacrificed on the altar
of reconciliation. The glorification of the Confederate cause held no outright
political challenge except to African Americans, whom white Northerners
had already largely abandoned. Although Southerners and Northerners
alike had viewed slavery as a major cause of the war in the immediate postbellum era, by the late 1880s whites in both sections saw it as only incidental

to the struggle. In 1870 GAR commander-in-chief John Logan bade his Memorial Day audience at Arlington National Cemetery not to forget "those who sealed the covenant of freedom with their blood, and broke asunder the chains and fetters of internal bondage and slavery! . . . the martyrs of freedom, who offered their own lives upon the altar of liberty." The first Lincoln monument in Washington, the Freedman's Memorial to Lincoln, erected through the efforts of African Americans, depicted the president freeing a slave, although this image was not without controversy. Some African Americans, including Frederick Douglass, who spoke at the unveiling, protested the choice of a black slave rather than a black soldier, but, as Kirk Savage points out, they lacked the money and "cultural privilege" to direct the building of monuments that represented their version of the war's story.[71]

After Reconstruction, former Confederates began to develop their arguments that the South had fought for liberty and Constitutional rights and to claim, as one Virginia orator did, that "slavery was an incident of, but not the cause of the war." White Union veterans in the late nineteenth century similarly came to deny the primacy of slavery and emancipation as causes of the war by emphasizing their status as the saviors of national union. Some Northerners did take issue with the erasure of slavery from the story of the war. An 1885 editorial in *Harper's Weekly*, for example, derided the claim that the war was over the nature of American government, saying that "[e]xcept for slavery, the exact nature of the government would have been a point of casuistry." A denouncer of Chicago's Confederate monument asserted that Union soldiers had performed the ultimate act of nobility in fighting for the liberty of African Americans.[72]

Missing even from these protests, however, was the recognition that African Americans had fought for their freedom as well, whether as Union soldiers or as civilians. The Freedman's Memorial to Lincoln was one of the few even to represent African Americans at all. The overwhelming majority of Civil War monuments, in the North as well as the South, depicted the American soldier as white, rendering black soldiers invisible once again. At the dedication for the Freedman's Memorial, Douglass noted with pride the slaves who had joined the Union army to fight for their freedom. White oratory, however, assumed that African Americans in the audience were all former slaves, who had come to express gratitude to the white Union soldiers who had died for their freedom. Although black veterans participated in Memorial Day exercises and thereby reminded white Americans of their role in the war, they remained largely invisible in the stories of the war.[73]

The Robert Gould Shaw monument, dedicated in Boston on Memorial Day, 1897, was the only nineteenth-century monument that depicted and acknowledged African Americans as actors in their own liberation. It was the exception in an era when memorial rituals and monuments emphasized the common battlefield experiences of white Union and Confederate soldiers. Booker T. Washington in his oration provided a rare voice in praise of the black soldiers who fought under Shaw. But he also asserted that equality "must be completed in the effort of the negro himself, in his effort to withstand temptation, to economize [sic], to exercise thrift, . . . to so grow in skill and knowledge that he shall place his services in demand by reason of his intrinsic and superior worth."[74] Steeped in bourgeois individualist ideology, Washington and those whites who supported equal rights made it clear that if the freedpeople did not succeed, it was their own fault. In that view, emancipation had removed the only external barrier keeping African Americans from achieving equality.

The majority of the freedpeople knew better from painful experience. By the 1890s federal exercises in the South were segregated, but even before this time some members of the GAR had made clear to African Americans their lack of welcome. When Pennsylvanian Theodore Bean spoke in 1888 at Seven Pines National Cemetery outside Richmond, he took for his theme the glories and superiority of the Anglo-Saxon race. One year later Maj. T. B. Edgington, another Northerner, arrogantly informed a largely black audience at the National Cemetery in Memphis that the Fifteenth Amendment had been a mistake. He suggested that most African Americans were incapable of intelligently exercising the franchise and should leave it to the "brave and cultured people of the Caucasian race," who "own nearly all the property and possess nearly all the intelligence" of the South. Edgington called for a revision of suffrage rights "to leave the white race dominant in every State in the Union," and concluded, "Let us see to it that the 'Lost Cause' was not the cause of white supremacy, or of civilization, or the cause of Christianity itself."[75]

Edgington's virulently racist address caused a national stir but not surprisingly won praise from white Southerners. His theme was amplified by former Confederates, who were beginning to devise ways to disfranchise African Americans. One orator justified the disfranchisement by explaining on Memorial Day 1909 that "free-thinking abolitionists" had negated the vision of the founding fathers by imposing black suffrage on the South and that disfranchisement was simply restoring the "Conservative Conception of Self-Government" of the founders.[76]

In the view of former Confederates, the freedpeople needed white guidance as much as they had when they were slaves. Although slavery had been just as hateful to white Southerners, they claimed, as to black, whites had brought some good out of the system by civilizing and Christianizing Africans. An 1896 article on Confederate Memorial Day ludicrously suggested that, in fact, the enslavement of Africans had somehow led to their emancipation. "[S]lavery in the South," the author asserted, "was the only elevating force which lifted [Africans] to civilization and freedom."[77]

When white Southerners postulated themselves as the "civilizers" of "barbaric" African Americans, they reaffirmed the principle of white supremacy. Few white Northerners protested disfranchisement and segregation, which was not surprising since few had ever supported black equality. Reconciliation was plainly for white Northerners and Southerners. On both the federal and Confederate Memorial Days, the manly ideal of the Civil War soldier, fighting courageously for a principle, was clearly white. Moreover, his Anglo-Saxon ancestry was an integral determinant of his manly character, according to Memorial Day orators, who recounted the history of the Anglo-Saxon race as one of resistance to tyranny.[78]

This racial ideology, given new force by scientific racism at the turn of the century, proved a particularly potent weapon in the hands of Southerners seeking to demonstrate that they were the truest Americans and heirs of the founding fathers. Memorial Day speakers declaimed on the purity of the Anglo-Saxon lineage of white Southerners, polluted neither by black blood nor by that of the so-called Mediterranean and Slavic races then pouring into northern cities. In 1909 an orator in Richmond boasted, for example, that Southerners had "resisted and prevented the legalized pollution of Anglo-Saxon blood." Seven years later Douglas Southall Freeman proclaimed Southerners to be "the Anglo-Saxons of the world, with blood as pure as that which flowed at Agincourt."[79]

Other ex-Confederates pointedly contrasted the Confederacy's Anglo-Saxon army to the Union's more polyglot one, which included large numbers of German, Irish, Norwegian, Czech, and other immigrants, in addition to native-born blacks and whites. A speaker in Savannah in 1895 asserted that "ex-Confederates of to-day are representatives of an American army—not an army made up largely of foreigners and blacks fighting for pay, but defenders of American principles as handed down by the forefathers of the Republic." The increasing immigration and concomitant nativism at the turn of the century led many white Northerners as well to idealize the Anglo-Saxon purity of the South as they celebrated the Lost Cause. T. B. Edgington provides an extreme example of a Northerner favoring white supremacy. Foreshadowing the paranoid fears of turn-of-the-century scientific racists, he warned of the danger facing the white South because of the disparity between the "fecundity of the negro race" and the less prolific "Anglo-American race."[80]

Even GAR posts were segregated along the color line, in the North as well as the South. Although officially maintaining the party line of racial equality, the national GAR, like the Republican Party, gave its tacit approval to the color line. White Union veterans in the former Confederacy moved to segregate their Memorial Day exercises in the late nineteenth century. By the 1890s the GAR exercises in the South's national cemeteries, like the burial plots themselves, were segregated, paralleling the Jim Crow laws being established. In Richmond, for example, black and white Union veterans had joined together for the ceremonies at Seven Pines National Cemetery in the two decades after the war, but this situation changed as white veterans reconciled in the 1880s. In 1890 the white Kearny Post traveled to Poplar Grove National Cemetery in Petersburg for Memorial Day, while the black Custer Post commemorated the day at Seven Pines National Cemetery. In subsequent years the two posts conducted separate exercises at Seven Pines at different times of the day.[81]

Although they belonged to segregated GAR posts, black veterans outside the former Confederacy did participate with their white counterparts in Memorial Day exercises. In Chicago African American veterans still marched with their white comrades-in-arms through the downtown streets on Memorial Day. The John Brown Post and its Women's Relief Corps continued to participate in the GAR exercises at Oak Woods, and on at least one occasion a local black minister delivered a Memorial Day address there. In 1912 African Americans were still a part of the general Memorial Day exercises. The black Eighth Infantry of the Illinois National Guard held Sunday memorial services that year and then joined the procession on Memorial Day.[82]

To counteract their invisibility in white veterans' stories of the war, black Union veterans presented their own stories in Memorial Day celebrations. African Americans cheered lustily for the black veterans who had fought for the right to fight for the Union. In 1886, for example, when General Sherman reviewed Chicago's parade, the *Chicago Tribune* reported that as the black soldiers marched by him, "an enthusiastic negro with a large tin horn . . . put all the lung power that he was capable of into that horn. This was followed by a round of cheers from the spectators." A black pastor in 1912 similarly congratulated the Eighth Infantry on "its manly deportment."[83]

African Americans also sounded almost the lone notes of protest against the apotheosis of the Confederacy. On the occasion of the Lee monument dedication in Richmond, John Mitchell Jr. delivered a scathing rebuke of the Lost Cause and questioned the professed loyalty of the former Confederates. "This glorification of States Rights Doctrine—the right of secession, and the honoring of men who represented that cause fosters in this Republic, the spirit of Rebellion and will ultimately result in handing down to generations unborn a legacy of treason and blood. There is lacking in all this display," he asserted, "the proper appreciation of the Union. There is evidence that the loyalty oft-expressed penetrates no deeper than the surface."[84] Such criticisms of the Lost Cause reached few white ears, however, particularly once Union and Confederate veterans reunited in battle in the Spanish-American War. White veterans continued to use Memorial Day as a touchstone of reconciliation and a forum for defining the essence of masculinity and femininity. These qualities they cast in a decidedly pale hue. It was left to African Americans and their few white allies to point out that the Lost Cause that Northerners had embraced, in its glorification of the Confederacy, vindication of secession, and endorsement of white supremacy, contained an inherent contradiction to the American commitment to liberty and equality promised by the Declaration of Independence and the Emancipation Proclamation.

2

EMANCIPATION DAYS

*O*N I JANUARY 1866 several thousand African Americans gathered
at the First African Church in Richmond to commemorate the third
anniversary of the Emancipation Proclamation. Black soldiers and ministers, teachers and farmers, men and women, the formerly free and the formerly enslaved, all joined in celebrating the freedom for which they had
long yearned and worked. As on the first federal Memorial Days, they
were joined by northern whites associated with the Union and the abolitionist cause, including ministers, journalists, schoolteachers, and representatives of the Freedmen's Bureau. Framed by "a super-abundance of
Union flags," a Massachusetts regimental band played, and a chorus of
children sang songs of freedom. The revelers offered cheers for Abraham
Lincoln, President Andrew Johnson and his cabinet, and John Brown,
whom one orator called God's "first instrument" of "delivery from auction-

blocks." As on the Fourth of July, the reading of the sacred document of freedom took center stage, and a Mr. Oliver of the Freedmen's Bureau read Lincoln's proclamation before the hushed crowd.[1]

White and black orators sounded a similar message of rejoicing and hope for the future. Although Lincoln had penned the proclamation, and soldiers had fought and died to make freedom a reality, several speakers reminded African Americans that they owed their ultimate thanks to God, a sentiment underscored by the inscription on the speaker's stand, which read "This is the Lord's work." The oratory painted an optimistic, if rather naïve, portrait of a racially harmonious postemancipation America. Fields Cook, for example, envisioned a peaceful and prosperous biracial future, in which "white and black children would grow up together in harmony," both receiving the education that would uplift them and America. He predicted boldly that, upon seeing the progress made by African Americans, "in ten years hence the white people who fought for slavery would celebrate the anniversary of freedom" with their former slaves. Heady in the flush of victory, Cook expressed his certainty that, with slavery dead, racism would soon follow. In his view, African Americans had been despised only because of black slavery; now that this stigma had been removed, he confidently proclaimed that "prejudice would be overcome."[2]

African Americans themselves had an important role to play in ensuring this outcome. Several speakers cautioned them not to work against their white fellow citizens but to forgive them and to live in peace with them. James Holmes, a former slave, modeled the proper behavior by announcing that "he forgave the white man for the wrongs he had done him." The orators propounded bourgeois values as the path to success for the freedpeople. One reportedly "exhorted the colored people to behave themselves." The onus was on the freedpeople, another warned, to "prove to the whites that freedom is not a failure."[3]

Although the celebration and the oratory were determinedly nonmilitant, there were inklings of future difficulties in implementing the envisioned postemancipation America. African Americans and their white allies recognized that this future necessitated the extension of full citizenship to the freedpeople, something most white Southerners opposed. One step toward claiming citizenship was participation in this public celebration of freedom.

That slavery was not the natural state of African Americans was proven, according to one orator, by the very "fact of their assembling to celebrate their freedom." Black orators explained what the freedpeople and other African Americans wanted from the government. "We want justice," Mr. Oliver declared simply, "and to be protected by the same laws that govern the white man."[4] The story of Emancipation Day in postbellum America is in part the story of the fight to fulfill these demands.

As a plethora of recent scholarship makes clear, African Americans in the non-slave-holding states had long celebrated various emancipation holidays, including the closing of the foreign slave trade, the abolition of slavery in various northern states, British emancipation, and the Haitian Revolution. On these days they called upon the United States to live up to its founding principles by abolishing slavery and extending the rights of citizenship to African Americans. In this way they publicly proclaimed that they were not only African Americans but also American citizens, who deserved all the rights and privileges that status entailed.[5] Only after the Civil War brought full emancipation, however, could African Americans nationwide freely and publicly celebrate their independence. They could celebrate the Fourth of July, knowing that the promise of the Declaration of Independence had finally been fulfilled. Like white Americans, they also honored the heroes of their struggle for liberty, including Frederick Douglass, who had devoted his life to the cause of abolition and rights for African Americans, and Abraham Lincoln, who had authored their emancipation. But the preeminent black holiday in the late nineteenth century was Emancipation Day.

How did emancipation affect black celebrations and their construction of African American identity? The postbellum era saw both change and continuity in the tenor of these celebrations. Emancipation celebrations, like their antebellum counterparts, celebrated freedom, but with a difference. American slavery had been ended; there was no longer any need to agitate for abolition on such occasions. One might assume that this meant African Americans could simply celebrate their independence, but as the Richmond emancipation exercises suggest, celebration and hope for the future bore the shadow of well-founded fears that emancipation might not mean full citizenship and equality. Thus, despite the very real gains brought about by emancipation, postbellum celebrations bore some striking resemblances to those before the war. They combined the celebration of freedom with the continuing need to show the disparity between American principles and the realities, if no longer of slavery, then of racism and second-class citizenship. African Americans continued to agitate at emancipation celebrations for the rights and liberties promised by the Declaration of Independence and the Emancipation Proclamation. They constructed an identity for themselves as black Americans, and they continued to strive for an expanded definition of America that would finally put to rest the notion of a "white man's country."

In building African American identity, black leaders focused primarily on the position and achievements of blacks in America rather than in their ancestral homeland. A few leaders did find a usable heritage for African Americans in ancient Egypt, claiming that Africans had been largely responsible for the progress of civilization. In his 1869 Emancipation Day oration, a California clergyman asserted that "[t]he Sphinx, the Pyramids, the Greek alphabet, the popular mythology of Greece and Rome . . . were African." The African race, he concluded, would "one day reassert the old power." But, as the latter statement suggests, even those who celebrated the African heritage drew a line between ancient and contemporary Africa and saw the modern progress of the race as occurring in America, not Africa. Most African American leaders at the time shared the sentiment of James Weldon Johnson's poem "Fifty Years," written for the semicentennial of emancipation:

> Far, far the way that we have trod,
> From heathen, kraals and jungle dens.[6]

On their holidays black Americans sought to redefine national identity to incorporate African Americans as full citizens of the republic established in 1776 and 1789 and won anew in 1865. Like white Americans, they interpreted the American Constitution and Declaration of Independence as the foundations of American liberty and democracy. In their reconstruction of American identity, they added to these documents the Emancipation Proclamation and the Fifteenth Amendment, which had made these principles real for African Americans. Holiday orators recounted the contributions of black men and women to American independence and to the nation's progress since 1776 and spoke out for their rights as American citizens.

Politics and class issues also shaped the emancipation holidays. Like the federal Memorial Day, Emancipation Day became intertwined with Republican politics. As long as and wherever the Republican Party remained viable, black and white Republicans agitated not only to expand black rights but also to maintain their own tenuous hold on power in the South. White politicians, ministers, teachers, and other allies, meanwhile, tried to remake blacks in their own middle-class image by preaching self-help, the virtues of hard work, and public decorum.

These were values with which bourgeois black leaders hardly disagreed. The African American ministers, journalists, politicians, professionals, and entrepreneurs who organized and took leading roles at black celebrations sought to construct a unifying African American identity that justified black claims to full American citizenship but also legitimized their own claims to leadership of the black community. John Mitchell Jr., who as a Republican politician, attorney, and founder and editor of the *Richmond Planet* stood among Richmond's black elite, advised his readers in 1890 to "educate your children, buy property, be religious." Above all, he told them, "[c]ultivate in them a spirit to work." Like their white counterparts, black leaders preached the gospel of the American Dream, which softened class divisions in the interest of African American unity. Although the majority of black politicians came from the ranks of the educated middle class, for example, Virginia congressman John Mercer Langston proclaimed at an emancipation celebration that it was "a good thing to go from the manger to the Halls of Congress."[7]

Despite the efforts of black leaders to build unity, conflicts emerged, beginning with a lack of consensus on which date to observe Emancipation Day. The official emancipation holiday sanctioned by the Republican Party after the war was 1 January, the date the Emancipation Proclamation went into effect. Another day observed in some areas and associated with Republican politics was 22 September, the anniversary of the preliminary Emancipation Proclamation. The Emancipation Proclamation, however, for all its noble sentiment, had had little practical effect on slavery in the Confederacy. Just as some antebellum blacks had chosen to celebrate deeds of black resistance in addition to or instead of the emancipation acts of whites, many African Americans after the war chose to celebrate "vernacular" emancipation holidays on dates more meaningful to their freedom. In defiance of Republicans and of other black leaders who endorsed the official celebrations, they commemorated dates such as 9 April, the anniversary of Lee's surrender, and 19 June, the date on which enslaved Texans had learned of their freedom. In Washington, D.C., on 19 April 1866 African Americans celebrated President Lincoln's April 1862 order releasing "certain persons held to service in the District of Columbia." Black Richmonders commemorated the anniversary of the fall of Richmond on 3 April 1865, when, as an orator at the official 1866 exercises explained, "the presence of the Union armies put the fact of freedom beyond a doubt."[8]

The difference between the official and vernacular celebrations lay in more than the dates commemorated. While the dominant narrative of emancipation pronounced by white speakers at official exercises focused on Lincoln's act—the white man freeing the black slaves—African Americans at vernacular celebrations were freer to articulate an alternative narrative that, while not disparaging the martyred president's role, incorporated blacks' contributions to their own emancipation as well as demands for citizenship. Although black politicians and community leaders supported the celebration of the official holiday, that does not necessarily mean that they accepted the dominant white narrative of emancipation.[9] Practical reasons for celebrating when the Republican Party ordered it surely suggested themselves; after all, the Republicans were the most likely government representatives to help African Americans attain their citizenship goals. Like their antebellum counterparts, black leaders in the postwar era had to straddle the line between the demands of their precious few white allies and the desires of African Americans. Many seem to have resolved the dilemma by simply adopting both the official and vernacular holidays.

RECONSTRUCTING AFRICAN AMERICAN IDENTITY

In late nineteenth-century Richmond, African Americans celebrated emancipation on both 1 January and 3 April. During Reconstruction the city witnessed a dramatic inversion of antebellum holidays, when white militia companies had paraded on Capitol Square and blacks, free or otherwise, had been barred from this space. On the Fourth of July, on Washington's Birthday, and on the two Emancipation Days, African Americans took over the

Emancipation Day parade in Richmond, 1905. Men, women, and children join the procession through the city streets. (Courtesy of the Library of Congress)

city's most important public space, while the majority of whites were conspicuous by their absence. On these holidays the Virginia Grays and other black troops paraded and drilled on the square before cheering African Americans and under the watchful eyes of Virginia's Revolutionary War heroes immortalized in stone. In 1875, for example, some six hundred holiday excursionists from the Staunton area joined black Richmonders on Capitol Square to watch the Fourth of July parade by black soldiers, heroes of the struggle for emancipation.[10]

White Richmonders did not take kindly to this usurpation of "their" holidays and public spaces. The *Richmond Times* in 1866 declared indignantly that the Fourth was "altogether a white man's affair," there being no "negro blood" in any of the signers of the Declaration of Independence. The newspaper suggested that African Americans celebrate their own holiday of Emancipation Day and leave the Fourth alone.[11] Although white Southerners accused black Southerners of dishonoring and destroying the nation's holiday, they had themselves abandoned it for all intents and purposes in the bitter aftermath of the war. If control of a city's public spaces and rituals reflects the larger political, social, and economic power structure, the takeover of the most sacred public space in Richmond by black troops and revelers looms as a suggestive indicator of the transfer of power (if only temporarily) from white to black.

The official Emancipation Day exercises demonstrated most clearly the newfound civic and political power of black Richmonders, gained in alliance with white Republicans, as well as the limits of that power. On 1 January 1867, on the eve of Radical Reconstruction, one orator on Capitol Square boldly called for the suppression of the Virginia governor and legislature and the state's conversion to a territory. The *Richmond Daily Whig*, aghast at the effrontery of the freedpeople, reported that "[t]he statues of those fine old slaveholders and rebels, George Washington, Patrick Henry, &c., looked down very tranquilly on the grotesque scene." Once the Reconstruction Act had passed, white and black Republicans continued to celebrate officially on 1 January, with a procession of black veterans and other black societies to Capitol Square. There the revelers called upon the governor to say a few words in honor of the day. Although Richmond's conservative white Republicans were nominally allied with African Americans, their leaders never pushed too far in the direction of black rights. In 1868 the governor blandly "express[ed] his sympathies with [blacks] and with the incentives which prompted them to celebrate this the natal day of their virtual release from thraldom." As this lukewarm endorsement suggests, white Republicans were hesitant to embrace too fully the cause of black equality. And the onus of successfully negotiating freedom was always on African Americans. In typical middle-class fashion, the governor told the freedpeople to court the virtues of "honesty and industry, virtue and patriotism," and felt compelled to remind them that "the only honest way of getting a livelihood was by 'earning their bread by the sweat of their brows.'"[12]

White Republicans did support African Americans in their fight for suffrage and full citizenship. Black and white holiday speakers agitated for the right to vote and educated their audience in the responsibilities of citizenship. In 1870 black Richmonders celebrated the success of this agitation with a procession and meeting to mark the passage of the Fifteenth Amendment. For whites, that amendment was not just the culmination but the end of the drive for black rights. By then a coalition of former Whigs, conservative Republicans, and Democrats calling themselves the Conservative Party had "redeemed" Virginia from Reconstruction. Governor Gilbert C. Walker, a Republican turned Conservative, had told African Americans when they called on 1 January that year that he hoped "they might appreciate and enjoy these rights and fulfil [sic] the destiny which had been appointed for them." He spoke of equality as if it were an accomplished fact, saying that the former slaves "now stood before him his peers, equal before the law and in politics, endowed with the same rights and privileges."[13]

Even the most bourgeois African Americans knew better, however. Peter Rachleff argues that black Richmonders in the 1870s and 1880s replaced the official celebration with commemorations of 3 April and of the April anniversary of the Fifteenth Amendment's passage. On these occasions they continued to call for the extension and implementation of black rights and liberties. Congressman John Mercer Langston told a holiday audience in 1890, for instance, "They say that this is a white man's government; I am here to tell you that it is a black man's government as well." He reminded revelers that the word "white" was not in the Constitution, the Declaration of Independence, or the Sermon on the Mount. The continuing celebration of 3 April, which black Richmonders saw as the true date of their emancipation, and of the Fifteenth Amendment stood as assertions of black citizenship and freedom from white control. Despite pleas from prominent Republicans, including Ulysses S. Grant, black Richmonders, freed by emancipation from the dictates of whites, chose to demonstrate that independence by celebrating on dates meaningful to them, not to white Republicans.[14]

THE 1890 EMANCIPATION CONVENTION

By the late 1880s a middle class of black businessmen and professionals was emerging in Richmond. Despite some philosophical differences, they generally agreed on the ultimate goals of racial solidarity, economic prosperity, and political and civil rights. Moreover, they considered themselves the natural leaders of the black community, perfectly positioned to lead the way to these goals. Perhaps inspired by the formation in January 1890 of the National Afro-American League, which sought to maintain black political and civil rights in the face of Democratic hostility and growing Republican indifference, they determined to revitalize and to institutionalize Emancipation Day as the flagship of African American identity. The first step was to establish one date on which Americans could unite to celebrate emancipation. A Richmond junk dealer named George Williams Jr. had begun a movement to eliminate the plethora of emancipation celebrations and to establish a single date that would be "a national Thanksgiving-Day for the whole people." He persuaded the leaders of Richmond's black community to endorse his idea, and in 1890 they organized a national convention to select this date and subsequently to petition Congress to declare it a federal holiday.[15] Such a declaration would lend governmental sanction to the freedom holiday and would demonstrate its significance to national identity for all Americans, not solely for black Americans. For, despite the 1866 speaker's hope that whites would celebrate Emancipation Day with blacks, the holiday remained in 1890 an overwhelmingly black one, particularly in the era of reconciliation between the blue and the gray.

Although the advertising for the three-day celebration and convention emphasized that it would be a national event, Richmonders not surprisingly took the leading roles in planning the events. The executive committee was composed of a cross section of the city's black leadership, including an attorney, a minister, a professor, a banker, a Sunday school leader, and a major with the state militia. All members and convention speakers were men; women played only supporting roles, such as decorating the convention hall. Mitchell and his *Richmond Planet* played an important role as well in publicizing and planning the celebration. In addition to setting a date for the emancipation holiday, the convention promised to provide a practical demonstration of the progress African Americans had made since winning their freedom. Visitors were invited to bring clothing and other relics of slave days, presumably to illustrate that progress. The program featured black speakers from across the nation, as well as essays and orations by young men and women "to show their intellectual improvement." Churches, schools, temperance organizations, fraternal and benevolent societies, and soldiers were invited to attend and to participate in the procession. Again reflecting the dissatisfaction with Republican politics, the organizers also invited "farmers alliances" to join the festivities. Finally, the advertisement underscored the organizers' emphasis on the role of African Americans in national history. It proclaimed that the convention would see "the largest gathering of the colored soldiers just as they appeared in the Union Army." These soldiers would reenact their courageous fight to win black freedom and save the Union in a sham battle.[16]

In the eyes of many black leaders, the lack of a single emancipation holiday was symptomatic of a lack of unity among African Americans, which hindered their ability to fight effectively for their rights as citizens. The organizers hoped that the convention would spur such unity, and the opening speaker, convention chairman Rev. J. A. Taylor, called upon the black community to learn from the Jewish nation, which remained united despite persecution and thus eventually triumphed. "The trouble with our race now," he scolded, "is that we don't stick together. Why, we stick to anybody but ourselves. We want race pride."[17]

Speakers suggested that racial solidarity was particularly necessary to protect political rights. The convention oratory showed the definite stamp of the National Afro-American League. Rev. Milton J. Waldron of Washington, D.C., a Civil War veteran and former Republican politician, asserted that whites would respect African Americans only when they were a political force to be reckoned with. That power would not come through blind allegiance to the Republican Party, which another speaker condemned for forming all-white clubs and sacrificing black rights in the name of white harmony. Rather, Waldron told his audience, they "must vote for the party that will recognize our manhood and protect our lives," whichever party that might be. "We have discharged our obligations to the Republicans and we never owed the Democrats anything," he continued, concluding that "[i]ndependence in politics is our only salvation." George T. Downing, a Rhode Island businessman, even announced that he had supported Democrat Grover Cleveland for president because he seemed to have "the ear of the South."[18]

The orators agreed that without unity African Americans would never secure their civil and political rights. They vehemently denounced white efforts to keep black Americans second-class citizens. Congressman Langston counseled African Americans to continue to fight for their rights, proclaiming, to great applause, "I sanction no color line against us. I sanction no oppression against us." As a first step in assertiveness, Waldron suggested that African Americans renounce the white-given appellation of "Negro" and choose their own identity. If whites were Anglo-Americans, he claimed, again reflecting the influence of the National Afro-American League, blacks should be Afro-Americans. In addition to its political connotations, this seemingly innocuous demand had tremendous implications for the goal of constructing African American identity. To claim the name "Afro-American" meant that blacks identified themselves as both African and American, with all the rights and privileges associated with the latter. Waldron even suggested that African Americans were more American than whites. "The Afro-Americans," he contended, "are more entitled to this land than the Anglo-Americans, as the white man stole the land, while the labor, the misery, and tears of the colored people were expended upon it."[19]

A grand procession on 16 October, led by chief marshal John Mitchell Jr., presented a practical illustration of racial pride and solidarity. Richmond's black GAR post, the First Battalion, local and visiting militia companies, and young cadets in Zouave uniforms joined bands and some sixty civic, fraternal, and religious societies in the line of march. The procession also featured the orators, the organizing committee, and other elites in carriages. Marchers carried both the American and Virginia flags to assert their loyalty to and full citizenship in nation and state. The Lincoln Beneficial Club bore a banner depicting Abraham Lincoln breaking the chains of slavery, and other groups carried banners with the likeness of the current president, Benjamin Harrison, despite accusations by some black newspapers that he supported the Lily-white Republicans. Another banner trumpeted the black progress that organizers wished to demonstrate: "In 1860 Slaves, in 1890 Bankers." The procession paused in front of the city hall, while marchers gave "loud hurrahs" for 9 April 1865, the date of Lee's surrender, and 22 September 1862, the date of the preliminary Emancipation Proclamation.[20]

Along with their political assertiveness, the black businessmen and professionals who sponsored the celebration espoused the bourgeois creed to which they attributed their own success. "Be frugal," George Downing exhorted his audience, "don't only make money but save it." Waldron advised African Americans to acquire land. One banner in the parade even suggested Booker T. Washington's approach to political agitation: "The dollar ballot is always counted; stick to finance."[21]

Despite the pleas for unity, the three-day celebration did not lack for either controversy or division. The most significant controversy surrounded the First Battalion, which almost did not participate in the procession, owing to dissent within the ranks and a feud with the executive committee. The conflict arose when a mass meeting of black civic societies appointed John F. Brown and Capt. Benjamin Scott of the Virginia Grays to request that the governor order a salute fired in honor of the occasion, a typical holiday event in the city. Because there were no black artillery units, white troops would have to fire the salute. Not surprisingly, the governor made it clear that "he would never order out a white company to fire a salute for such an occasion." The executive committee subsequently disavowed any connection with the fiasco, contending that it had never authorized the request. One member informed the *Richmond Times* that the action had been "the height of folly and bad judgment" and assured whites that "it did not meet with the approval of any of the intelligent or better class of the colored people." Banker and clergyman W. W. Browne condemned the request for a rather different reason, claiming that "the colored people didn't wish any white folks to fire any salutes for them. They would fire their own salutes."[22]

This controversy suggests the limits of black unity and the range of black views. Although their speeches might be militant, the actions of the black leadership often fell short of the desires of ordinary African Americans. Black elites had to tread a dangerous line between militance and acquiescence to the practical reality of white supremacy, and they often divided on how to do so. While some sought to mollify the white power structure to win practical gains, others sought its recognition of blacks as equals through overt gestures such as the salute. Still others, such as Browne, called for self-reliant separatism.

The salute controversy underscores the desire of African Americans for the respect of white Americans and for white recognition of blacks as their equals. While it is tempting to view the request as an act of incredible naïveté, it seems unlikely that Richmond blacks really expected the governor to comply. Rather, the act of requesting a holiday salute was a symbolic demand for white recognition of black equality and legitimation of the holiday. White Richmonders, not surprisingly, read the request as an incredible presumption. The *Richmond Dispatch* editorialized on the "Impudence Extraordinary" of the African Americans who requested the salute, claiming it was just "another proof that as a people if they are given an inch they will start out to take an ell." Despite the executive committee's haste to dissociate itself from the salute controversy, it had made its own similar symbolic gesture by inviting the governor and the mayor to make welcoming addresses to the convention. Both men not surprisingly pleaded prior engagements, and the *Richmond Times* reported that "they had not given their consent to speak, nor had they any idea of doing so." The governor sent a perfunctory note, failing to endorse the celebration or even to congratulate the revelers. "That you should rejoice on the day from which you date your freedom and celebrate it in a proper manner is right and natural," he allowed. The rest of the message paternalistically warned them to be sure that "each day's proceedings are characterized by good order and dignity."[23]

Underscoring the transformation of Emancipation Day into a black holiday, the *Richmond Dispatch* reported that only four whites attended the convention; two were reporters, and the other two were a professor and a president at black colleges. White Republicans, the putative allies and defenders of African Americans, were conspicuous by their absence. That whites remained hostile or indifferent to black overtures does not make those gestures any less significant; the symbolic power of the requests for white recognition lay in the very requests themselves. Artillery salutes and speeches by local officials were common features of important holiday celebrations. Both the governor and the mayor of Richmond had attended German Day exercises less than two weeks before, for example, and the mayor had also attended the St. Patrick's Day banquet earlier that year.[24] By their requests African Americans asserted that their commemoration was just as significant as any offered by whites and just as deserving of official recognition.

On 17 October the delegates met to deliberate on the convention's purpose, selecting a national date for the celebration of emancipation. Again, conflict intruded on the proceedings. The election of a permanent national holiday committee composed of three Richmond men, including George Williams Jr.

and John Mitchell Jr., drew vocal dissent from the non-Richmonders present. Another delegate complained that the vote was invalid because women had voted, a charge the chairman denied indignantly. While the election was proceeding, W. W. Browne attempted unsuccessfully to seize control of the meeting. The choice of a date was no less controversial. Delegates voiced strong support for 22 September, 3 April, and 20 April, as well as 1 January. Richmonders tended to favor 3 April; delegates from northern states thought that 22 September would be more convenient, given the weather of northern winters, than 1 January; while delegates from the lower South charged that both the September and April dates would interfere with the cotton crop. The convention eventually, perhaps inevitably, settled on 1 January as the most logical date to establish as a national holiday. Although 1 January did not resonate with many African Americans in the same way as 19 June or 3 April, those dates held more local than national significance. Moreover, 1 January bore the weight of tradition; a delegate from Norfolk declared that using any other date would be like changing the Fourth of July. Finally, 1 January had practical benefits not lost on the bourgeois delegates. A local businessman had noted that "I have to close up on that day anyhow, and the colored people have holiday anyway and won't lose any time from business."[25]

With its main order of business thus concluded, the convention ended. Although it had attracted national attention to the effort to make Emancipation Day a federal holiday, the convention was a decidedly mixed success. Like the veterans and women who sponsored Memorial Day exercises, the organizers had to deal with public indifference to their project. While Jim Crow laws and disfranchisement efforts made it impossible for African Americans at the turn of the century to take their freedom for granted, that did not guarantee large turnouts on holidays. Just as veterans scolded Americans for not keeping Memorial Day sacred, Richmond's convention organizers lambasted African Americans for neglecting what should be the most hallowed of their holidays. In an advertisement the sponsors deplored "how ungrateful and unthankful the colored citizens have been that they have failed to establish a National Thanksgiving-Day."[26]

The convention and celebration did little to change the opinions of most African Americans. Although the convention featured some of the most distinguished African Americans in the nation, most of the sessions were not well attended. Those events with the most crowd appeal—the parade and the convention appearance of the wildly popular Langston—did very well, drawing an estimated ten to fifteen thousand spectators apiece. The other convention sessions, in contrast, drew audiences of less than five hundred. Undoubtedly the poor attendance was in part the result of the admission fee, which was twenty-five cents, a not-inconsiderable sum for working people. Even on the final day, when convention-goers voted on the date for the holiday and the executive committee lowered the admission fee to ten cents, most African Americans in Richmond reportedly elected instead to spend their hard-earned money on the "apples, cakes, fried chicken, and sweet potato pie" sold by vendors outside the hall, rather than watch or participate in the proceedings.[27]

Not surprisingly, the date selected by this minority of African Americans failed to create a national consensus. Despite the efforts of the convention organizers, their declaration of 1 January as the national holiday had little effect on emancipation celebrations. Although it remained the most widely observed date and the closest thing to an official Emancipation Day, Congress never sanctioned it as a federal holiday, and many black communities stubbornly clung to their traditional dates of celebration. Alexandria, Virginia, for example, which had one of the largest annual festivities, continued to celebrate on 22 September. In 1895 some ten thousand people attended the exercises, and a broadside advertising the 1896 celebration noted that the military procession would be reviewed by "the Mayor, U.S. officials and other distinguished people" and that speakers would include vice presidential candidate Garrett A. Hobart.[28]

Even though it meant doing without such signs of white approval, other African Americans resolutely persisted in commemorating the dates they deemed most significant in winning their freedom. Thus, African Americans in Texas continued to celebrate 19 June, or Juneteenth, and black Richmonders continued to commemorate the date when Richmond fell, in agreement with William Bell, who had told the *Richmond Planet* in 1890, "I am in favor of April 3d when Richmond fell because that was the day that I shook hands with the Yankees." There was even a movement in Richmond to overturn the efforts of the 1890 convention. In 1905 the *Richmond Planet* reported that African Americans in Richmond and neighboring Manchester, under the leadership of Capt. Benjamin Scott, had organized the American Freedmen's Association "for the purpose of celebrating the 3rd of April as the national day that the Negroes were set free." As late as 1918 Richmonders were still celebrating the April date. That year the *Richmond Planet* noted that editor John Mitchell Jr., who had done so much to get 1 January established as the holiday, was set to speak at the April exercises.[29]

The continuing celebration of the date of Richmond's fall demonstrates that elites cannot declare holidays by fiat, without the support of ordinary people. A holiday intended to commemorate a specific event must have a solid connection to that event, particularly when it lies within living memory of those celebrating. Although 1 January and 22 September clearly stood as significant dates in the abolition of slavery, the dates when emancipation had been practically effected resonated much more strongly with those who had won their freedom.

THE SEMICENTENNIAL

As for most white Americans, even 1 January no longer excited interest. Southern (and many northern) white Republicans had succumbed to the lily-white virus by the 1890s, as the white North and South reconciled on the old, sure footing of white supremacy. By its lack of action on a federal holiday to mark the end of slavery, Congress withheld recognition of emancipation as a nationally significant event. State legislatures likewise failed to establish an emancipation holiday, illustrating whites' lack of interest in, if not outright hostility toward, celebrating the event that had gone so far toward fulfilling the promise of equality of the Declaration of Independence. The racial gulf in America, which the revelers in 1866 had optimistically believed was on the verge of healing, had become a chasm once again. Most white Americans again stood opposed to an Americanism that incorporated African Americans in any significant manner.

Even on the semicentennial of emancipation in 1913, the *New York Times* gave the occasion only one line of an editorial, acknowledging that it was the "greatest anniversary of the new year." It also published James Weldon Johnson's "Fifty Years." The *Nation* contributed an editorial praising the advances of African Americans in art and industry in the fifty years since emancipation. While the holiday went virtually unnoticed in many white papers, the *Daily Jewish Courier* in Chicago did "endorse the holiday of the free," explaining that Jews had "endured enough persecution as a race and as individuals, to understand the philosophy of freedom" celebrated on Emancipation Day.[30]

Amid this climate of white indifference, African Americans across the country jubilantly celebrated the anniversary throughout 1913. That summer in New York City, for example, W. E. B. DuBois wrote and directed *The Star of Ethiopia*, a pageant of African and African American history. In one Pennsylvania town African Americans combined the semicentennial with their Memorial Day ceremonies. As with the emancipation holiday, African Americans chose to commemorate the semicentennial on days that were meaningful (or convenient) rather than be bound to the official date of 1 January.[31]

The city of Chicago witnessed a remarkable interracial celebration of the semicentennial. A number of Jewish Chicagoans, along with native-born white reformers such as Jane Addams, joined African Americans in that city for one of the largest semicentennial celebrations held outside the former Confederacy. The Bethel Literary Club had begun the push to raise black awareness of the upcoming anniversary at the Bethel Church's 1911 New Year's Eve service, where members presented addresses on white antislavery activists Wendell Phillips and Harriet Beecher Stowe and on emancipation. The *Chicago Defender* reported approvingly that the oratory about "[t]his very important event in race history, neglected on every hand, inspired a large audience to increased interest in their own people and the importance of the Emancipation of the American slaves." The club followed up with a triple celebration of the February birthdays of Abraham Lincoln, Frederick Douglass, and Richard Allen, founder and first bishop of the African Methodist Episcopal Church.[32]

The stage was thus set for the semicentennial celebration in 1913. Rather than hold it on 1 January, Chicagoans chose the 12 February birthday of Illinois's favorite son and the author of the Emancipation Proclamation. The fledgling National Association for the Advancement of Colored People (NAACP) organized the program for the interracial celebration, and the committee of arrangements included "wealthy business and professional men" and local representatives of "the race" such as Ida B. Wells-Barnett and Dr. Charles E. Bentley. Judge Edward Osgood Brown presided over the exercises, and the *Chicago Defender* reported that the audience included "earnest, thoughtful, justice-loving people of every nationality and of every creed." The commemoration drew a stellar cast of national reformers and race activists, who spoke on emancipation and racial issues between interludes of choral and organ music. W. E. B. DuBois, a founder of the NAACP and editor of the *Crisis*, took the podium as the main speaker and had to wait through a full ten minutes of applause before commencing. Antilynching and woman suffrage activist Wells-Barnett organized the "emancipation choir" of 150 women and 50 men, while Bentley received the great honor of reading the Emancipation Proclamation to the crowd. Rabbi Dr. Emil G. Hirsch echoed the *Daily Jewish Courier*'s empathy with the struggle of African Americans for freedom, and Jane Addams admonished whites to cultivate the virtues of "[p]atience, charity, humility." The *Chicago Defender* reported that three thousand attended the celebration and another three thousand were turned away for lack of room.[33]

The semicentennial exercises bore the mark of the NAACP's advocacy of civil and political rights and rejection of the rhetoric of Booker T. Washington. Although the emphasis was on the progress of the race in the fifty years since emancipation, the revelers did not hesitate to express their dismay at continuing racism and other threats to that progress. The *Chicago Defender* noted pointedly that "[i]t is not always easy to be optimistic regarding the race question." The paper deplored the fact that the Emancipation Proclamation "has meant so little in some parts of this country especially in late years." Like a good Progressive, DuBois denounced "irresponsible oligarchy in the power of corporate wealth, and the ruthless manipulation of government by shrewd and conscienceless men," who were "determined to thwart any expression of the popular will," but he saved his harshest condemnation for the "widespread flouting of democracy" by southern disfranchisers. In contrast to the Richmonders who prohibited women from voting at the 1890 convention, he called boldly for "a democracy based on the franchises of all men—and all women—regardless of their wealth, or their race, or the color of [their] grandfathers[.]" The most radical proposition of the day, however, came from a white professor of biblical literature at the University of Chicago, who proclaimed that "amalgamation," not segregation, was the only solution for America's race problem.[34]

DuBois's emphasis on political rights reiterated the most common theme of emancipation celebrations: African Americans were Americans and demanded their full rights and privileges as American citizens. Indeed, DuBois contended that the denial of citizenship rights to black Americans threatened the very existence of American democracy. "When eight states deliberately disfranchise so many of their white and black citizens," he warned in his conclusion, "the very foundations of democracy are in danger." Once again, African Americans asserted their claim to full citizenship in the American nation. Although they defined themselves as African Americans, the emphasis was on their Americanism. In the celebration's only reference to African roots, the emancipation choir performed "Ethiopia," an original piece composed by chorus director J. A. Mundy. The choir closed the exercises, however, with "My Country 'Tis of Thee."[35]

Chicago's semicentennial celebration was remarkable for its interracial program and audience. Unfortunately, it was also rare. Despite the best efforts of African Americans, Emancipation Day did not become a federal holiday, nor did it become a generally observed occasion outside black America. The Emancipation Proclamation stood as a sister document to the Declaration of Independence only in the eyes of African Americans. Kirk Savage has noted that the Freedman's Memorial to Abraham Lincoln in Washington, D.C., "assigns the subject [of emancipation] to black memory instead of national memory." Likewise, Emancipation Day became a black rather than a truly national holiday, despite the 1866 orator's naïve hope that former masters and former slaves would celebrate emancipation together.[36]

African Americans went to great lengths on Emancipation Days to show that they had played and continued to play a vital role in American history and that they were full citizens. The initial sympathy of white Republicans and abolitionists to these assertions, demonstrated in the biracial official celebrations, fell before the tidal wave of resurgent racism and white reconciliation. By the early twentieth century most white Americans were indifferent, if not actively hostile, to African American demands for full citizenship, and their definition of American identity remained lily white. As on the federal Memorial Day, Reconstruction-era integration on Emancipation Day had dissolved by the end of the century into separatism and segregation. The labor movement demonstrated a similar trajectory in the postbellum era, both in its struggle for acceptance of its vision of America and in its move away from interracial cooperation.

3

LABOR'S DAYS

*I*N HIS HOLIDAY EDITORIAL for the Fourth of July 1866, Andrew
C. Cameron, editor-publisher of the National Labor Union's *Workingman's Advocate*, outlined the struggle facing the nation's laborers in the aftermath of the Civil War. While workers had been away fighting in the
Union army for no other reason than "the love of country," according to
Cameron, capitalists had been busily accumulating "their ill-gotten wealth
by selling shoddy clothes, and tainted food to feed the army." Now that
the war was over, the nation's laborers must prevent their old enemy from
enslaving them. The postwar conflict, Cameron asserted, pitted workers,
"the men who make the country—who saved it," against the "bloated
monied aristocracy ... whose carriage spatters the dirt on you as you pass
by."[1] In this holiday editorial, Cameron and the union he represented
called upon workers to revive the spirit of 1776 by declaring their inde-

pendence from capital and thus fired one of the initial salvos in the class conflict that would mark the late nineteenth century.

Four years later, in an address to black voters, representatives of Chicago's Labor League, led by none other than Cameron, amplified this antagonistic position toward capital in urging African American workers to unite with their white counterparts: "We recognize the existence of but two classes— the robbers and the robbed, the men who labor and the men who live off the products of others' labor. . . . With one of these classes your interests are identified." The National Labor Union took the position that "the interests of labor demand that all workingmen should be included within its ranks, without regard to race or nationality." That did not mean an integrated union, however. Although the National Labor Union boasted of "admitting colored delegates" to its congress "on terms of perfect equality," African Americans chose to organize the parallel Colored National Labor Union. They recognized the complexities that the National Labor Union did not admit, that white workers as well as employers barred black workers from certain occupations and that, as a result, the interests of black and white workers were in practice not always identical. The black union's platform called for "the establishment of co-operative workshops . . . among our people as a remedy against their exclusion from other workshops on account of color, as a means of furnishing employment, as well as a protection against the aggression of capital."[2]

As the actions of the National Labor Union and the Colored National Labor Union suggest, organized labor welcomed the end of the Civil War as the dawn of a new era for American workers. David Roediger has argued that the postbellum labor movement "saw the liberation of Black slaves as a model" for the emancipation of workers from wage slavery. There were even physical links between the two crusades; for example, Ira Steward, father of the eight-hour movement, had been an abolitionist. In 1776 Americans had declared war on political slavery, in 1861 on chattel slavery, and in the late 1860s labor leaders declared war on the wage slavery that kept workers from enjoying the fruits of their labor. After the Civil War leading union men such as Steward and Cameron launched the new emancipation crusade with a struggle to free workers from the bondage of long working hours.[3]

Like the Union veterans of the Grand Army of the Republic, labor unionists began the postwar period in a biracial alliance. As the invitation of the Labor League suggests, organized labor not only welcomed but also encouraged African American workers to unionize and to support the fledgling eight-hour movement. This alliance, however, like that within the GAR, was marked on the part of white union leaders and members by continuing racism and deep-seated ambivalence toward anything approaching true equality for black workers. For their part, black workers, like black veterans, retained the hope of attaining equality yet were realistic about the racial attitudes of their white counterparts. In yet another similarity to the GAR, the National Labor Union and the later Knights of Labor were biracial but not integrated unions; local chapters organized straight down the color line.[4] Nevertheless, the very use of emancipation as a model and the recognition of common cause between black and white workers demonstrated a significant change in white views toward black workers. Always fragile, this biracial alliance, like that among Union veterans, was doomed to crash on the rocky shoals of the hardening color line. By the end of the nineteenth century, only the radicals—socialists and anarchists—among organized labor still clung to the biracial class unity that formed such an elemental part of their ideology.

Strident anticapitalist rhetoric and the appeal across racial as well as ethnic lines typified the postwar labor movement in burgeoning industrial cities. Although individual unions remained segregated along racial, ethnic, and gender lines, labor leaders recognized the necessity of uniting workers in a larger common movement. German, Scandinavian, and Czech immigrants, many exiled because of their socialist activities, brought to the United States radical ideologies and a tradition of labor activism, which combined with the increasing disillusionment of many native-born workers to form a pungent critique of the industrial system. Workers' declining control over the conditions of their labor, employer intransigence on hours and wages, the tremendously skewed distribution of wealth, and the brutality of the state militias and police toward workers stoked the fires that made postbellum America the scene of the most volatile and violent class conflict in the nation's history. The era also saw a flourishing of unions, which sought to direct the challenge to capitalism and to liberate workers through less violent means, such as demonstrations, strikes, and legislation. Trade unions in major industrial centers federated into umbrella labor organizations that coordinated general strikes and demonstrations and pushed for legislative action; in large cities such as Chicago and New York, competing federations even emerged, with one led by socialists and the other by more pragmatic craft unionists. At the same time, to compete with businesses that had become national corporations, labor leaders established new national labor organizations, beginning with the National Labor Union and moving on to the cooperationist Knights of Labor, the radical Socialist Labor Party and the International Working People's Association, and the pragmatic American Federation of Labor (AFL).[5]

Although these organizations differed greatly in ideology and tactics, there was a great deal of movement between them in the Gilded Age, and socialists retained a strong minority voice within even the AFL well into the twentieth century. All the late nineteenth-century unions shared the goal of bettering the condition of American workers, and all supported the eight-hour movement. To help accomplish their goals, city and national labor federations sponsored a series of eight-hour demonstrations, used established holidays such as the Fourth of July to espouse the workers' cause, and created two new holidays, Labor Day and May Day.

Just as veterans at Memorial Day celebrations constructed the story of the Civil War, so labor leaders used their holidays to explain the ongoing labor wars. On these occasions labor leaders of divergent ideological convictions articulated their notions of the proper relationship between labor and capital, the ultimate goals of labor organization, and the place of the working class in America. Above all, the holiday celebrations furnished forums for debate over working-class Americanism and American identity itself. Like the veterans, labor union members of various ideological stripes could agree on certain elements of the story. As James Barrett has pointed out, civil rights and liberties, including the right to an "American standard of living," and a rough cultural and racial pluralism (in principle if less often in practice) were basic ingredients in organized labor's version of Americanism. Moreover, just as Civil War veterans depicted an America epitomized by themselves and their fallen comrades, veterans of the labor movement constructed an America in which workers constituted the central actors. In addition to disagreements over ideology and ultimate goals, however, radical and pragmatic unionists conflicted in their definitions of the working class in terms of ethnicity, race, gender, and occupation or skill level. The National Labor Union invited the membership of black and immigrant workers, as did the Knights of Labor and socialist unions. The latter organizations also encouraged female workers to join and organized unskilled laborers as well. Thus, although in practice most leaders of these unions were white, male, and skilled, their working ideology and membership practices defined the American worker in broader terms. The AFL, in contrast, restricted its membership to skilled crafts workers. Because of the various barriers that excluded African Americans and women, as well as many immigrants, from most skilled trades, the AFL's definition of the American worker was much more restrictive than that offered by the other unions.[6]

Not surprisingly, industrial cities such as Chicago figured prominently in the development of public celebrations as vehicles for the construction of labor and class identity. In smaller towns and less industrialized regions, particularly the South, unionization and the acceptance of labor holidays proceeded more slowly. In the South the race problem inevitably complicated matters, although the Knights of Labor made inroads into some southern cities, including Richmond, where the union organized both black and white workers in the 1880s.[7] Labor activists had long known the potential of public demonstrations and strike parades to bring their causes before the public, to recruit members, and to build solidarity. As unions grew over the course of the Gilded Age, they institutionalized such activities into annual displays of working-class strength on new labor holidays.

What of the majority of American workers, who belonged to no union at all? Organized labor counted among its members a much smaller percentage of working-class Americans than the major veterans' organizations did of Civil War veterans. Like the leaders and members of these groups, however, those of unions presumed to speak for all workers. In addition to their many other purposes, holiday celebrations served unions as recruitment tools. Like the veterans, however, union leaders found their celebrations competing with the allures of commercial recreation and private forms of celebration; by the late nineteenth century many unions had trouble gathering even their own members for holiday parades and picnics.

Gilded Age Chicago provides a particularly revealing window on the holiday construction of working-class Americanism. The city ranked among the nation's fastest growing; its population soared from 109,000 in 1860 to almost two million in 1900. The majority of that growth came from immigrants and their children, who filled most of the positions opening in the city's factories, mills, and stockyards. This tremendous population growth fueled the development of one of the country's most vibrant labor movements, which encompassed a broad variety of ethnic groups and represented all shades of working-class ideology, from trade unionism and cooperationism to socialism and anarchism. At the height of late nineteenth-century union activity in 1886, an estimated 12 percent of the city's 250,000 wage workers were affiliated with unions.[8] Chicago was thus in the forefront of the labor movement in the late nineteenth century, and in 1867 its unions sponsored the first May Day demonstration in favor of the eight-hour day.

THE FIRST MAY DAY DEMONSTRATION

Despite the anticapitalist tone of rhetoric such as Cameron's, organized labor began its fight after the Civil War with more limited ends than the overthrow of capitalism. The eight-hour day emerged as the initial focus of labor's efforts. Workers created eight-hour organizations in cities across the United States, and labor papers such as the *Workingman's Advocate* supported, promoted, and publicized those organizations' efforts. Eight-hour proponents couched their rhetoric in the traditional artisan republican terms, which received fresh meaning on the heels of emancipation. At its first congress in 1866, the National Labor Union proclaimed that the eight-hour law was necessary "to free the labor of this country from capitalistic slavery." As a result of the agitation, six states, several cities, and Congress had passed (short-lived) eight-hour legislation by 1868.[9]

One of those states was Illinois, where the legislature had passed an eight-hour law in 1867. On 1 May, the day it was to take effect, forty-four Chicago unions staged a procession and mass meeting to celebrate the triumph and to demand strict adherence to the new law. Marching workers, foreign born as well as native born, made it clear that the eight-hour day represented a fulfillment of American principles. The wagon of a unionized German toy-making shop, for example, linked the movement to its antebellum predecessor with a banner proclaiming that "[f]rom 12 to 10 [hours] and from 10 to 8 is but a national progress." The Journeymen Stone Cutters Association enlisted George Washington on the side of trade unionism by displaying a banner depicting "The Father of Our Country." The banner redirected the cry of the leaders of the American Revolution, "In Union There Is Strength," to the organization of the nation's workers. Like the Revolutionary War generation before them, workers would have to fight to build a union. Echoing the artisan processions of the early republic, the unions' floats illustrated the centrality of skilled labor to the nation through the reenactment of their respective trades. Ship caulkers caulked a ship dubbed "Banner State," the tanners dressed skins, the marble cutters cut marble, the iron moulders cast moulds, and the hamsewers sewed hams.[10]

Although the procession celebrated the triumph of the eight-hour day, the unions knew full well that the war was not yet over. Legislators sympathetic to employers had succeeded in amending the state's eight-hour law to make eight hours a legal day's work only "in the absence of a written contract to the contrary," and most Chicago businessmen had been hastily drawing up such contracts. The employees of the railroad corporations, which were being particularly intransigent, made no bones of their determination to see the eight-hour day enforced, with banners reading "Eight hours and no surrender" and "Eight hours or no work."[11]

At the lakefront mass meeting that followed the procession, speakers affirmed the unions' eight-hour cry. Hon. A. J. Kuykendall, the orator of the day, asserted that it was only natural that the day should be divided equally so that workers might have sufficient time to exercise their rights and duties as American citizens. He called for "eight hours for labor, eight hours for rest and eight hours for the improvement of the mind" necessary for the citizens of a republic to study the principles of government. A second speaker perhaps better reflected the desires of workers when he divided the day into eight-hour periods for sleep, labor, and "recreation and amusements."[12]

Like the workers in the procession, the speakers framed their arguments with the republican ideology of slavery and citizenship that had fueled the American Revolution and the Civil War. "A contest is now going on between capital and labor," Kuykendall told his audience that May afternoon. Kuykendall made clear the parallel between this struggle and the one that had resulted in the emancipation of American slaves: "If [workers] do not control capital it will own labor as slaves. . . . If all the wealth is produced by labor it ought to be subservient to labor; otherwise labor is as completely the slave as the African ever was. We must not stop with freeing the African and allow ourselves to be slaves." In contrast to such fiery prolabor sentiments, the mayor urged gradualism, cautioning workers not to press their employers too rapidly for enforcement of the law.[13]

The next morning, eight-hour advocates heeded Kuykendall's image of war rather than the mayor's counsel of conciliation. Thousands of workers stayed home, and groups of eight-hour men visited open shops and factories encouraging, and in some cases forcing, employees not working the eight-hour day to join their general strike. Although the eight-hour day was already a dead letter for most workers, given the law's emasculation, the general strike sounded the death knell of the first eight-hour movement in Chicago. In a fit of righteous indignation that the workers would dare to attempt to enforce the new law, the antilabor *Chicago Tribune* alleged that "rioting" eight-hour men had made the city's streets as well as its factories unsafe for law-abiding citizens. The eight-hour laws were not enforced in Illinois or elsewhere, and unions had to continue to fight employers on a piecemeal basis through strikes for the eight-hour day. By the mid-1880s, a work shift of ten or more hours was still standard in most industries.[14]

But the great May Day demonstration of 1867 had reinforced for organized labor the efficacy of public processions and meetings in publicizing its demands and demonstrating its power and unity to the employing classes. The failed general strike showed the foolhardiness of making such demands without sufficient strength behind them. Unions set to work to build their membership and transformed demonstrations and holiday celebrations into tools for recruiting and educating unorganized workers. As a result, it became even more important for unions to articulate clearly their vision of working-class Americanism on such occasions.

HOLIDAYS AND CLASS CONSCIOUSNESS

Long before the advent of formal labor holidays, labor unions made use of public venues—city streets, squares, and parks—to create and demonstrate class solidarity, to voice their demands, to gain public support, to recruit new

members, and to indoctrinate and educate workers. In addition to strikes
and demonstrations, more social occasions served these purposes. For union
members, picnics, balls, and holiday celebrations built fraternal bonds and
raised money for the movement as they entertained.[15]

The Fourth of July, as the nation's birthday and the only summer holiday
for most workers, provided a prime occasion for constructing working-class
culture. Unions sought to impose order on the rowdy holiday traditions of
gunfire, fireworks, and drinking and to use the holiday to promote their own
ends. They moved the celebration off the streets (except for processions) and
into the more controlled atmosphere of picnic groves. They offered something to entice every worker, including parades and picnics that featured
rhetoric along with races, athletic contests, dancing, and food and alcohol. In
1866, for example, the Trades' Assembly of Chicago sponsored a holiday picnic outside town. In an effort to appeal to those who preferred merriment on
their holidays, the celebration focused on recreational activities rather than
oratory. The day's events included dancing, a game of quoits, and a number
of races, including a ladies' race and a wheelbarrow race. The *Workingman's
Advocate* indignantly disputed the reports in the mainstream press of rowdi-
ness on the part of the union attendees. It blamed an outside "band of rowdies" for the problems and asserted that "[a] more orderly, better conducted
class of people never left our city" than the Trades' Assembly members who
gathered for the picnic.[16]

The labor organizations had to compete on the Fourth with ethnic associations, whose celebrations proved more attractive to many nonunion workers. The Chicago *Turngemeinde* (a nationalist gymnastic organization), for
example, sponsored a well-attended celebration of the centennial in 1876,
which focused on recreation and recitations of German contributions to
American history and culture and avoided mention of class. Unions themselves generally organized along ethnic lines, however, which meant that
holiday celebrations often blended ethnic and working-class culture. That
same year the German Journeymen Tailors' Union invited other German
and some Scandinavian unions to participate in a centennial procession and
picnic, which featured oratory (in German) and "other amusements peculiar
to the German community."[17]

Socialist and anarchist unions proved themselves most adept at fashioning the Fourth and other holidays into forums for defining and expressing working-class Americanism. They blended ideology and entertainment to make their celebrations both educational and amusing. In Chicago, which had a particularly strong radical movement, such events drew large crowds in the 1870s. The Workingmen's Party of Illinois, forerunner of the Socialist Labor Party, sponsored a centennial celebration on the eve of the Fourth. The *Lehr und Wehr Verein*, a paramilitary club formed a year earlier to protect workers against police assault, led a grand procession of socialist unions and turners (or gymnasts). The parade featured "a beautiful girl whose classic features were surmounted by a 'cap of liberty,'" a clear link to the symbolism of the American and French Revolutions.[18]

Despite the presence of this republican allegory, the purpose of the parade and the exercises that followed was not to extol simplemindedly the progress of American liberty in its first century. Rather, Chicago's socialists sought to remind the workers that the American Revolution had not yet been completed. The highlight of the oratory was the reading, in both German and English, of an alternative declaration of independence, which called for "a radical reform throughout our entire social and political system" so as to secure for workers their "inalienable rights" of "life, liberty, and the full benefit of their labor." The workers present voted unanimously to adopt this declaration, before adjourning for the typical picnic fare of food and beer, contests, games of chance, dancing, and fireworks.[19]

Three years later the Socialist Labor Party staged a three-day Fourth of July *volksfest* that featured a drill by the Bohemian Sharpshooters, a Czech militia group, a procession of socialist unions, music by bands and ethnic singing societies, and speeches by labor activists such as Peter J. McGuire, a carpenter and founder of the Social Democratic Party. Ira Steward, who had organized eight-hour leagues across the country, presented another declaration of independence that specifically linked the eight-hour movement to American liberty. "Resolved," Steward announced, "that while the Fourth of July was heralded a hundred years ago in the name of Liberty, we now herald this day in behalf of the great economic measure of Eight Hours."[20]

In addition to their Independence Day celebrations, radicals in Chicago commemorated annually the March anniversary of the Paris Commune, their model for the social revolution. These commune festivals infused with revolutionary ideology the traditional holiday events of music, gymnastics, song, dance, drama, recitations, and oratory. Tableaux and plays that reenacted the events of 1871 reinforced these lessons, as did the customary singing of the "Marseillaise," which socialists had adopted as their hymn. In 1902 the *Chicago Daily Socialist* advertised a "Grand Commune Festival" to be sponsored by the Socialist Party and the combined German singing societies. In addition to music, recitations, and dancing, the celebration was to feature "Living Pictures Portraying the most thrilling scenes in the famous Commune of Paris." At these festivals, speakers addressed the ethnically mixed crowds in English, German, Czech, and Norwegian, retelling the history of the great working-class uprising as an inspirational lesson to American workers. They also used the commemoration to support the international socialist struggle. "So while we Socialists meet here to revere and honor the memory of the revolutionists that died in the Commune of Paris," Thomas J. Morgan told revelers in 1905, "we also give our ready sympathy and encouragement to the living revolutionists in Russia and wish them complete success in their efforts to destroy Russian despotism." In 1909 Chicago socialists combined the commune festival with a commemoration of Karl Marx's death. The *Chicago Daily Socialist* noted that the crowd included Germans, Scandinavians, Poles, Czechs, Jews, and Italians, in addition to native-born Americans.[21]

At the commune festivals, socialists constructed an international working-class identity and advocated revolution. On the Fourth of July, they also called for revolution while they created an American working-class identity that encompassed both socialism and American revolutionary principles. With the alternative declarations, as well as their appropriation of the symbolic phrygian (liberty) cap, the citizens' militia, and the national holiday itself, socialists redefined America in terms of class and placed workers in the contemporary role of their revolutionary forefathers, fighting to extend the liberty won in 1783.

THE ORIGINS OF LABOR DAY

The socialist belief in the efficacy of holiday celebrations in building class identity and solidarity played an instrumental role in the establishment of a distinct labor holiday. In New York City in 1882 the Central Labor Union, an umbrella association of Knights of Labor assemblies and socialist unions, sponsored a massive demonstration that became the first Labor Day. The holiday grew out of plans by socialist members of the Central Labor Union for a "monster labor festival" to be held in early September to coincide with the national conference of the Knights, whom they wished to win over to the socialist cause. Various other motives animated the union organizers of the festival as well. They sought both to raise money to begin a union newspaper and to impress the more conservative trade unionists and Knights with their strength. At the same time, they wished to demonstrate the common bonds that united the workers in the city, whatever their affiliation, and so invited the other organizations to march with them and to share the speakers' podium at the picnic afterward. Just as importantly, they hoped the celebration would show both the political parties and capitalists the power of an organized and united labor force. In a statement two days before the parade, grand marshal William McCabe made clear this purpose: "Let us offer to monopolists and their tools of both political parties such a sight as will make them think more profoundly than they have ever thought before." Finally, the festivities were to serve as a recruiting and educative tool for unorganized workers, whom the Central Labor Union invited to march in the parade and encouraged to come hear the speakers.[22]

The organizers of the first Labor Day had ties to the Knights of Labor and trade unions as well as to socialism. Machinist Mathew Maguire and tailor Robert Blissert, both of whom were Knights as well as founders and officers of the Central Labor Union, led the drive for the demonstration. Carpenter Peter J. McGuire, who later, as vice president of the AFL, claimed sole responsibility for the inauguration of labor's great day, played a less instrumental role, but he did attend the Central Labor Union's meetings about the demonstration, sat on the reviewing stand for the procession, and was one of the featured speakers at the picnic. The organizers' cross-affiliations with trade unions, the Knights of Labor, and the Central Labor Union illustrate the still fluid nature of the various labor organizations in the early 1880s. Although the socialist Central Labor Union sponsored the festival, socialists, Knights, and trade unionists shared the reviewing stand, the line of march, and the rostrum. The Central Labor Union did not invite politicians to play any role in the day's festivities, another indication of the socialists' leading role in planning the affair.[23]

An estimated ten to twenty thousand workers of all ideological stripes marched in the first Labor Day parade on Tuesday, 5 September 1882. Some twenty-five thousand New Yorkers jammed a local park after the procession for a picnic lunch and speech making. The speakers included Blissert, McGuire, a German-language orator, and newspaperman and labor sympathizer John Swinton of the *New York Sun*. After four hours of oratory, the workers and their families ate their lunches, drank beer, listened to German singing societies and Irish fiddlers, danced to union bands, and viewed fireworks displays in the evening.[24]

Although the socialist, cooperationist, and trade unionists marched and picnicked together on 5 September in a grand demonstration of labor solidarity, the harmony of the day was short lived. Beneath the surface, the growing tensions between the three groups seethed. The Knights of Labor, backing away from the militantly anticapitalist rhetoric of the radicals, began to rid themselves of socialist and anarchist members. Indeed, less than two months after the first Labor Day, Maguire and his Advance Labor Club were expelled from the Knights of Labor.[25]

Despite the rising tensions, the Central Labor Union judged the "Labor Day" enough of a success to repeat it a year later, again on 5 September. In 1884 the organization resolved to make the holiday an annual affair and set its observance for the first Monday in September rather than the fifth of the month, making Labor Day the nation's first Monday holiday. Since the majority of workers then labored six days a week, the holiday would give them a rare two-day weekend. The Knights of Labor endorsed this plan at its annual convention, as did the Federation of Organized Trades and Labor Assemblies (the predecessor of the AFL), at the instigation of Andrew Cameron. Unions in other industrial cities adopted Labor Day starting in 1885, and organized labor began to push to make the day a state and federal holiday.[26]

At these first Labor Day celebrations, organized labor's desire to present a united front and to demonstrate the power of the working class ran headlong into the sharpening ideological divisions within the movement. In Chicago, stronghold of the revolutionary socialist and anarchist movement, Labor Day from the start could not contain these tensions. The craft union–dominated Trades and Labor Assembly, under Andrew Cameron's leadership, sponsored the city's first Labor Day celebration in 1885. Cameron, like many of those who had spoken the rhetoric of class war in the 1860s, had backed down from this language in the wake of the Paris Commune and the rise of a socialist movement in the United States. Whether from political conviction or to avoid antagonizing capital, the Trades and Labor Assembly apparently forbade the carrying of the red flag in procession, leading the socialist and anarchist unions of the Central Labor Union to withdraw in protest. Instead the Central Labor Union held its own exercises and parade, in which "the red flag can be carried without objection," on Sunday. The city's Knights of Labor joined the Trades and Labor Assembly's celebration rather than that of the Central Labor Union.[27]

The fourth division of the Trades and Labor Assembly's procession featured "[i]ndustrial firms represented by trucks, wagons, etc.," demonstrating the trade unionists' desire to separate themselves from the revolutionary ideology of the Central Labor Union. The *Chicago Tribune* reported that "[s]everal enterprising firms in town took occasion to advertise their goods by sending curiously-arranged carts bearing huge inscriptions, to be drawn in the procession."[28] In the combined celebration of the Trades and Labor Assembly and the Knights of Labor, capitalists were no longer simply the audience to be persuaded of the validity of workers' demands; they had actually been invited to play an integral part in the demonstration. The advertising carts represented a dramatic symbolic capitulation to the employers' longtime argument that capital and labor were not of necessity opposed but rather had a shared interest, although the craft unions interpreted this dictum rather differently than did the capitalists.

The socialist and anarchist unions would have none of it. It was not just the ban on the red flag to which they objected but precisely the conciliatory approach of the other organizations toward the enemy, capital. They saw the invitation to businesses as a shocking breach of labor solidarity. At the Central Labor Union's celebration, prominent radical Sam Fielden, later to be charged in the Haymarket Square bombing, castigated the Trades and Labor Assembly for its servile attitude toward the employing classes, telling the crowd, "There is going to be a parade tomorrow. Those fellows want to reconcile labor and capital. They want to reconcile you to your starving shanties." In a further affront to the socialist vision of working-class Americanism, the trade unionists had even invited representatives of the capitalist system—including a judge, a congressman, the mayor, and a general—to speak rather than representatives of labor, to whom the day rightfully belonged.[29] By inviting the representatives of the political and economic power structure to participate, the Trades and Labor Assembly may have lent legitimacy to the labor holiday, but in the radicals' eyes, this invitation only demonstrated an unwholesome and unmanly subservience to capital.

Both celebrations included processions followed by picnics featuring oratory, games, and dancing. Although both the Knights of Labor and the radicals organized women workers, neither celebration included such unions. The only women in the Trades and Labor Assembly's procession were "invited guests," who rode in carriages in traditional fashion, and the girls on a commercial float, dressed in traditional allegorical fashion "to represent the different nationalities of the earth." Although they did not participate in celebrations as members of unions, women did play more than a decorative role in the socialist exercises. The *Chicago Tribune* reported that "about fifty girls and women bearing a banner with the inscription . . . 'American Corps'" marched in the Central Labor Union's procession. And at the picnic that followed, radical journalist Lucy Parsons made a speech comparing workers to slaves and calling for revolution against their capitalist masters. That she was herself a former slave lent the words a chilling resonance.[30]

The banners carried by the marchers in the Central Labor Union's procession served a similar exhortative and educational purpose, with mottoes such as "Hail to the social revolution!"; "Down with government, God, and gold!"; "Lawlessness means equality for all!"; and "Every Government is a conspiracy of the rich against the people." Radicals intended such slogans to educate and to indoctrinate Chicago's workers to the need for socialist revolution or, in the latter three cases, for anarchy. In contrast, the messages of the trade unionists and Knights eschewed class war to focus on pragmatic issues such as convict labor and the ongoing struggles for the eight-hour day and better wages. The stonecutters, for example, carried a banner proclaiming the by then traditional slogan "[e]ight hours for work, eight hours for rest, eight hours for recreation." While one group of marchers echoed the traditional labor verity "[c]apital springs from labor," another adopted the more conciliatory "[c]apital and labor should go hand in hand."[31]

THE TOBACCO FLOAT

Labor Day in New York City. Union men bear banners asserting their centrality in the American republic. (*Leslie's Illustrated Newspaper*, 1887; courtesy of the Library of Congress)

The placating tone of the procession continued at the Trades and Labor Assembly's picnic. The politicians who spoke expressed sympathy for organized labor, but one warned that "the poor must understand that the rights of the rich must be respected, and the rich must appreciate the duties they owe to the poor and to society." Mayor Carter Harrison warned his audience to fight through the ballot box, not in the streets, and asserted that "[l]abor and capital may seem antagonistic, but they are in fact the best of friends. Make it friendly by organizing and teaching capital that its interest is to pull with you." The main goal of Labor Day, in the mayor's formulation, was neither to educate unorganized workers to the benefits of unionization nor to demonstrate labor solidarity to the public and particularly the employing classes. Rather, it was to educate capital and labor that their interests were mutual and best served by working together. By 1885 nonsocialist organized labor in Chicago was on the verge of accepting its own version of this belief. The debacle of the Haymarket Square bombing and the formation of the AFL the next year only hastened this reconciliation. A sure sign of the growing conservatism of Chicago's nonsocialist unions was the *Chicago Tribune*'s praise of their Labor Day celebration.[32]

On the other hand, the paper went out of its way to portray the radicals as wild-eyed, unwashed, ignorant, and fanatical foreigners and began its account of the Central Labor Union's celebration in inflammatory fashion: "With the smell of gin and beer, with blood-red flags and redder noses, and with banners inscribed with revolutionary mottoes, the anarchists inaugurated their grand parade and picnic yesterday morning." The *Chicago Tribune* described the participants as "workingmen, organized and unorganized, and tramps," as well as "some sorts of women." A German band the paper called "[s]ome twenty unwashed musicians." The writer noted that the revelers "were nearly all foreigners of the most ignorant stripe," conveniently forgetting that the vast majority of Chicago's working class was foreign born or had parents who were. This attack on the radicals was hardly unique. The probusiness *Tribune* simply mouthed the xenophobic stereotypes that had already become central to capital's campaign to discredit the radical labor movement by depicting it as inherently un-American.[33]

In contrast to the radical celebration, that of the Trades and Labor Assembly and the Knights of Labor demonstrated that those unions had by

1885 extricated themselves for the most part from the ideology of social revolution or even confrontation with capital. The shift was not yet complete, however. Albert Parsons, for example, retained his membership in the Knights of Labor up until his execution for his alleged role in the Haymarket Square bombing. That socialists still exerted a pull over the membership of trade unions was evident by the fact that the president of the stonecutters' union had felt it necessary to announce publicly before Labor Day 1885 that "this body will not take part in the Socialists' parade, but will join the Trades Assembly procession Monday." In concession to its socialist or sympathetic members, however, the union did not forbid their participation in the earlier procession as individuals, not as union members. Socialists continued to proselytize for converts and for control of the labor movement from within the Knights of Labor and AFL into the twentieth century.[34]

THE SECOND MAY DAY

In 1885 and 1886 the various labor groups in Chicago came together in a fragile unity for a final time in a renewed campaign for the eight-hour day, which ended in the tragedy of the Haymarket bombing and further fragmentation of the labor movement. The Federation of Organized Trades and Labor Assemblies, forerunner of the AFL, resolved at its 1884 convention in Chicago to give the eight-hour movement, stagnant since the depression of the 1870s, a new national push. The next year the federation proposed that its member organizations vote for a universal strike on 1 May 1886. The seemingly more obvious choice for the demonstration, Labor Day, was probably not chosen because it was not yet celebrated outside of New York City in 1884. The choice of 1 May is more obscure. Aside from being the traditional May Day, which celebrated rebirth and fertility, 1 May was also by custom Moving Day, when all leases began. More to the point, 1 May had become a day for workers in the building and allied trades, which had been dormant all winter, to rally to demand union wages and hours under threat of strike.[35] Finally, there was precedent for an eight-hour demonstration on this date in the Chicago demonstration and strikes of 1867.

In 1885, with the support of sixty-nine of its seventy-eight member unions, the Federation of Organized Trades and Labor Assemblies drew up an eight-hour agreement that employers might sign with unions to avert the strike. Some members of the federation took a more confrontational tone in an appeal to workers to join the demonstration. "Arouse, ye toilers of America!" one broadside exhorted. "Lay down your tools on May 1, 1886, cease your labor, close the factories, mills and mines—for one day in the year. One day of revolt—not of rest!" This circular expressed a contempt for capital that demonstrated that socialists still had influence within the federation. May Day was to be "[a] day on which labor makes its own laws and has the power to execute them! All without the consent or approval of those who oppress and rule."[36]

Chicago's unions embraced the idea. All wings of the labor movement used the year of planning for the demonstration to recruit new members to their unions. As a result the labor movement saw tremendous growth across the board. Chicago's Central Labor Union, for example, grew from eight member unions in 1884 to twenty-four in 1886, membership in the Knights of Labor soared in 1886 alone from ten thousand to more than twenty thousand, and the Trades and Labor Assembly doubled from twenty-five unions in October of 1885 to fifty just five months later. On 1 May 1886 some thirty to forty thousand Chicago workers struck, and thousands of others took an unscheduled holiday, causing hundreds of local factories and workshops to close. Various unions paraded through the streets, bearing banners demanding the eight-hour day or, in a few instances, praising their employers for complying with this standard. Some one thousand woodworkers, for example, paraded through the labor districts of the north and west sides carrying "numerous banners bearing words of praise for such of their employers as had given them shorter hours with the regular pay." The ideological sympathies of the woodworkers were revealed by their cheers as they passed "the Socialists' headquarters." The employees of one sash, door, and blind factory likewise marched with banners lauding their employer, who had revised the wage and hour scales to their liking.[37]

Many Knights of Labor assemblies ignored the national no-strike rule and went out on strike as well on May Day. An assembly of meatpackers, for instance, struck and won the eight-hour day without loss of pay. And on 3 May hundreds of girls and women, derisively dubbed "Shouting Amazons" by the *Chicago Tribune*, left their sewing machines and paraded exuberantly through the streets, waving eight-hour banners and accompanied by a brass band. They stopped at workshops along their route to recruit additional strikers. At the end of the day, the women formed a new Knights of Labor assembly, claiming that they were not socialists or "red-flag" people but merely wished to better their condition.[38]

One of the most impressive demonstrations of the day was that of radical lumber workers. Thousands of Czech, Polish, and German lumber hands staged a procession through the lumber district, waving the red flag and calling upon their few comrades at work to join them. The *Chicago Tribune*, in typical fashion, described the assemblage as a "blood-thirsty mob of Anarchistic strikers," who carried an upside-down American flag and "rags that had just been soaked in fresh blood." Reflecting the then-current stereotypical association of immigrants and radicalism, the paper sniffed disdainfully that the marchers looked "as if they had just landed from the old country." After their procession, the strikers listened to anarchist speakers, who allegedly exhorted them to burn the lumberyards of noncomplying employers. The *Chicago Tribune* further fanned the flames of the fear of radicalism by noting that an anonymous socialist had reported that radicals were pleased with the progress made by the strikers, adding that "Chicago was the best place in the country to start the movement, and we expect it to spread all over the country."[39]

While the eight-hour demonstrations in Chicago were dominated by socialists and anarchists, that was not the case everywhere. In Cincinnati, for example, the Knights of Labor and crafts unions were in charge, and in New York City crafts unions led the way. In Louisville, Kentucky, the May Day procession included some six thousand members of the interracial Knights of Labor. Samuel Gompers invoked symbolism of the American Revolution when he proclaimed that "May 1st would be forever remembered as a second declaration of independence," but events were to prove his prediction wrong. Thousands of striking workers did win concessions of eight hours of work for eight, nine, or ten hours of pay, and although many manufacturers attempted to rescind these gains once the crisis had passed, the trade unions had been strengthened and were able to maintain many of the gains. In exchange, however, they largely repudiated socialism and radicalism. Two incidents helped to strengthen this resolve. On 5 May state militia troops opened fire on striking Polish American Knights of Labor in Milwaukee, who had refused to stay off the streets in the wake of the Haymarket bombing. Nine laborers were killed.[40]

More significant for the labor movement was the Haymarket Square bombing, where the anarchists' violent rhetoric appeared to be coming to fruition. The tragic events outside the McCormick Reaper Factory on 3 May 1886 and at Haymarket Square the following day hastened the break within the labor movement. Workers and policemen were killed and wounded, although the *Chicago Tribune* largely ignored the working-class casualties. The men arrested, with the exception of Albert Parsons and Oskar Neebe, were, conveniently, foreign-born radicals. The Haymarket bombing gave Chicago's business leaders the ammunition they needed to rid the city of the trouble-making anarchists. Historians have argued persuasively that the eight men eventually made to stand trial for the Haymarket bombing were chosen not so much on the basis of their actual deeds or ideas as because of their leadership in the radical labor movement.[41]

Although radicals faced job loss and severe repression in the aftermath of Haymarket, in Chicago and elsewhere they refused to concede defeat. To underscore their continued commitment to revolution, they maintained their annual commune festivals. Moreover, they made 11 November, the anniversary of the executions of four of the Haymarket defendants, the holiest of their holidays, with graveside exercises in Chicago and meetings, music, and oratory elsewhere. As on Memorial Day, women carried floral wreaths to lay on the martyrs' tomb and speakers extolled the heroism of the slain. Much as the former Confederates on their Memorial Days, holiday orators sought to vindicate the Haymarket martyrs and their cause. Echoing Memorial Day speakers, an orator at Chicago's 1890 exercises implored his listeners to "[r]emember that those boys stood there and sacrificed their lives for the freedom of those left behind." Anarchists averred that they were the truest Americans. Voltairine de Cleyre asserted that the martyrs' only crime was a uniquely American one. They had preached "that real justice and real liberty might come on earth; that it was all false, all unnecessary, this wild waste of human life, . . . this turning of people into human rags." To make their pleas for vindication and remembrance more plaintive, the anarchists, like the Civil War veterans, trotted out their own veterans, widows, and orphans. In

Chicago in 1893, Albert Parsons Jr. unveiled the monument to his father and the other Haymarket martyrs. Oskar Neebe, who had been pardoned in 1893, presided over the 1895 Martyrs' Day meeting in Chicago, and the widowed Lucy Parsons was a regular speaker on this and other anarchist holidays.[42]

AN ALTERNATIVE LABOR HOLIDAY

In addition to staging their own commemorations, the radical labor unions continued their bid to capture the trade union movement from within. One way they did so, as in 1886, was to participate in (and to seek to control) mass labor demonstrations such as those for the eight-hour day. In 1889 the AFL renewed agitation for the shorter day and inadvertently set in motion the forces that would culminate in the first international May Day. The federation set 1 May 1890 for a general strike for enforcement of the eight-hour day. To build support for the movement, the federation followed the time-honored tradition of lending it legitimacy by linking it to the American revolutionary past, scheduling rallies for Washington's Birthday 1889 and 1890, the Fourth of July 1889, and Labor Day 1889. On the first of these occasions, some 240 mass meetings across the nation endorsed the AFL's action, including one sponsored by the Trades and Labor Assembly in Chicago, which featured speeches by Henry Demarest Lloyd and two local ministers, all of whom endorsed the movement for higher wages and shorter hours. The fourth speaker, E. S. Darrell, appeared to harbor some misgivings about the trade unions' new practical philosophy, as he stressed that, while the eight-hour day was a big step in the right direction, it was not a permanent solution to the labor question. The speakers made no overt connection between George Washington and the eight-hour movement, apparently allowing the symbolism of the date to stand alone.[43]

The AFL sponsored more than three hundred meetings and demonstrations around the country on the following Fourth of July. Chicago's prominence in the labor movement was evident by the presence of AFL president Samuel Gompers on the speakers' stand. Joining him to demonstrate the various forces uniting behind the eight-hour movement were the city's mayor, a congressman, Lloyd, and two radical socialists. Once again the speeches centered on the benefits of the eight-hour day more than its overt connections with American independence, although Mayor DeWitt Cregier, obviously trying to walk the political tightrope between labor and capital, "confin[ed] himself to some patriotic remarks about Independence Day" and hoped his presence would suggest more. The socialists, who spoke in German and Danish, took a typically more aggressive stance; one avowed that he was "tired of hearing these theories. Let us, at last, have action." The movement accelerated with the coming of Labor Day, which occasioned more than four hundred demonstrations nationwide, including separate parades and picnics in Chicago by the Trades and Labor Assembly and the Knights of Labor. The final holiday before 1 May, Washington's Birthday 1890, saw another blitz of meetings.[44]

Socialists joined the 1889–90 eight-hour movement relatively late, but once they did, they supported it enthusiastically. In 1889 the newly established Second International adopted the resolution of a French delegate for a "great international demonstration" for the eight-hour day to take place on 1 May 1890, the date the AFL had already selected. The AFL, meanwhile, had begun to back away from the general strike, which had the potential to turn violent, as in 1867 and 1886, and might easily spin out of the federation's control. The national organization dropped the plan for a general strike in favor of a more practical strategy, in keeping with its support of tactical strikes. The union with the best chance of winning would strike on 1 May, and on each succeeding May Day another union would strike, until all trades had won the eight-hour day. The Brotherhood of Carpenters and Joiners, which had a large strike fund, was chosen to inaugurate the May Day strikes.[45]

A good portion of Chicago's laborers turned out for the city's demonstration on 1 May 1890. If the 1886 demonstration had been dominated by radicals, this time the pragmatic trade unionists controlled the day. As promised, the carpenters were the only men on strike in Chicago, and Michael Hardy of the Bricklayers' Union took great pains to assure his audience from the speakers' stand that "[t]he present movement was not a strike." An estimated ten thousand workers, accompanied by bands, paraded through the city's streets, and some twenty-five thousand listened to sympathetic politicians and labor leaders discourse on the justice of the eight-hour movement and the need for political solidarity among labor. Although the Central Labor

Union cosponsored the demonstration with the Trades and Labor Assembly, the oratory and overall message bore the strong imprint of the trade unionists. The speakers emphasized the peaceful resolution of labor problems and praised the lack of violence in the carpenters' strike, and the marchers demonstrated their patriotism, as they had in recent Labor Day parades, by waving the red, white, and blue. This Americanism extended to language as well; although some German unions bore placards in their native tongue, all the speeches at the lakefront were in English. W. H. Kliver of the striking union perhaps best summed up the links between organized labor, capital, and patriotic citizenship that the AFL had begun to forge: "Capital cannot get along without labor any more than labor without capital. We did not want to strike. We were forced to it."[46]

Organized labor, Kliver suggested, sought not to overthrow capitalism but only to take labor's rightful place in the system. The villain of the day was not capital but only the president of the Carpenters' and Builders' Association, who had refused to grant the striking carpenters the eight-hour day. Another villain was Mayor Cregier, who after his lukewarm support at the Fourth of July rally the year before failed to appear at the May Day demonstration. Speakers damned him as a coward who would not address the workers who had helped him win the previous year's election. The mayor apparently received the workers' message loud and clear, as he made himself visible at the following Labor Day celebration. The damage had been done, however; he was not reelected. Instead, Hempstead Washburne, who had spoken in favor of the eight-hour day at the 1890 Washington's Birthday rally, became the city's next mayor.[47]

There were dissenters from the rosy picture of labor-capital cooperation. In addition to the inevitable opposition of socialists and anarchists, the upcoming world's fair, the World's Columbian Exposition, came under fire from some workers. The fair, said one speaker, would benefit not the workingmen but "the railroad corporations, the hotelkeepers, the saloonkeepers, and the millionaires who control the land that surrounds us." The minimal impact of this viewpoint on the Trades and Labor Assembly, however, was demonstrated by its invitation to the fair's "millionaire directors" to review its Labor Day parade four months later.[48]

Although Chicago had one of the largest May Day demonstrations, the city was by no means alone. The messages of the day ranged from the conciliation with capital preached by Chicago's trade unionists to calls for social revolution by socialists and anarchists in New York City, Berlin, and Madrid. The AFL's strategy appeared to pay off, as more than forty-six thousand carpenters nationwide won the eight-hour day as a result of the 1890 strike. This success led to the spread of May Day throughout the industrialized world. By 1891 Samuel Gompers was calling May Day an "institution" and a "new Independence Day," and the AFL continued throughout the 1890s to promote 1 May as a time for renewal of eight-hour agitation.[49]

The *Chicago Tribune*, never a friend of labor, expressed uneasiness with this newest labor holiday, for it was already considered such. "[N]ow May-Day has taken on a new complexion," it mused in 1890. "It asserts itself as the new Labor-Day. It is the day on which labor rises up and makes demands. It wants eight hours for a day's work now. It makes no promises as to what it will want in the future." The paper's misgivings bore fruit as, despite the AFL's backing, May Day quickly became an international socialist holiday. In Chicago in 1891, for example, the music of choice in the procession was the socialists' hymn, the "Marseillaise." In contrast to the previous year's demonstrations, workers heard speeches in German, Czech, and Polish as well as English. The crowd unanimously adopted resolutions acknowledging the international character of the labor movement and calling upon the city to enforce its eight-hour ordinance. The *Chicago Tribune* predictably wrote disparagingly that "[t]he labor celebration of May day lacked the enthusiasm that makes the Sept. 1 hurrah of the Chicago workingman a thing to be remembered," attributing this to the fact that the "procession was distinctively socialistic in character."[50]

TWO VISIONS OF WORKING-CLASS AMERICANISM

May Day was never recognized as a legal holiday in the United States on the state or national level, and as it became more closely associated with international socialism, nonsocialist trade unions withdrew from the celebration. Because American unions had already established a holiday for labor, it was perhaps only natural that May Day as an annual holiday was less popular than in other nations. By contrast, American workers adopted Labor Day quite rapidly and painlessly as the American labor holiday in the 1880s and 1890s. In 1887 Oregon became the first state to legalize the holiday; by 1894, when the federal government made it a legal holiday, thirty-one states had recognized Labor Day.[51]

Like the AFL, Labor Day was the beneficiary of the post-Haymarket repression of radicalism. May Day, like socialism, became its victim. The federal government's endorsement of Labor Day sealed the fate of May Day as an interest group holiday in the United States, tainted by its connection with socialism. By enacting the holiday, the states and the federal government made a symbolic concession to the rights of workers in exchange for their eschewing of the theory of social revolution that animated the socialists and their sympathizers. Government officials thus gave tacit support to the AFL's policy of practical unionism. The Labor Day legislation may also be read as clever political strategy. By sanctioning the holiday, federal and state lawmakers recognized and catered to the growing power of the workers' vote, but the legislation did nothing to force employers to grant their workers a paid holiday. "All admit," the *Chicago Daily Socialist* noted in 1909, "that when a man knocks off work on Labor Day his time is also knocked off the time sheet." Legislators thus effectively straddled the line between the demands of labor and capital. Socialists recognized the complicity of labor and capital involved in the legalization of the holiday and abhorred it as destructive to the spirit of Labor Day. "The original idea of an assertive working class demonstration," the *Chicago Daily Socialist* editorialized in 1903, "has been destroyed by the demagogues who made it a 'legal' holiday."[52]

The two holidays diverged in the 1890s, paralleling the widening gulf between the craft unionism of the AFL and the radicalism of socialist unions. While socialists made May Day an occasion to preach social revolution, the self-consciously apolitical AFL, which accepted the permanence of industrial capitalism and sought primarily to improve the condition of skilled wage earners, emerged as the leading force behind Labor Day and transformed it into a vehicle for its pragmatic philosophy. Thus, by the turn of the century, each holiday had become a forum for the construction of a working-class Americanism that embodied the ideology of its sponsoring unions.

In the late 1880s and 1890s, leaders of the declining Knights of Labor and the surging AFL united with their employers and elected officials to make

Labor Day a microcosm of the new pragmatic labor ideology. Therein lies the secret of the rapid acceptance of Labor Day. It became an occasion to celebrate the American laborer, who was in partnership with capital rather than opposed to it, who used nonviolent strikes as tactical maneuvers to gain practical benefits, not to attack industrial capitalism, and who prided himself on being a patriotic, flag-waving American, who would not tolerate the red flag of radicalism. And "himself" it was in general; the craft unions of the AFL remained for the most part closed to women, as well as African Americans and semiskilled and unskilled workers.

On May Day, in contrast, socialists and anarchists condemned capitalism and called for its overthrow, whether by peaceful political means or by revolution. "The spirit of May Day is revolutionary," asserted Ralph Korngold in the *Chicago Daily Socialist* in 1911. "It speaks defiance to the capitalist class."[53] May Day revelers waved the red flag proudly and made common cause with workers all over the industrial world. The international character of the day, in an age in which internationalism was a suspect philosophy, and its adoption as an alternative Labor Day by socialists made May Day suspicious in the eyes of many Americans. The nativism that dogged the socialist movement played a prominent role as well in May Day's failure to catch on in the United States. The dominance of the day by socialists, anarchists, and immigrants made it easy for most Americans to dismiss May Day as a socialist and foreign holiday.

Americans thus ended up with two Labor Days that reflected the growing divisions within the labor movement and that offered disparate visions of working-class Americanism. The pragmatic and the radical unionists' visions did dovetail on several critical points. Both enshrined productive labor as the key to American prosperity and to the very success of the nation, and both claimed to be the true heirs of the American republican tradition. Craft unionists and socialists each sought for workers the rightful fruits of their labor. They agreed that labor unions were necessary to attaining the latter goal, and despite socialist ideology, both movements were dominated by skilled craftsmen. Perhaps most significantly, both posited unions as the sine qua non of working-class identity and solidarity.

The pragmatic and the radical unionists diverged most sharply on labor's relationship to capital. The AFL sought employers' acknowledgment of the indispensability of labor, especially skilled labor, for which radicals accused the federation of bowing submissively before capital. The AFL saw the situation differently. Although the federation accepted the legitimacy of capital, it took the position that labor constituted an equal partner of capital, not a junior or submissive partner. When capitalists reviewed Labor Day processions, that signified to the AFL capital's acceptance of the equal partnership and of the centrality of labor. In the socialist view, no such partnership was possible. Capital could only be the enemy of labor and thus of the republic and, as such, must be eliminated. To socialists, then, to have capitalists review workers' processions made a mockery of working-class Americanism.

The AFL's determinedly nonideological, practical focus made for an oddly classless working-class identity, devoid of the oppositional consciousness of socialists and anarchists. Nevertheless, it was clearly a working-class identity, albeit one that privileged an elite subset of labor, the skilled craftsman, as the quintessential worker. Unskilled laborers, far from sharing a common identity with skilled workers, posed a threat to their class identity. Radicals, in contrast, remained adamantly ideological, insisted on the overthrow of capitalism as the ultimate goal of all workers, and defined workers much more inclusively as those who worked for wages, whether skilled or unskilled, male or female, black or white, immigrant or native born.

The central feature of both Labor Day and May Day was the procession of unions, with members wearing uniforms, bearing the tools of their trades, and occasionally reenacting those trades on floats. Union leaders intended the massed workers to show the strength of organized labor to capitalists and politicians, as well as to unorganized workers whom they sought to recruit. Making a strong showing on labor holidays was so important that some unions fined members for not participating. In Chicago in 1900, for example, the Building Trades Council threatened to fine members $5 for not marching in the Labor Day parade.[54]

As this action suggests, the procession constituted the most significant element of both Labor Day and May Day celebrations, because it was the central vehicle for conveying working-class Americanism to unorganized workers and persuading them to join the ranks of organized labor. However they differed ideologically, all unions posited union membership as the core of this identity. To organized labor, the union was synonymous with working-class unity and strength. Visiting Scottish socialist Keir Hardie told Labor Day celebrants in 1895 that socialists "believe in the organization of labor in the trade unions" and warned that any worker who was "not a member of the union of the trade to which he belongs . . . is practically ranging himself on the side of the millionaire, on the side of the sweater, on the side of every enemy of honest labor." Not only union membership but also the consumption of union-made products became a test of working-class loyalty and solidarity. At the Labor Day picnic sponsored by Chicago's Knights of Labor and Trades and Labor Assembly in 1886, for example, union men attacked and demolished a stand whose proprietor was allegedly selling nonunion cigars. Radicals as well condemned workers who failed to support unions. The bakers' banner in Chicago's 1891 May Day procession asserted that "[u]nion men should eat only union bread."[55]

In addition to affirming the centrality of unions, banners revealed the ideological divisions within the working class. Whereas socialists favored banners with such revolutionary sentiments as "He who would be free must strike the blow" and "Workers of the World Unite," practical unionists preferred to focus on unionism's compatibility and partnership with capitalism. The *Chicago Tribune* reported approvingly of the 1886 Labor Day procession that "the strongly-worded mottoes and transparencies so common in former labor demonstrations were not to be seen." The paper noted that the banners of the Trades and Labor Assembly and the Knights of Labor bore prolabor but noncontroversial slogans such as "Cooperation Is the Remedy for Strikes" and "Organized Labor Is the Bulwark of the Republic." In the wake of Haymarket, those unions also redoubled their efforts to demonstrate the patriotism of organized labor. Steamfitters in Chicago's 1890 Labor Day parade suggested that patriotism and unionism were indivisible with a red, white, and blue banner bearing the inscription "We are Union men and carry Union colors." In the wake of the Spanish-American War, patriotism even took pride of place over unionism; an 1898 Labor Day banner proclaimed, "Our country will ever be first; our union next."[56]

The uniforms worn and accessories carried by union members further emphasized the unity and discipline of the working class. Some wore actual work clothes or variations thereon, but virtually all unions had some identifying clothing or badge. Members of individual unions thus presented a

Tinsmiths in the Pullman, Illinois, Labor Day parade, 1901. The tinsmiths wear tin hats and carry tin umbrellas, thus demonstrating their craft. (Courtesy of the Chicago Public Library, Special Collections and Preservation Division)

striking vision of solidarity, marching as a uniformed group, much as Civil War veterans did on Memorial Day. Painters dressed in the white overalls of their trade, blacksmiths wore their leather aprons, and butchers looked jaunty in their freshly washed red and white checked smocks. Other unions chose fancy attire rather than work clothing. Printers in Tucson, for example, donned white suits and hats that could not have withstood an hour in the print shop, while bridge and structural ironworkers in Chicago struck a dandified note in 1898 in "blue flannel blouses and brown fedora hats, red, white, and blue cravats, and a boutonnière and silk badge." Marchers also carried or wore indicators of their trade to demonstrate their pride in their class and craft. Some carried tools of their trade; plumbers bore turnkeys, for instance, while boilermakers shouldered their hammers like muskets. Others showed the products of their labor: cigarmakers carried cigars; brushmakers displayed their brushes; and tin, sheet-iron, and cornice workers carried tin umbrellas they had crafted.[57]

Rather than displaying their tools or carrying their products, other unions chose to demonstrate physically the vitality and importance of their trade by having selected members enact their craft on floats. Blue-jeaned machinists in one Tucson Labor Day parade operated a lathe on their float, which also included a functioning engine spouting smoke. Not to be outdone, boiler-makers noisily riveted a boiler. In other processions, horseshoers shod horses, barbers gave shaves, plasterers plastered walls and ceilings, and brick-layers laid bricks. In Detroit caulkers caulked the deck of a small boat, and in Chicago one year typecasters handed out souvenirs, reportedly pelting the crowd "with lowercase 'm's' and 'w's.'" In the smaller May Day processions, the story was similar. On May Day 1891, for example, German printers printed and distributed handbills advocating the eight-hour day.[58]

These holiday performances by skilled workers had a long history in the United States, dating back at least to the artisans who constituted the central feature of the Constitution ratification processions in 1788.[59] By demonstrat-ing their crafts before unorganized workers, capitalists, and other parade-goers, union members showcased their contribution to the American repub-lic—the skilled labor that literally made it work. While industrialists and financiers might congratulate themselves at world's fairs for the nation's moral and economic progress, organized labor knew better. On their holiday floats, they showed that the printers who kept the presses going, the machinists who kept the industrial machinery turning, the bricklayers who laid the very foun-dations of American business were the ones really responsible for that progress. Since the Revolution, America had been defined in terms of useful citizenship, and on their holidays unions showcased the productivity that they asserted made the working class the most useful group of citizens and thus the epitome of Americanism. The irony that many of the traditional crafts were currently under assault by industrialists seeking to increase pro-ductivity was not lost on organized labor and, indeed, lent urgency to the in-sistence of the holiday demonstrators that their crafts remained a vital and es-sential component of national progress.

Although both Labor Day and May Day processions centered on masses of uniformed workers and craft floats, the parades sponsored by radical and practical unionists sported notable differences, not least of which was the trend among the latter of inviting representatives of capital to participate. In a move undercutting the message of their craft floats, some trade unions began to invite businesses to enter advertising floats in Labor Day parades. Chicago's Trades and Labor Assembly had done so at its first parade in 1885. Although these floats displayed products made by workers, the emphasis had shifted from the process of making the product (the labor) to the object itself as something to be consumed. In 1886 the assembly announced that the "principal feature" of its Labor Day procession was to be not the union marchers themselves but "a grand industrial parade, to which a cordial invitation is extended to all manufacturers and business firms to participate and thereby exhibit their productions." By giving this advance notice, the celebration committee trusted "that no inconvenience to business will result."[60]

Some of the unions also demonstrated the shift in emphasis to consumption by showing what their products would do for consumers rather than the skill that went into making them. The soapmakers' float in 1886, for example, bore a washtub in which sat "a young negro stripped to the waist and buried beneath a layer of soap suds," who was being scrubbed by "a good, fat, and very black 'aunty,'" to the general hilarity of the crowd. Through this display the union itself seemed to accept the switch from a producer ethos to a consumer ethos then gaining steam in the United States. The float played on a well-worn racial stereotype of African Americans as dirty, one that would be used with great success in the N. K. Fairbanks Company's Gold Dust Twins advertisements. African Americans were relegated by the soapmakers, as they would be by the emerging profession of advertising, to the role of comic relief for the spectators. In the craft union vision of working-class Americanism, African Americans, who remained barred from joining most trade unions, could play only a supporting role. In the South this was overtly stated. On Labor Day 1890, for instance, the *Richmond Dispatch* praised the new holiday, explaining that "Richmond has as much pride in the excellence of her white working people as in any other of the many clear advantages she possesses."[61] Even in Chicago, however, the color line was drawn as early as 1886, as the soapmakers' float makes clear.

The introduction of advertising cars into Labor Day parades seemed to relegate even the skilled white workers honored on Labor Day to the supporting role of consumers in the world of goods being fashioned by manufacturers and retailers. Some unionists apparently saw more clearly than the soapmakers that this trend of glorifying the product of their labor, rather than the labor itself, deemphasized and ultimately devalued the laborer's craft. That same year the Pullman Knights of Labor assemblies declined to celebrate with their Chicago compatriots because of their disinclination to march before one of George Pullman's cars. A "prominent union man" at the postparade picnic sided with the company, however, not the workers. "The Pullman Company was not to blame for [the workers' absence]," he asserted. "To be sure they wanted a magnificent car they were building displayed in the procession, and the men kicked against that on the supposition that it would be giving glory to a corporation." But, he concluded, "this was foolish, for whatever attention the car, because of its beauty, would attract, could only reflect credit on the men who fashioned and built it."[62] This position implied a subtle but serious alteration in the working-class identity propounded by pragmatic unionists. It was but a short step from workers parading behind the product they had made to the advertising floats that held only the product, removing the worker entirely from the notice of spectators.

Although advertising floats remained a relatively minor part of Labor Day processions, they altered the day's purpose in another serious way as well. If the unions targeted the unorganized workers who watched the parades as potential union members, the businesses who sponsored advertising floats clearly saw both spectators and marchers as potential consumers of their products. The products they displayed grew increasingly divorced from the workers who had made them. In Tucson the 1905 Labor Day procession prominently featured the massed display of consumer goods, including furniture, clothing, shoes, and hardware, by a local department store. Department stores were becoming the central institutions of the emergent consumer society and the ones most responsible for the consumer society's illusion that products appeared magically from nowhere, produced by no one.[63] Such exhibits, whose blatant promotion of the consumer society seemed to undercut Labor Day's focus on the workers who produced the goods, were anathema to socialists and anarchists, who refused to share their holiday space with the capitalists they opposed. To many, if not all, pragmatic unionists, however, advertising wagons, like capitalist parade reviewers, demonstrated the interdependence of capital and labor and the partnership between employers and employees.

The flags and music of the holiday processions provided additional evidence of the ideological nature of the participants' class identity. Bearing the U.S. flag demonstrated that workers were patriotic Americans who contributed to American prosperity. The socialist red flag proclaimed workers' commitment to socialism, the internationalization of the working class, and the belief in the opposition of capital and labor. And the foreign flags sometimes flown by ethnic unions demonstrated their pride in their ethnicity and continued attachment to their homelands. These flags mingled at early Labor Day parades and continued to do so at May Day celebrations. After the Haymarket Square bombing, however, Labor Day took on a definitive red, white, and blue cast, as pragmatic craft unionists discouraged other flags, particularly the red flag of socialism, and sometimes banned them outright. The *Chicago Tribune* reported in 1886 that "[t]he Stars and Stripes fluttered at the head of all the leading organizations, but not a red flag was to be seen." Moreover, the German American branch of the Typographical Union "[t]o show their loyalty to American principles . . . carried only the Stars and Stripes at their head." These displays of patriotism increased in the 1890s as patriotic societies proliferated and created new rituals of flag veneration. Pragmatic unionists jumped on the bandwagon, eager to adopt this visible badge of Americanism. The *Chicago Tribune* reported that in the Trades and Labor Assembly's 1893 Labor Day parade "there was but one flag—the Stars and Stripes. . . . There were no black flags [of anarchy] or red flags, no emblems of violence, incendiarism, murder and revolution." Marchers not only waved American flags but also dressed in the national colors. Ironworkers wore red, white, and blue cravats; junior steamfitters carried red, white, and blue umbrellas; and others bore badges and insignia in the American colors.[64]

If partisans managed to sneak flags other than the Stars and Stripes into Labor Day celebrations, other union men or spectators dispensed patriotic justice. For example, at a Labor Day parade in Pittsburgh in 1890, the German American Bakers' Union carried a German flag. Members of the Junior Order of United American Mechanics demanded that they furl the flag, and when they refused, a free-for-all ensued between the bakers and mechanics.

Woodworkers in the Pullman, Illinois, Labor Day parade, 1901. The prominent placement of the American flag demonstrates organized labor's patriotism. (Courtesy of the Chicago Public Library, Special Collections and Preservation Division)

The Germans, although assisted by a German American police officer, lost the fight and watched as the patriotic mob tore the offending flag to shreds, shouting "America for Americans" and "the Stars and Stripes the only banner on our streets." In Chicago two years later the vice president of the Trades and Labor Assembly warned on the eve of Labor Day that "[i]t won't be the police or military, but the strong arm of organized labor that will take any man by the throat and strangle him tomorrow if he attempts to trail the Stars and Stripes in the dust."[65]

The frenzied patriotism of the 1890s drove some socialists to condemn the American flag they had always defended. Like the American government, gripped in the vise of the capitalist parties, the American standard had become the captive of the enemy. At 1895 May Day exercises, Thomas J. Morgan denounced the flag waving of the nonsocialist unions, declaring that "[t]he American flag . . . was invented by the bosses to act as a sort of new suit for them to dress their slaves in." In reaction against this hyperpatriotism, socialists turned more exclusively to the socialist banner. In 1910 the *Chicago Daily Socialist* noted that "crimson flags waved aloft over all" in the

May Day procession. Marchers and spectators sported red boutonnieres, ribbons, sashes, handkerchiefs, and hatbands. Showing their colors even on such occasions subjected socialists to unwelcome scrutiny. The *Chicago Tribune* complained in 1895 that celebrants at the Socialist Labor Party's Sunday Labor Day picnic "flaunt[ed] a red flag" given to the party by socialist women. City officials, fearing that the socialists would try to parade the banner through city streets, sent a detachment of police to the picnic grounds "to see that no red flag parade started out from that point."[66]

The music played by marching bands further defined the unionists' America. On May Day the air filled with the strains of the French revolutionary hymn, the "Marseillaise," the favored anthem of socialists. After Chicago's 1910 procession, the *Chicago Daily Socialist* reported, "[o]ne organization after another entered the gates of the park singing the 'Marseillaise.'" In contrast, at the Labor Day celebrations of the pragmatic unions, such patriotic airs as "America," "Hail Columbia," and the national anthem prevailed. But radicals appropriated American patriotic songs as well, for they continued to believe themselves to be truer to American principles than capitalists were. On May Day 1891, for example, members of the socialist Cloakmakers' Union in Chicago played and sang "America" and "John Brown's Body" in procession. Although the *Chicago Tribune* had little use for the celebration, it did express gratitude that the cloakmakers sang "so stoutly that the chorus of the 'Marseillaise' was almost drowned."[67]

The pragmatic unionists' emphasis on their patriotism was more than a ploy to avoid attacks in the wake of Haymarket or an indication that workers were swept up in the patriotic delirium of the 1890s. They, like socialists, craved acceptance of themselves and their unions as an indispensable component of American society and economic progress. One way of acquiring such legitimacy was through the recognition of capitalists and major party politicians. Socialists rejected out of hand the authority of both and thus wanted them only to view socialist celebrations from a distance, with fear and trembling for the future of capitalist America. But to the pragmatic unionists, who accepted capitalism and still sought to work through political channels to achieve their ends, acceptance and even approval were necessary. Thus, whereas the organizers of the first Labor Day had refused to invite representatives of capital or government to their celebration, AFL-affiliated city trade councils invited both to review their Labor Day processions. In one of the most stunning examples, Chicago's Trades and Labor Assembly in 1890 invited the "millionaire Fair Directors" (of the 1893 World's Columbian Exposition) to sit on the reviewing stand. Rather than viewing this invitation as submission, as socialists did, nonsocialist workers reveled in the power such reviewers imputed to organized labor. The president of the Chicago Federation of Labor claimed in an 1898 Labor Day speech that "Labor day was not inaugurated for the purpose of giving the workingman an opportunity for recreation only, but for the additional purpose of showing the upper crust of society that laboring men [are] not slaves."[68]

As the potential political power of unions increased, mayors and congressmen found it an essential campaign strategy to accept such invitations. After being castigated as a no-show at Chicago's May Day demonstration in 1890, for example, Mayor DeWitt Cregier put in an appearance at Labor Day exercises, giving an impromptu speech in which he reinforced the pragmatic unionists' classless vision of class by telling them that "under this broad and starry banner there is no caste." By the 1890s gubernatorial and even presidential candidates were reviewing Labor Day parades in major urban industrial centers such as Chicago and New York City. In one of the most stunning instances of courting the labor vote, vice presidential candidate Theodore Roosevelt and presidential candidate William Jennings Bryan sat together in the reviewing stand on a Chicago Labor Day just two months before the 1900 election.[69]

Socialists, who derided party politicians as agents of capital, refused to invite any but avowed radicals to review their processions, and they steadfastly refused to parade "as slaves before the plutocrats and capitalists." Instead, socialist leaders such as New York City journalist John Swinton and Chicago politician and labor leader Thomas J. Morgan reviewed their Labor Day and May Day marchers. Socialists fought tooth and nail against trade federation plans to have capitalists review joint parades. In 1892, for example, Chicago's Cloakmakers' Union vehemently protested the Trades and Labor Assembly's plan to parade before "politicians of the capitalistic parties" and withdrew from its Labor Day procession. A violent argument ensued on the floor of the assembly, but the pragmatists won the battle, and the assembly's president announced that any organization that insulted the flag or the speakers would be barred from the parade. Socialists refused to believe that parading before capitalists could do anything but degrade workers and make a mockery of their holidays. In 1903 the *Chicago Daily Socialist* noted with disgust that at the Building Trades Council's Labor Day celebration "an aspirant for the Republican nomination for governor and a colonel of the militia will orate to the fool workers whose celebration has become a sham."[70]

Despite their ideological conflicts, socialist and pragmatic unions agreed that one of the most important aims of Labor Day and May Day processions was to recruit unorganized workers to the union fold. The unorganized majority played the part of spectator on the holidays, imbibing, if not necessarily accepting, the scripted construction of working-class Americanism and the absolute indispensability of unions to it. Socialists most blatantly used the holidays as occasions to proselytize the unorganized as well as nonsocialist union members. In 1902, for example, the *Chicago Daily Socialist* reported that most of Chicago's socialist orators had been engaged to speak before trade unions on Labor Day. The paper explained that the unions had two reasons for parading on Labor Day. The first was "to show the employers the strength of union labor," and the second was "to encourage the thousands of unorganized laborers who turn out to view the parade to be part of it the following year." For socialists, simply providing a model to the spectators was not sufficient. In addition to parading, they actively worked on labor holidays to recruit workers to the cause. Each year the *Chicago Daily Socialist* published a huge run of special Labor Day and May Day issues, which it exhorted radical workers to purchase (at $7.50 per one thousand) and to distribute to marchers and spectators. "Let every Socialist do his part in the distribution of literature and papers," the paper urged, "and the seed planted on this Labor Day cannot fail to bring a splendid harvest." In 1902 socialists reportedly gave out forty thousand copies along the parade route in Chicago.[71]

After the work of marching and proselytizing, union members and spectators retired to picnic grounds for speeches, food and drink, and various amusements. The twin aims of building working-class unity and recruiting new workers made oratory a central feature at both socialist and pragmatic picnics. The politicians who shared the reviewing stand with labor leaders also shared oratorical duties at the postparade exercises. In Richmond in 1900, for example, the mayor and the Virginia attorney general spoke to

Labor Day parade, meat cutters, Yards, 1908. The butchers of Chicago's stockyards wear their colorful red and white checked smocks. Among the crowd socialists are no doubt seeking converts. (Courtesy of the Chicago Historical Society, negative number DN-53253)

Labor Day celebrants. That same year both Theodore Roosevelt and William Jennings Bryan addressed the Chicago revelers. Socialist picnics likewise featured the oratory of sympathetic politicians such as Scottish socialist and former member of Parliament Keir Hardie, Chicago's own socialist mayoral candidate, Thomas J. Morgan, and Wisconsin's socialist candidate for Congress, Victor L. Berger. In addition to the politicians, the main holiday orators at both socialist and nonsocialist celebrations included union leaders such as Morgan, Samuel Gompers, and Andrew Cameron. At Chicago's 1886 Labor Day exercises, for example, Knights of Labor Grand Lecturer A. A. Carleton shared the rostrum with Congressman Frank Lawler and other politicians. Carleton praised the patriotic "industrial army of peace" and asserted that, unlike the anarchists, they sought "not to destroy or tear down, but to build up." In contrast, socialist speakers, according to the *Chicago Daily Socialist*, "told the toilers to take all they are entitled to." Speakers at socialist celebrations included anarchists Lucy Parsons, Voltairine de Cleyre, and, after their pardon, two of the surviving Haymarket defendants, Oskar Neebe and Michael Schwab. In 1902 the *Chicago Daily Socialist* advertised that Mother Jones was to speak at the Labor Day picnic sponsored by the Women's Alliance of the Socialist Party.[72]

Despite the fact that a significant percentage of union members in Chicago were not native English speakers, the oratory at the celebrations of pragmatic trade unions and Knights of Labor was typically in English only. In contrast, at radical picnics one was as likely to hear addresses in German, Czech, Norwegian, and a variety of other foreign languages as in English. The *Chicago Daily Socialist* noted that at the Socialist Party's 1910 Labor Day picnic, for example, "addresses were made in all languages." Although socialist unions may have drawn a larger proportion of their members from among immigrant workers, given their more inclusive membership policies, that alone cannot explain this discrepancy. Certainly nonsocialist trade unions and the Knights of Labor counted many German Americans and Scandinavian Americans among their members. The more mainstream the politicians were who spoke at unions' celebrations, one imagines, the less likely they would be to orate in a foreign language; one can hardly picture Theodore Roosevelt addressing the crowd in German or Norwegian. The deliberate use of English might also have been part of the same strategy as the proliferating American flags—to show that workers were just as patriotic and just as American as capitalists. The socialists' convention of having speakers address the workers in a variety of languages similarly had ideological and strategic functions. That gesture expressed the internationalism of the movement while it also addressed the problem of trying to spread the word to immigrant workers whose grasp of English was often minimal at best.[73]

Although oratory composed an essential characteristic of the picnics, unions knew that workers had no desire to spend an entire afternoon listening to speakers. After all, the union celebrations faced the same competition for revelers' time and money as did Memorial Day exercises. The picnics thus featured recreational activities designed to appeal to workers' craving for amusement in their rare free time. For a good many workers, "eight hours for what we will" meant more time for entertainment and play. Many were loathe to devote their holiday from work to marching and listening to speeches. Indeed, one reason why unions instituted fines for not parading on Labor Day was low participation. Despite the fine threatened by the Building Trades Council in Chicago, for example, only about one-tenth of the membership marched in 1900. Acceding to their members' demands, unions had by the turn of the century begun to decrease the number of speakers and to incorporate more games, sporting events, and other amusements into their holiday celebrations. As the Nashville Banner observed in 1892, laborers preferred to watch "feats of physical strength and endurance rather than have their minds burdened with some intricate question relative to the solving of the labor problem."[74]

As early as 1887, the pragmatic unionists bowed to the nonideological nature of the new trade unionism and the realities of the popular taste in amusements. In Chicago that year, the Trades and Labor Assembly and the Knights of Labor "decided at the last moment to have no speech-making," as the crowd of thirty-five thousand that filled the picnic grove "was in no mood to listen to vague platitudes about the labor movement." Rather, the workers jammed the dance pavilion, the wheels of fortune, and the beer stands. As with Chicago's Memorial Day bicycle race, sporting events became an increasingly important part of labor holidays, whether within or outside of the confines of union celebrations. In Boston woodcarver Charles E. Adams watched but did not participate in the 1887 Labor Day procession. Afterward, he noted in his diary that he and a friend "went out to see the ball game between the Boston and the Philadelphias." In Richmond in 1890, members of fourteen white trade unions united for a Labor Day procession and then gathered afterward for food and a baseball game, eschewing oratory. Tucson's 1905 celebration featured a variety of races, a boxing match, a baseball game, and dancing in addition to the parade and speeches.[75]

Although the ideological and evangelical nature of socialism all but demanded oratory at holiday picnics, the number of speakers declined even at socialist celebrations. In 1909, for example, the Chicago Daily Socialist noted that there would be only one address at the Labor Day picnic because "picnickers are not much given to listening to speeches." Instead, the socialists of the twenty-second ward issued a challenge to any indoor baseball team willing to play against them at the picnic. The following year's Labor Day amusements included dancing, races, a tug of war, and a professional wrestling exhibit.[76]

Despite such appeals to workers' thirst for amusement over education, attendance at Labor Day and May Day processions and picnics dwindled, except in times of labor crisis. Chicago socialists in the early twentieth century had stopped sponsoring regular May Day processions; only the crisis fomented by the use of injunctions to crush organized labor spurred the parade in 1910. In the 1890s, not only did Chicago socialists and pragmatic unionists hold separate Labor Day celebrations, but also the Knights of Labor and various individual unions opted out of the Trades and Labor Assembly's exercises as well. In 1890, for example, the curriers and leather workers eschewed the assembly's procession for their own picnic, as did the Typographical Union and the Knights of Labor. The fragmentation of the Labor Day celebrations continued. In 1910 the city's AFL-affiliated unions failed to hold a Labor Day procession because only seventeen of the fifty-eight member unions had voted in favor of one. Similarly, Richmond's Central Trades and Labor Council had decided to drop its parade in 1895, instead urging workers "to regard the day as a day of rest." By the early twentieth century, the council's Labor Day celebration had become purely a recreational affair, featuring dancing, games, a sham battle, a baby contest, and bicycle, motorcycle, and horse races. The Central Trades and Labor Council had completely capitulated to workers' demands for amusement. In doing so, organized labor in Richmond had traded the ideological power of the holiday for the mass attendance of commercial recreation; in 1910 the council charged a ten-cent admission to its celebration.[77]

In addition to the ideological struggle for control of America's labor movement and the ongoing efforts to attract new members, organized labor had to fight the apathy of its own constituents on labor holidays. Not only could the various factions of the labor movement not agree on a definition of working-class Americanism, they could hardly get the bulk of the nation's workers to care. While workers certainly cared about their rights and wanted to improve working conditions, most did not see joining a union, an admittedly risky proposition at the turn of the century, as the best way of doing so. The seeming preference of many organized and unorganized workers for amusement over edification suggests that constructing working-class Americanism was less important to the rank and file than it was to union leaders. And as if ideological conflict and commercial competition did not provide sufficient threats to the development of class consciousness, organized labor had to face the compelling (and competing) pull of ethnicity on the growing majority of the working class who were immigrants or their children.

4

ETHNIC HOLIDAYS

*I*N 1911 AN EDITORIAL in a Chicago Polish-language newspaper, *Dziennik Zwiazkowy*, explained that the "[p]urpose of our [p]ublic [a]ddresses" on Polish national holidays was "to elevate the sleeping spirit of our compatriots, to stimulate and encourage them to be religious, to awaken in them a love for progress, enlightenment, and the homeland, and especially to present historical facts to the young people born on American soil." To the latter end, it was particularly important to "have school children and young people recite poems and sing during com-memorations," because "in this way they are encouraged to attend, thus becoming acquainted with Polish history and traditions." If that was not sufficient inducement to the second generation, the editor suggested that priests might bribe children to remember these holidays by offering them candy.[1]

Although the editorialist's topic was holiday oratory, he might have been speaking about ethnic holidays in general. Like the Fourth of July, the national holidays of immigrants and their children served first and foremost to construct national identity and to cultivate patriotism to the homeland. Ethnicity, particularly in the late nineteenth and early twentieth centuries, was closely related to nationalism. Indeed, recent scholarship has suggested that ethnicization in this period was in part a process of nationalization. While political refugees and many urban professionals and artisans came to America as ardent nationalists, most immigrants in this period, particularly peasants from southern and eastern Europe, possessed little sense of national identity. Rather, identities based on church and village allegiances prevailed. When immigrants came to America, ethnicity was ascribed by outsiders—Sicilians and Neapolitans became "Italians," for example. But the most significant source of nationalism came from within, from leaders of immigrant communities, who constructed ethnic nationalism out of the materials of their homelands and their adopted land.[2]

For emigrants separated from their homelands even more than for native-born Americans, the nation of origin constituted, in Benedict Anderson's words, an "imagined community." Immigrant nationalists worked to make that imagined community real by creating a unique heritage for their nation of origin out of carefully selected and interpreted history.[3] They taught this heritage on their national holidays, which, for immigrants as for Americans, served as the premier vehicles for constructing and articulating national identity. On such occasions the abstract imagined community was made temporarily concrete. Although the nationalists who sponsored such celebrations sought the participation of all members of a perceived ethnic group, the most crucial target, as the editorial suggests, was the younger generation, which lacked direct ties to the homeland. If they could not be reached, ethnic nationalism would die a swift death in America.

The close relationship between nationalism and ethnicity does not mean that they were synonymous, however. Because immigrants lived in America, ethnicity could not be purely about national identity but was also a product of the immigrant experience and aspirations in America. Ethnicity, in part, was about becoming American—not assimilating in the classic sense but showing that immigrants' heritage and values were congruent with American culture and so need not be discarded.[4] Like African Americans, immigrants sought to demonstrate that, despite their ethnic ties, they were just as American as native-born whites. Thus, ethnicity was inextricably linked to America as well as to the homeland. On ethnic holidays immigrants and their children did not simply create ethnic national identities; they constructed versions of ethnic Americanism. Their ethnicity informed the way they constructed American identity, but their understanding of American culture and values also shaped their ethnic identity.

Turn-of-the-century nationalism and, thus, ethnicity were preeminently middle-class phenomena. Immigrant nationalists, like their American counterparts, espoused a liberal bourgeois vision of the nation that linked progress, enlightenment, and middle-class morality. The fraternal, musical, military, religious, and gymnastics organizations that sponsored ethnic celebrations tended to be middle class in membership, leadership, and outlook (with the exception of socialist organizations). Although most members of these groups were no doubt sincere in their ethnic nationalism, and many fought in a variety of ways to liberate their homelands, that should not blind us to the more pragmatic functions of ethnicity. Even if only temporarily, these individuals lived in the United States, and their promotion of ethnicity also served as a strategy of adjustment to this situation, by unifying the ethnic community into a cultural, economic, and political power base and legitimizing their leadership of it.[5] Just as the leaders of veterans' organizations and labor unions presumed to speak for their constituencies, so the leaders of ethnic organizations took it upon themselves to define ethnic Americanism for their ethnic groups.

As the Polish editorial suggests, the ethnic press, another predominantly middle-class institution, played a signal role in promoting nationalism and ethnic celebrations.[6] Editors suggested what types of celebrations would be appropriate, pushed immigrant leaders to arrange them, and often served on arrangement committees and spoke at holiday exercises. They educated immigrants in nationalism by publishing accounts of their homeland's struggle for independence and biographies of its heroes. They promoted national holiday celebrations to arouse public enthusiasm and advised immigrants on how to celebrate properly by publishing programs and instructions for participants. Afterward they printed descriptions of celebrations and the texts of the speeches.

Although they presented ethnic Americanism as primordial and consensual on ethnic holidays, ethnic leaders, like Civil War veterans and labor unionists, actually constructed this identity and often disagreed vociferously on its tenets. We tend to speak of ethnic communities as if they were monolithic, and nationalists sought to portray them as such, but they were no more so than other groups. Within the ranks of nationalists, various factions competed for leadership and sought to win the hearts and minds of the majority to their vision of the nation and ethnic group. The *Dziennik Zwiazkowy* editorial suggests one of these divisions in its admonition that holiday orators stimulate and encourage religious belief. Polish American nationalists quarreled vehemently over the proper relationship between Catholicism and Polish nationalism, and advocating religious belief on a national holiday placed the newspaper squarely within the Catholic nationalism of the Polish Roman Catholic Union. Religion was, for most groups, the most volatile issue of ethnic nationalism; however, other conflicts intruded on the nationalists' project as well, from different conceptions of the shape of the nation to lifestyle issues such as temperance.

These intragroup struggles over nationalism played a formative role in the construction of ethnic Americanism. Victor Greene, in his study of Polish and Lithuanian immigrants in Chicago, argues that intraethnic tensions were much more important than interethnic ones in building ethnic consciousness. The process of choosing sides in the debates among immigrant leaders was, Greene contends, an ethnicizing one.[7] And national holiday celebrations provided the most visible and trenchant arena for presenting one's side of the debate.

Nationalists also faced ideological competition for the hearts and minds of the working class from socialists, who condemned bourgeois attempts to repair class conflict with the glue of nationalism. Socialism and nationalism were not necessarily mutually exclusive. As Eric Hobsbawm has suggested, socialists could be ardent nationalists who imagined the nation in egalitarian and reformist terms, which held more appeal than liberal bourgeois nationalism for many working-class immigrants.[8] One has only to look to American socialists, who on labor holidays told of an America whose principles would come to their fullest fruition under socialism.

Socialism never attracted more than a minority of immigrants, however. More significant obstacles to nationalists' success lay in a persistent strain of indifference to the ethnic project, at least as the middle class defined it, and the meteoric rise of popular commercial culture, which competed directly and most attractively with nationalists' celebrations for the scant free time and attention of immigrants and their children. Ethnic leaders, like labor unionists, sought to combat the lure of popular culture by incorporating some of its features into their celebrations, but that provided a limited solution. Not only did these additions tend to dilute the message of the celebrations, but also, as frequent lamentations over poor attendance suggest, they failed to provide much competition for commercial culture.

CONSTRUCTING A NATIONAL HERITAGE

Most immigrant groups celebrated at least one national holiday, either brought from their homeland or created in the United States. Poles in America commemorated annually the anniversary of the doomed constitution of 3 May 1791 and the November 1830 and January 1863 Risings against Russia, which they interpreted as evidence of a widespread Polish national spirit and thirst for liberty, and they celebrated Tadeusz Kosciuszko as Poland's George Washington, who had fought for freedom for Poland as well as America. Irish Americans honored not only St. Patrick but also the Protestant United Irish martyr Robert Emmet. Filipinos commemorated the anniversary of the 1896 execution of nationalist José Rizal by the Spanish colonizers. Czechs celebrated Jan Hus, a fifteenth-century Reformation leader who had promoted the use of the Bohemian language and worked to halt the Germanization of Bohemia, and Karel Havlíček, a journalist who had been imprisoned by Austria for his nationalist politics during the era of the 1848 revolutions. Zionists celebrated various Jewish anniversaries, from Passover and Chanukah to Lag b'Omer, which commemorated a Jewish revolt against the Romans. "The historical festivals," asserted the *Reform Advocate* in 1891, "unite in the spirit the dispersed sons of Judah."[9]

Those immigrants whose homelands had already achieved nationhood observed the anniversaries of their independence. Greeks observed the anniversary of their 1821 independence annually on 25 March, whereas Italians celebrated the anniversary of the constitution that united Italy, as well as the patriots Giuseppe Garibaldi and Giuseppe Mazzini, who had fought for unification. Norwegians commemorated the Seventeenth of May, the date of the 1814 Eidsvoll constitution that formalized Norway's independence from Denmark. Mexicans celebrated the anniversary of their independence on the Sixteenth of September, the anniversary of Father Miguel Hidalgo's *grito de dolores*. Irish Protestant Unionists, in reaction to the Irish republicans, began after the Civil War to celebrate the Twelfth of July, the anniversary of William of Orange's victory over James II in the Battle of the Boyne. German veterans of the Franco-Prussian War celebrated their victory and the unification of Germany.

The main purpose of these holidays was to create bonds of ethnicity that would unify immigrants in America in support of the homeland and for the good of its emigrants in America. Immigrant nationalists first had to deal with the local allegiances of many of their countrymen, transforming these into patriotism to the more abstract nation. They had to make that "imagined community" as concrete in the eyes of immigrants as the village or family. One way of doing so was to appropriate and to transform the dances, music, and costumes of folk culture into national culture. This appropriation was doubly ironic given that the folk, or peasant, revival in Europe was largely a reaction against the homogenization of culture brought by the urban, industrial economy that bourgeois nationalists embraced. In America, as in Europe, middle-class nationalists seized upon the peasant revival to build nationalism.[10]

Consequently, at Polish commemorations musicians played the polonaises transformed and made famous by Chopin. Scots listened to bagpipers on St. Andrew's Day, Czech holiday dancers performed the Beseda, and cantors sang Zionist folk songs on Jewish holidays. Norwegian Independence Day celebrations featured folk festivals, and children on German Day played "German national games," such as "chicken-pulling." Irish and Scottish nationalists revived so-called traditional Celtic sports—hurling and Gaelic football in the Irish case and Highland games in the Scottish case—and held contests or exhibitions at their celebrations.[11]

One of the most important nationalizing forces was the development of a national language to overcome the multitude of dialects that divided people from different regions. Nationalists thus presented holiday speeches, recitations, and songs in the national language. Singing stirring national anthems in the national language united holiday revelers in a sentimental patriotism. In the case of the Irish, the overwhelming majority of whom spoke English as the first language, this patriotism took the form of a revival of the Gaelic that the English rulers had so brutally suppressed. Although few Irish Americans understood Gaelic, a song, recitation, or St. Patrick's Day sermon in the language provided a pungent symbol of the nationhood that the British had stolen from the Irish people. Similarly, Zionists made the ancient Hebrew, rather than the Yiddish that most Eastern European Jews spoke, the language of Jewish nationalism.[12]

As proponents of the liberal political principles of the age and their adopted land, immigrant nationalists constructed their nations as models of liberal democracy and their people as inherently liberty-loving and virtuous. "We are the children of a people in whom love of liberty and country constitute striking traits of character," one orator informed his Chicago audience at a 1911 celebration of Norwegian independence. In his 1905 St. Patrick's Day oration before the Ancient Order of Hibernians, a Richmond priest enumerated at great length the qualities of the Irish people, which included statesmanship, military skill, moral courage, "vigor of mind," and physical perfection. Moreover, he observed, "the true son of Erin never fights in an unjust cause" but is ever ready to lend a hand "at the cry of freedom." Throughout history, he concluded, the Irish had been "pioneer[s] . . . sowing the seed of future civilization and enlightenment."[13]

Such people could not help but create democratic nations. A 1912 holiday editorial in *Scandia* proclaimed that the Seventeenth of May was "a 'day of the people,' of equal importance to merchant, farmer, manufacturer, lawyer, and laborer," because the constitution enacted on that date had meant "the end of power, of pomp and splendor, . . . of material and spiritual oppression" by the clergy and nobility. "Under this constitution," the editor explained, "all are equal." Similarly, *Dziennik Zwiazkowy* construed Poland's 3 May constitution as "a momentous act of voluntary sacrifice on the part of the nobility, in favor of the middle classes and of the peasants." That these interpretations were not necessarily historically accurate did not much matter. Indeed, a doomed constitution such as Poland's, which had never had to withstand the demands of governance, could be shaped into almost anything. What American Polish leaders constructed from it was a prototypically liberal society that had been crushed by the forces of tyranny in the form of Russia and Prussia. In reality, the Polish nobles had extended citizenship rights only to the small class of German burghers, not to the bulk of Polish peasants and certainly not to serfs, neither of whom those nobles considered to be Poles. Polish nationalists simply omitted this problematic bit of history. The image created by this act of collective memory making, not its accuracy, was the important thing.[14]

And that image was, above all, one of unity, the devotion of all classes to the same nation and principles. According to Tony Bennett, the very purpose of a national heritage is "to enfold diverse histories into one," which may necessitate the erasure of past divisions in the service of contemporary unity. Thus, nineteenth-century nationalists pointedly incorporated ordinary people into the national heritage they were creating, ignoring the fact that many of the heroes they celebrated had not recognized peasants, serfs, or even artisans and shopkeepers as members of the nation. The American Irish fraternal Ancient Order of Hibernians, descended from the Catholic agrarian secret societies that had joined the United Irishmen's 1798 uprising, constructed and celebrated the peasant as nationalist. Likewise, Polish nationalists combined the May constitution with Kosciuszko's 1794 insurrection to find a precedent for working-class nationalism in the peasants who, armed with scythes, assisted Kosciuszko's army of nobles at the Battle of Raclawice. Just as importantly, those nationalists painted the November 1830 and January 1863 insurrections as popular uprisings, conveniently forgetting that they were the work of the upper classes, not the peasantry, who in some instances had even aided authorities in repressing the revolts.[15]

Immigrant nationalists created long and heroic histories to mask the fact that these various nations were in reality new phenomena in the process of construction. Norwegian holiday orators, for example, recounted "the Northland's struggle for liberty since the saga times and the days of fair-haired Harold, who defeated the numerous petty kings and united the nation under a single crown in 872 A.D." Mexican Americans traced their fight for independence back beyond 1810 to the Aztec struggle against the conquering Spanish. And an 1895 St. Patrick's Day sermon, delivered in Gaelic, disputed England's civilizing claims, tracing "the children of Er" to ancient Greece and Rome, claiming that they had given Christ to the world and were the ancestors of "the Aryans, the white race."[16]

In addition to building political heritages for their nations, nationalists sought to weaken or to destroy the bonds of localism by creating national heroes such as Kosciuszko, Rizal, and Garibaldi; national flags and anthems such as the Czech "Kde Domov Muj" ("Where Is My Home") or the Polish "Boze Cos Polski" ("God Save Poland"); national poets such as Adam Mickiewicz and Robert Burns; and national organizations such as the Ancient Order of Hibernians and the German and Norwegian turners, Czech Sokols, and Polish Falcons, which were gymnastics associations that preached nationalism through physical fitness. Certain foods and drinks even became symbolic of the nation. Scottish Americans in Chicago, for instance, ate haggis at a St. Andrew's Day banquet while listening to a sung version of Burns's poem "To the Haggis."[17]

Nationalists incorporated all these elements into their holiday exercises. On Rizal Day Filipinos heard the martyr's last poem, "Ultima Adios," composed on the eve of his execution, while Mexicans thrilled each year to the ritualistic reading of Hidalgo's *grito*. Orators told of the heroic exploits of Hus and Emmet and Kosciuszko in the service of the nation. Uniformed turners executed gymnastics drills, and costumed dancers performed the newly national dances of Norway or Scotland. And all revelers joined together to sing the national anthem in the national language. Benedict Anderson suggests that this communal singing, more than the other holiday events, created, at least temporarily, the "physical realization of the imagined community" of the nation.[18]

That creation was not a one-way process, from those who scripted holiday exercises to a passively receptive public. Rather, it required the active participation of that public, if only to sing along with the national anthem or to watch the procession. Nationalists exhorted their compatriots to support the national project in word and in deed. They could demonstrate their patriotism not only by attending and participating in the holiday rituals but also by working for the national cause, in the homeland or in the United

Dedication of the Havlíček statue by Czech Chicagoans, 1911. Ethnic Americans built monuments to their national heroes and then gathered around them to celebrate their holidays. (Courtesy of the Chicago Public Library, Special Collections and Preservation Division)

States. At celebrations nationalists collected money to fund ethnic philanthropy, to build monuments to national heroes, and even to pay for the holiday exercises. *Dziennik Chicagoski* suggested, for example, that Poles should erect a monument to Kosciuszko to commemorate the centennial of his 1794 insurrection, and nationalists on subsequent holidays collected money for this undertaking. As an inducement to giving, some newspapers published lists of donors. In Tucson, for instance, *El Fronterizo* published the names and donations of those who contributed to the 1887 Mexican Independence Day celebration.[19]

It was particularly crucial for immigrants to aid their homeland's struggle for liberation. Irish republicans solicited funds for the Irish Republican Brotherhood and for famine relief and even raised an ambulance corps in 1900 to aid the Boers in their war against the English, on the theory that anything that hurt England helped the Irish cause. Zionists collected money for the Palestine fund. Merely participating in "routine festivities" for the national holiday was not sufficient to demonstrate patriotism, the *Greek Star* informed Chicago Greeks in 1908. Rather, they were duty bound "to contribute morally and materially for the liberation of the Greeks of Macedonia," which was "a cultural and ethnological Greek territory."[20] Participation in ethnic holiday celebrations thus became not merely a symbolic illustration of republican citizenship but a demonstration of such citizenship in action.

REACHING THE NEXT GENERATION

It was never too early to learn this active citizenship. As *Dziennik Zwiazkowy* had made clear, the sponsors of ethnic holidays, like those of Memorial Day, wished above all to ensure that the next generation imbibed their messages. In language that would have sounded familiar at GAR Memorial Day exercises, an orator at an 1887 German celebration urged veterans of the Franco-Prussian War to "uphold their native language and customs, and to educate their children, though born in this country, in the patriotic spirit which has made the German people one great and strong nation." Recognizing that active learning was superior to passive observation, ethnic nationalists incorporated children into virtually every facet of their celebrations, save oratory. Children marched in procession with school or Sunday school groups, as members of cadet and turner organizations, and with junior versions of temperance and fraternal organizations. They learned national songs and folk dances to perform at holiday exercises. They recited national poetry and performed in holiday plays and tableaux. At school exercises to honor Kosciuszko in 1894, Polish children even swore an oath to love Poland, to help and pray for her, and to guard the Polish language and faith.[21]

Children regularly took part in holiday processions. The *Daily Jewish Courier* reported in 1919 that on Herzl Memorial Day, which commemorated the founder of the modern Zionist movement, "all the children from the Talmud Torahs marched in parade to the Herzl School," where they listened to speakers who told them the significance of the day. Norwegian churches sponsored a special children's procession and festival for the Seventeenth of May, and children also participated in the general procession. In 1890, for example, young turners wearing white sailor shirts and caps banded with the Norwegian red, white, and blue joined marchers, while twenty-four girls in Norwegian costumes rode in a special chariot in the parade. As the latter suggests, girls began to take on the allegorical role long reserved for women on American holidays. The most beloved element of the annual procession for Mexican Independence Day was the allegorical float bearing "thirty little girls from eight to twelve years, dressed in white, with laurel crowns and tri-color sashes" with the names of the Mexican states and territories etched in gilt. The most honored place was reserved for the three girls who represented "America," "the United States," and "Mexico."[22]

In addition to parading, children took active roles in holiday exercises. They sang and recited poetry and prose, they performed national dances, and they dressed in national costumes. Tucson's *El Fronterizo* reported in 1887 that little Juan Franco had provided an object lesson in patriotism by recit-ing "an exquisite poem dedicated to the National Flag" at Mexican Indepen-dence Day exercises. The same celebration also featured "a precious choir of little girls singing the National Hymn." Students at Chicago's Free Thought schools celebrated the quincentenary of Jan Hus's death with a detailed pro-gram for their parents and the rest of the Free Thought community. Carry-ing Czech flags and dressed in national costumes, the children paraded to Pilsen Park, where they and their teachers presented recitations, Czech songs, and tableaux of Czech history. Girls, like their mothers, also took on more symbolic and decorative roles. When Norwegian Chicagoans arranged a tribute to their national hero, Leif Eriksson, to counter the Columbian quadricentennial in 1892, it featured "[p]retty little girls with red frocks and garlands in their hair [who] gave away grapes to the guests out of big baskets to commemorate the discovery of Vineland the Beautiful."[23]

Like their parents, children learned and even taught lessons of their na-tional history on holidays. The *Sunday Jewish Courier*, for instance, in 1919 pub-lished a child's composition on the significance of Lag b'Omer, which provided an encapsulated version of Zionism. "Many, many years ago," it began, "Jewish people lived, in their own land, Palestine. They were happy and content for many years. Then came a bad, wicked enemy, a people called Romans, who de-stroyed the country." The lessons of history, not surprisingly, often pointed out the villains responsible for the nation's suffering. Polish nationalists made these lessons particularly visceral to young children. A children's choir at exer-cises commemorating the 1894 centennial of Kosciuszko's insurrection sang "People Are Tormented by the Cruel Muscovite," and a little girl recited "The German Tortures Polish Children" at November exercises in 1916.[24]

Ethnic holiday sponsors often aimed the lessons of national history squarely at the community's children. The November insurrection, for example, provided lessons particularly relevant to Polish youth. As World War I raged in 1916, one speaker told them that "the virtue with which the youth of Wilno University distinguished themselves upholds the national spirit and leads the nation toward freedom." If young Polish Americans emulated the students who participated in that rebellion, he concluded, the national spirit could not help but triumph. Other holiday orators linked their instruction on national duty to lessons on proper deportment. Rev. Jens C. Roseland told Norwegian children in 1911 that the main purposes of the Seventeenth of May were "honoring our ancestry" and inculcating in "our youth a knowledge of some of the principal events in Norse history." He warned, however, that they must also fight social impurity and intemperance, the latter of which was "a more destructive foe than war, pestilence, and famine combined." Polish Catholic nationalists of the Polish Roman Catholic Union bemoaned attempts by its rival, the Polish National Alliance, to lure Polish youth into "camps of debauchery and idleness, camps of prodigality and family disorganization, camps of false patriotism."[25]

ETHNICITY AND MIDDLE-CLASS VALUES

While this moral warfare was particularly pronounced in the struggle for the allegiance of the younger generation, it played a vital role in the construction of ethnic Americanism at the turn of the century and points up the decidedly bourgeois nature of ethnicity. Holiday celebrations presided over by ethnic nationalists were subject to the same codes of public behavior as other middle-class institutions. Ethnic leaders revealed a preoccupation with order and proper behavior on holidays and throughout the year. A Norwegian minister, for example, explained to children at a 1905 independence celebration "the necessity of obeying the law and keeping order." It was not sufficient to police one's own behavior at celebrations; good citizens were expected to watch each other's behavior because they cared how the community represented itself. In a 1917 editorial on an upcoming commemoration, *Dziennik Zwiazkowy* implored Poles "to maintain the dignity that such an event requires," explaining that it was "the concern of each individual to see to his own proper behavior, and that of the next person, . . . [so] that we may not be taken as a disorderly mob."[26]

The evolving holiday calendar of Mexican Americans in late nineteenth-century Tucson provides a dramatic illustration of the triumph of liberal bourgeois nationalism. One of the highlights of the year had long been the traditional fiesta honoring St. Augustine, Tucson's patron saint. But in the last two decades of the century it came under attack from middle-class Mexican Americans, joined by their European American counterparts. The fiesta was problematic because its affirmation of traditional local and religious allegiances and hierarchies undermined the creation of national identity. Just as importantly, its carnivalesque disorder and its flouting of the bourgeois value system were anathema to middle-class nationalists.[27]

In traditional fashion, the fiesta comprised two parts, the sacred and the profane. The sacred fiesta consisted of two days of church services and religious processions led by the clergy and what *Las Dos Repúblicas* called "the most select of our society." These services and processions reproduced and validated the social hierarchy and the central role of Catholicism in Mexican life. The profane feast that followed lasted almost three weeks, temporarily overturning the social order by promiscuously mixing classes, races, and genders in a kaleidoscopic whirl of food, alcohol, dancing, games, and, increasingly, gambling. At the gambling enclosure, one observer reported that "[t]he Chinese cooks and laundrymen are bucking against faro, the ladies of the demi-monde venture a little on *rouge et noir*, and all classes . . . try by some lucky throw or turning of a card to double their wealth."[28]

Criticism centered on the profane fiesta's lack of order and perceived immorality. Newspaperman Carlos Velasco condemned the "festive vice" and proclaimed that "[w]e have always been opponents of such public fiestas, because . . . there is always an element of disorder however much they are guarded, and they leave no benefit of value to the place where they are celebrated." Critics viewed gambling as the most noxious of the fiesta's diversions. One observer reported a middle-class horror story observed at the fiesta: "We witnessed . . . a little girl not more than ten or twelve years old [gambling]. That little girl, if she lives, may become a wife and mother, and what a low and degraded race must spring from her." After more than a decade of attacks on the fiesta, its bourgeois opponents finally convinced the territorial legislature to kill it by connecting it to antigaming measures. In 1891 the legislature passed "an Act to prevent gambling at any fiesta."[29] As gambling had become the economic mainstay of the profane fiesta, it was no longer profitable to produce it, and it disappeared, leaving only the religious services in the cathedral.

Mexican American leaders did not have to look far for a replacement for the fiesta. In contrast to the religiosity and carnivalesque anarchy of the fiesta, Mexican Independence Day was a model of orderly patriotism. The *junta patriótica* that planned the celebration reflected the bourgeois character of Mexican nationalism; regular members included journalists, ranchers, merchants, professionals, and entrepreneurs. The celebration followed the pattern set by countless other national commemorations. Mexican Americans gathered for a massive civic procession, followed by literary exercises consisting of patriotic recitations, the reading of the *grito*, patriotic music, and speeches recapitulating Mexico's struggle for independence. The program presented an array of national symbols, from the *grito* and Hidalgo to the ubiquitous national tricolor and the virginal representatives of the republic. It also contained abundant opportunities to demonstrate one's patriotism, by singing the national hymn, marching in the procession, presenting a recitation, or even making an impromptu speech, a symbol of the nation's democracy and the only element of spontaneity in the celebration. Equally important, Mexican Americans showed their love for their homeland by contributing funds for the celebration.[30]

Orators reinforced the national sentiment created by the more visceral elements of the exercises, and they directed it to a liberal bourgeois conception of the Mexican nation. The spirit of liberty, they proclaimed, was indigenous to Mexico and the heritage of the Aztecs, not the brutal Spanish conquistadores. Orators took pains to identify themselves with their Aztec forebears, echoing the revolutionary hero José María Morelos, who had seen independence as the reestablishment of the Aztec empire. The young "Goddess of Liberty" in the 1887 procession was, appropriately, "dressed in the typical garb of the ancient Aztec." Once they had established the roots of Mexican liberalism, nationalists avowed that national progress depended on the liberal government, capitalist development, and bourgeois values. In an 1877 holiday editorial, *Las Dos Repúblicas* called for "tolerance, industry, and self-

Maria Soto Audelo dressed as Mexico for the
Fourth of July procession in Tucson, 1917. Women
and girls most typically played allegorical roles in
holiday processions, impersonating Mexico,
America, and Liberty. Maria wears a banner of
the Mexican tricolor and a liberty cap. (Courtesy
of the Arizona Historical Society/Tucson,
accession number 69759)

denial" as the keys to progress for Mexican Americans. A speaker two years
later praised Mexico's political, moral, and intellectual progress and reminded his audience "that extensive commercial relations [between the
United States and Mexico] are the very best kind of annexation."[31]

Although the fiesta and independence holiday had coexisted peacefully in
Tucson throughout most of the nineteenth century, the liberal bourgeois

Mexican nation being created by Porfirio Díaz and his adherents after 1876 left little room for traditional fiestas. They featured the sorts of amusements that violated bourgeois morality, they strengthened local and religious loyalties and hierarchies, and they did nothing to create a sense of national identity. Rather than attempt to transform the fiesta, Tucson's Mexican American leaders destroyed it, leaving the Sixteenth of September as the primary source of Mexican American identity. Although traditional feasts remained viable in some ethnic communities, ethnic leaders across the nation, like those in Tucson, focused their efforts on the national holidays that had proven to be more conducive to the construction of nationalism and ethnic Americanism.[32]

NATIONALISTS DIVIDED

Although bourgeois leaders agreed, for the most part, on the fundamental tenets of ethnic Americanism—liberal democracy, capitalism, and bourgeois morality—they disagreed vehemently on other issues affecting the construction of ethnicity. The role of religion in ethnic nationalism constituted a particularly nasty bone of contention. The Chicago celebration of the anniversary of an event deemed seminal in the construction of the Polish nation provides a case in point. In May 1891 Polish Chicagoans held a four-day extravaganza to commemorate the centennial of the Polish constitution of 3 May 1791. On 2 May Polish societies from across the city stepped out in procession to begin the celebration. Led by Polish police officers, a cornet band, and the Second Regiment of Polish Independents, a militia group, the marchers included parish-based affiliates of the Polish National Alliance, other nationalist organizations such as the King Jan III Sobieski and King Jagiello Societies, the Holy Trinity Singing Society, the Pulaski Guard, and Polish tailors and carpenters. Youth participants included the St. Stanislaus Cadets and a group of boys bearing "sickle-shaped swords," who represented the peasant scythe-men of Kosciuszko's 1794 rebellion. After the marchers, members of women's auxiliaries rode in decorated carriages.[33]

The procession wended its way from Haymarket Square to Central Music Hall, where Judge Murray F. Tuley presided over exercises that featured nationalist music played by Polish bands and sung by Polish singers, including the "Polonaise of May 3, 1791," "Our Fatherland," "Polish Serenade," and "Polonaise Triumphale," which had been composed for the occasion. The musical selections also reinforced the American part of ethnic Americanism, including the "Star-Spangled Banner" and "Hail Columbia." The audience listened to addresses, in Polish and English, on the Polish constitution and Polish nationalism. A recitation of "Poland's Destruction" and a magic lantern show featuring stereopticon views of "Polish Historical Events" rounded out the program.[34]

On the actual centennial Sunday, after special morning masses at Polish parishes, schoolchildren performed a program of recitations and music in the afternoon, followed by an evening concert and speeches in Polish by "prominent laymen and clergymen." Boleslaus Klarkowski, the main orator, praised the constitution they celebrated and recounted its sad history. Although Poland was down, Klarkowski emphasized, it was not out so long as the "spirit of the Constitution" lived within Poles. He placed the responsibility for the resurrection of Poland squarely on the shoulders of American Poles; if Poland perished, he told them, it would be because they had allowed it and thus were unworthy of a fatherland.[35]

The commemoration continued Monday with a Catholic mass for the dead, "for the repose of the souls of the departed who died in the defense of Poland," and another evening meeting. It concluded on Tuesday, 5 May, with a pontifical mass at St. Stanislaus Kostka, celebrated by Archbishop Patrick Feehan. A procession of uniformed men of the parish societies and schoolgirls in the Polish colors, white dresses with red sashes, led the way into the church. In the afternoon delegates from across the nation convened for a "strictly nationalist conference" to decide the proper interpretation of the constitution and how to create solidarity among American Poles. The final act of the long celebration came that evening with an address titled "Our Holy Patriotic Duty" by a priest visiting from Michigan and a six-act play, the "Siege of Czestochowa."[36]

Upon first reading, this four-day jubilee appears to present a coherent and unified vision of Polish nationalism, organized around the premier national symbol of the 3 May constitution. Speakers such as Klarkowski explicated the constitution as a model of enlightened liberalism and egalitarianism. They also reminded revelers, however, that it had fallen not only through the efforts of Russia and Prussia but also through the betrayal of Poles themselves. They warned that there were Poles today who were just as guilty of treason. For, although the *Chicago Tribune* reported that the first day's parade featured "all the various Polish societies in the city," Chicago Poles were so divided in 1891 that they had actually sponsored two separate celebrations.[37] The first day's procession and exercises were the work of the Polish National Alliance (PNA), while the subsequent three days came under the auspices of the Polish Roman Catholic Union (PRCU). Each saw the other as betraying Poland much as had the traitors of the 1790s. Rather than Polish American solidarity, a close reading of the text of the centennial reveals serious conflicts over the shape of Polish nationalism, centering on the role of religion in defining ethnicity.

The PRCU-PNA debate was of long standing in Chicago, dating from the 1860s. It embraced the role of the clergy in the nation and the role of Catholicism in Polish identity. Much of the debate, as Victor Greene has demonstrated, was over the ownership of church property and the question of to whom Poles owed first allegiance, church or nation. The religionist camp of the PRCU, led by the clergy and its lay supporters, contended that nationalism and ethnicity were subordinate to religion and also that a non-Catholic could not be a Pole. In the words of Chicago's chief religionist, Rev. Vincent Barzynski, "second to the love for God is the love for our fatherland." The nationalist camp of the PNA, in contrast, subscribed to the liberal-bourgeois view that religion was not a defining characteristic of the nation. Its members were predominantly Catholic, but they espoused a nationalist Catholicism in which church was subordinate to nation.[38]

The PNA condemned the clergy as the main obstacle to the nationalist project and refused to cooperate with the PRCU's 1891 celebration, which the PNA newspaper, *Zgoda*, dubbed treasonous and "a farce."[39] Therefore, it held a separate celebration the day before the centennial. Although the revelers included parish-based PNA affiliates, the PNA exercises took on a decidedly secular cast. The parade did not begin or end at a church, exercises took place in a secular institution, none of the orators were clergymen, and the music and addresses were strictly nationalist, with no religious overtones.

The PRCU castigated the PNA for its nonparticipation in the three-day PRCU celebration. Klarkowski pointedly asserted that the partitions of

Poland had occurred "when we were not in harmony with God." It was the PRCU that had sponsored the national conference, although it noted defensively that priests served only as "observers and advisors," not participants. The PRCU condemned the PNA for behaving unpatriotically by refusing to participate in the conference. The delegates to the conference, unhindered by the PNA, interpreted the 3 May constitution to fit their definition of Polish identity; they concluded that it dictated that Poles must remain Catholic in the United States. They also resolved that any slander against the clergy or the church should be considered a crime against Poland. They decried the lack of patriotism of nationalist Poles and requested that priests instruct their parishioners in their patriotic duty. Finally, they asserted that those Poles who sent their children to public schools or failed to teach them Polish "violate[d] their national honor."[40]

The PNA-PRCU rift endured into the early twentieth century, fracturing the very holidays on which nationalists sought to convey national harmony. Unlike the massive centennial celebrations, the annual exercises for the constitution, the two insurrections, and Kosciuszko's Birthday generally took place on the parish level. Affiliates of each organization sponsored separate celebrations, sometimes at the same parish. For example, the PNA societies of St. Adalbert's parish held exercises commemorating the November insurrection on 30 November 1895, while the same parish's PRCU organizations celebrated on 24 November. At the latter exercises, the president of the PRCU told his listeners that if they continued their belief in God and church, God would "certainly" return their fatherland. The Reverend A. Nowicki then spoke on "true patriotism" and defended the right of priests to do national work.[41]

Other ethnic communities saw similar conflicts over the relationship between religion and nationalism. Within the Czech American community, for example, Freethinkers, Protestants, and Catholics squared off. Both Freethinkers and Protestants celebrated the martyred Jan Hus as their chief national hero, but the former focused more on his work as the "great Bohemian patriot and advocate" than on his role in the Czech Reformation. The Free Thought biography of Hus praised his efforts to check the German influence on Bohemia by deporting Germans, as well as his use of the Czech language for his writings and sermons. Freethinkers and Protestants in Chicago each sponsored celebrations of the 1915 quincentenary of Hus's martyrdom. Despite their concentration on his Reformation work, Czech Protestants made clear that they also celebrated Hus as a national hero. Girls in Czech national costumes sang a hymn composed by Hus, and a minister who spoke linked Hus to the long-awaited resurrection of the Czech nation, exclaiming that "[a]fter five hundred years he will rise from his ashes—in a liberated nation! That should be the culmination of the observance of this great anniversary!" For Catholic Czechs the Reformation leader and Free Thought hero was an impossible symbol. Lacking a viable national hero to celebrate, they passed on the national language and traditions at parochial schools and in the Catholic gymnastics organizations they established to rival the Freethinkers' Sokols.[42]

Irish immigrants in Chicago also battled over the proper relationship between religion and nationalism. After the potato famine and the failure of the 1848 Young Ireland Rebellion, a growing number of Irishmen, at home and abroad, embraced republicanism. Although they remained a minority in Ireland, exiled republicans took a leading role in constructing Irish nationalism in America. Catholic nationalists, like their Czech and Polish counterparts, put church before nation. A prime arena for this conflict was St. Patrick's Day. For a time after the Civil War members of the Fenian (from Fianna, an ancient Irish warrior) Brotherhood headed the annual St. Patrick's Day parades in Chicago. The Fenians, many of whom were exiled Forty-Eighters, were the American wing of the Irish Republican Brotherhood, a society devoted to gaining Irish independence through revolution. In 1870 the Catholic Church condemned and excommunicated the Fenians, and that same year "a strong undercurrent of feeling among the [Catholic] Temperance Societies against the Fenians" in Chicago led to their ouster from their customary position at the head of the St. Patrick's Day parade. Refusing to take second place, the Fenians, accompanied by four carriages of Fenian Sisters, marched in a separate procession one hour before the main parade.[43]

One reason for the Catholic animosity toward the Fenians, aside from the church's condemnation of secret societies, lay in the Fenians' religious neutrality. Although the Fenians soon faded from prominence, the conflict did not. The Clan na Gael Guards, a new republican organization, supplanted them as the main champion of Irish nationalism and independence. The

Clan na Gael promoted the republican cause by sponsoring the celebration of three holidays: Robert Emmet's birthday, the anniversary of the 1867 execution of several Fenians dubbed the Manchester Martyrs, and the feast of Our Lady Day in Harvest (the Assumption of Mary), which was also the anniversary of two sixteenth-century victories over England. As the elevation of the Protestant revolutionary Robert Emmet to heroic status suggests, the Clan followed Emmet's United Irishmen in insisting on religious neutrality. Orator John Finerty, for example, closed exercises in 1878 commemorating the centennial of Emmet's birth with a plea for Catholic-Protestant unity, without which the Irish would never rid themselves of "the hated yoke of England."[44]

The Clan's chief rival was the Ancient Order of Hibernians (AOH), whose members had to be of Irish birth and Roman Catholics of good standing. While the republican societies focused on Emmet's birthday and the other two holidays, the AOH and Catholic sodalities and temperance societies took a bigger role in the celebration of St. Patrick's Day. The Catholic clergy, abetted by the temperance societies, campaigned to change the celebration of St. Patrick's Day to a more sober and religious one. Attentive to the latter change, if not the former, the AOH began to attend mass as a group on the holiday. The clergy took on a more active role in these celebrations as well; at a St. Patrick's Day reception in 1885 Rev. Maurice J. Dorney delivered an address titled "The Position of the Priest Among the Irish People."[45]

Adding a further dimension to Irish religious divisions was the emergence of the Irish Protestant Unionist movement in the late nineteenth century in reaction against the republican and Home Rule movements. In 1867, the same year the Clan na Gael originated, Unionist immigrants established the first American lodge of the Loyal Orange Institution and began to celebrate the Twelfth of July or Boyne Day as their national holiday. Even as in Northern Ireland today, the Orangemen's July marches provoked violent reactions from some Irish Catholics, who hanged effigies of Orangemen and harassed the marchers. In 1871 the governor of New York ordered the state militia to protect the marchers, but a confrontation led to tragedy when soldiers fired into the hostile crowd, killing dozens. The *Chicago Tribune* blamed the Irish Catholics for the deaths, asserting that the main problem was that they had "refused to become Americanized" and had carried to America "the feuds which have disgraced their native country for centuries."[46]

Religion and temperance also split the Norwegian American community. In Chicago Lutheran ministers and allied temperance organizations clashed with religiously neutral Norwegians on the Seventeenth of May. The conflict reached a particularly nasty juncture in 1911. That year the Norwegian churches arranged a children's procession and exercises, while the Norwegian National League sponsored a parade, folk festival, and other exercises at Brand's Park. The main orator at the religious celebration was the Reverend Jens C. Roseland, who told the children present that Norwegian youth must fight "[i]nfidelity, [i]ntemperance, [s]ocial [i]mpurity, Sabbath [d]esecration, [p]rofanity." The religious celebration and its clerical organizers came in for sharp criticism from nationalists, who asserted that "practically all our people" thought that the children's parade had been "a miserable exhibition, brainlessly planned and arrogantly defended by the pastors." *Scandia* voiced its agreement with these critics, claiming that the "shame and embarrassment of Norwegian youth" by such a poor showing would hurt the nationalist cause among the very people who were its primary targets. The paper concluded that "our Norwegian colony will, hereafter, see to it that the preachers are left on the shelf as far as May 17th is concerned."[47]

Although religion provoked the greatest number of conflicts, it was never the only divisive element in ethnic nationalism. In 1900, for example, disputes over the use of union musicians and over who would conduct the orchestra had marred the Norwegian National League's downtown exercises and led a splinter group to hold an opposition celebration in a Norwegian neighborhood hall. And the variety of other exercises indicated that many Norwegians ignored both of these celebrations in favor of the gymnastics exhibition, dancing, and speeches offered by the Norwegian Turner Society; the speeches, folk songs, and play at the Society Fram social; the Norwegian music offered by two singing societies at the Sons of Norway exercises; or the religious exercises offered at the Norwegian Lutheran Trinity Church. Meanwhile, disagreements over the politics and control of the Clan na Gael and the Ancient Order of Hibernians split Irish American republicans into two factions in the 1880s. Until they called a truce in 1897, the factions sponsored separate, parallel holiday celebrations, at which they spent the majority of their time denouncing their enemies within the movement rather than the enemies of Irish independence.[48]

Such religious, political, and ideological conflicts wracked the nationalist movements within each ethnic community, belying the image of unified nationalism that the sponsors of ethnic holiday celebrations sought to perpetuate and revealing the contestation that went into the construction of ethnic Americanism. In addition to this strife, leaders of ethnic communities faced challenges to their authority on the topic of nationalism from outside the middle class.

CHALLENGES TO THE BOURGEOIS VISION

The liberal ethnicity of middle-class nationalists had no place for workers as a class. The nationalists' holiday processions rarely featured labor unions. Ethnic Americans could participate as schoolchildren, as police officers and soldiers, as band members, or as members of nationalist, fraternal, military, temperance, or religious organizations. Unions, however, which identified workers as members of a distinct class, were, for the most part, not welcome.

There were some exceptions to the invisibility of organized labor. Polish carpenters and tailors marched in the Polish National Alliance's centennial parade in 1891, and freethinking Czech butchers, carpenters, and building trades workers marched with their unions for the Hus quincentenary in 1915. Germans, with a strong artisan tradition in the United States, were most likely to incorporate unions into national celebrations. The 1871 peace procession in Chicago, for instance, featured five divisions of artisans, from brewers, butchers, and bakers to chimney sweeps and house painters.[49] For the most part, however, labor remained invisible at middle-class celebrations, which sought to perpetuate the myth of class harmony under the national umbrella.

Socialists refused to go along with that illusion. Far from being invisible at socialist commemorations, workers were celebrated as workers, as nationalists, and as revolutionaries. German singing societies in 1902 sponsored a commune festival to commemorate the Paris Commune, which socialists viewed as the opening salvo of the socialist revolution. And in 1906 ethnic socialists united in Chicago to commemorate the first anniversary of the Bloody Sunday massacre of Russian revolutionaries. After a procession, marchers listened to speeches in Russian and Yiddish, heard the German singing societies' rendition of the "Marseillaise," and gave money to aid the revolutionaries' cause. Ethnic socialists in Chicago also celebrated May Day, the new international labor holiday. In 1905 the Italian Socialist Club sponsored musical exercises and a ball in honor of the day, and the German Socialist Saengerbund held a May festival. The Jewish Amalgamated Clothing Workers sponsored a musical program and speeches in 1920, and the Poale Zion organization held exercises the following year at the National Socialist Institute. Immigrants also joined the general May Day processions. The 1910 parade, for example, featured a division of Jewish unions and organizations and a Czech division that included labor unions, Socialist Party branches, turners, and socialist educational clubs named for Karl Marx, Ferdinand Lassalle, and Karel Havlíček.[50]

Just as Catholicism's first loyalty to Rome did not preclude nationalism, neither did socialism's first loyalty to class. Socialists in Chicago constructed their own brand of national identity at separate national celebrations. Italian socialists, for example, celebrated Italian unification and its architect, Giuseppe Garibaldi, whom they embraced as the preeminent national hero of Italy. They celebrated the centennial of his birth in 1907 with a meeting at the foot of his statue in Lincoln Park, where they laid a wreath of red flowers bearing the slogan "The International Is the Sun Rise of the Future." A socialist journalist sneered at the nonsocialist observance of the anniversary, proclaiming that "[i]f Garibaldi could have arisen from his grave and seen how he was profaned by the commemoration which the Italian officials of Chicago celebrated today, alas! how he would have laughed."[51]

Some socialists even criticized middle-class nationalists, as they did the pragmatic trade unions, for their lack of true patriotism. Italian socialists, for example, condemned the semicentennial celebration of two battles in the Italian unification struggle. Noting that only one hundred people attended the exercises and that the lone Italian flag was hidden by three huge American flags, *La Parola Dei Socialisti* scorned that the event "demonstrate[d] merely that Italian patriotism is lacking in America." Despite their internationalism, socialists proclaimed themselves to be more loyal to their homeland than nonsocialists. The Italian Americans at the celebration, the paper charged, sought to conceal their heritage; the men "display[ed] the clean-shaven upper lip of Americans, and . . . their offspring remain absolutely ignorant of their mother tongue." The only part of the exercises that drew any enthusiasm, *La Parola* contended, was the singing of Garibaldi's hymn and the "Marseillaise," because they were hymns of international revolution.[52]

Immigrant socialists also attacked nationalists for their embrace of the clergy and of the capitalist corruption of true democratic principles. A speaker at a socialist commemoration of the anniversary of Italian unification in 1913 deplored "the modern patriots who did not give rightful recognition to this historic day in order to avoid hurting the clerical-sabandist capitalist order," the "black-frocked party" that was "insidiously spreading its propaganda in the schools." The German *Chicagoer Arbeiter-Zeitung* castigated the 1889 centennial of George Washington's inauguration as "a real miserable affair" that revealed how the American Constitution had been overthrown by the "perfidy" of the capitalist class, and implied that only socialism would return America to its founding principles. The paper upbraided those Germans who had participated in the exercises, reserving its praise for those "smart enough not to participate in the whole humbug."[53]

Although socialism presented the clearest ideological challenge to bourgeois ethnic nationalism, it had relatively few adherents among American immigrants. A much more serious threat to the nationalists' project lay in the competing pull of commercial entertainment. Particularly during the summer months, holiday exercises faced stiff competition for workers' precious free time and money from circuses, amusement parks, taverns, baseball games, and packaged excursions. To combat these attractions, some nationalists incorporated controlled elements of amusement that did not offend bourgeois mores. Most holiday celebrations offered fireworks displays and dancing, for example, and many offered pageants or folk festivals, which attempted to marry nationalism and entertainment. By the turn of the century, this trend had accelerated. Like the holiday picnics of labor unions, those of ethnic organizations featured games, races, shooting galleries, and beer and ice cream stands. An 1895 celebration of the November insurrection, for example, incorporated entertainment technology with a magic lantern show featuring slides of Polish patriots.[54]

In Tucson Mexican American leaders in the early twentieth century began to incorporate into their Mexican Independence Day festivities events that contributed nothing to the construction of Mexican nationalism. These activities, which offered only amusement to holiday revelers, included bicycle and horse races with monetary prizes, games and races for children and adults, balloon ascensions, exhibition boxing matches, a queen contest, and dance competitions.[55] The problem with adding such features was that they inevitably diluted the nationalist message. Although the decline of oratory was less noticeable on ethnic holidays than on Labor Day, the ethnic middle class, like union leaders, had to appeal to a populace increasingly less interested in edification than in amusement on its infrequent holidays. Thus, although the middle class took the lead in shaping national identity, ordinary people influenced it as well by their tastes and their willingness to participate.

A final, and perhaps the most serious, enemy of middle-class nationalists was indifference to their projects. Few immigrants brought with them a strong sense of ethnic or national identity, and probably few believed that this was necessary to success in America. It was middle-class leaders, for the most part, who viewed nationalism as important and sought to excite an interest in it among their compatriots by sponsoring lavish ethnic holiday celebrations. The persistence of a level of indifference to their cause was evident in chronic low attendance at such functions, aside from special celebrations such as centennials. Ordinary people expressed little interest in oratory and bourgeois uplift. This indifference led the press and holiday orators into periodic jeremiads. In an article on the Gymnastic Union Sokol's 1880 commemoration of Jan Hus's death, *Svornost* lamented the "comparatively small audience present" at the exercises: "We cannot refrain from saying, with warranted bitterness, that the cancer of disinterest is beginning to eat into the enthusiasm and life of our community." More than twenty years later the Czech press in Chicago was still lecturing Czechs on their apathy; *Denní Hlasatel* in 1906 noted that "[m]any were absent whose duty it was to attend the [Havliček] celebration, but let them settle that with their own conscience."[56]

CONSTRUCTING ETHNIC AMERICANISM

If duty did not always call ethnic Americans to middle-class nationalists' celebrations, it did increasingly bring native-born politicians seeking the ethnic vote. Although African Americans in Richmond could not attract any white officials to their emancipation exercises after Reconstruction, for example, the mayor, governor, and other officials regularly attended the annual German and Irish celebrations. When the governor was too ill to attend the German Day celebration in 1895, he sent a holiday message that detailed Virginia's pride in "her adopted sons and daughters," who came from "a high and exalted race." German Richmonders, for their part, recognized and accepted the privileges of race. The president of the German-American Association in 1890 thanked the governor and mayor for attending the celebration, noting that "by their presence [they] prove . . . that they honor our devotion, for are we not all of one Anglo-Saxon race?"[57]

In Tucson, where Mexican Americans composed the majority population until after 1900, and in large cities such as Chicago, where immigrant groups formed sizable voting blocs, politicians and other officials were even more likely to make the rounds of ethnic holiday observances. Indeed, politically powerful groups such as Irish Americans could afford to snub elected officials when displeased. In 1895, for example, marchers in the Chicago St. Patrick's Day parade refused to salute or otherwise acknowledge the mayor as they passed his reviewing stand, allegedly because he had forgotten to wear the green. "So far as the marchers and spectators were concerned," the Chicago Tribune reported, "Mayor [John] Hopkins and his friends might as well have been in Greenland." A high-water point of political acknowledgment of ethnic power came in 1910 when President William Howard Taft traveled to Chicago for the Irish Fellowship Club's St. Patrick's Day celebration. Not surprisingly, the occasion drew a star-studded cast of politicians, including the governor, lieutenant governor, mayor, several senators and congressmen, judges, state legislators, and aldermen, whose presence stamped the holiday and the Irish cause with the utmost legitimacy. "The coming of the President of the United States to a St. Patrick's Day celebration at this juncture in Irish history," the club proclaimed in its resolution of thanks to Taft, "was significant testimony given to the whole world of his classification of Irish-American citizenship and his knowledge of the capabilities and the loyalty of the Irish race."[58]

Although electoral power undoubtedly constituted the main reason for such attention from political leaders, it was not the only one. Even before disfranchisement, African Americans had trouble drawing whites to their celebrations. Despite rising nativist sentiment at the turn of the century,

European immigrants, particularly Germans, Scandinavians, British, and Irish, benefited to a certain extent from the privileges of perceived whiteness. Native-born whites welcomed them, through attendance at their holiday celebrations, with much more enthusiasm than they showed to African Americans. Like African Americans, ethnic Americans defined their ethnicity as congruent with Americanism, and they constructed a pluralistic Americanism that incorporated them fully and on their own terms. The guest lists of ethnic holiday celebrations demonstrate that this ethnic Americanism was more palatable to native-born white Americans than the similar demands of African Americans for acceptance as Americans.

At the Irish Fellowship Club's banquet, Michael J. Faherty, the club's president, had assured Taft that he was not among strangers. In his telling, Irish Americans were the prototypical Americans. Like African American orators, he pointed to the Irish military contributions to the nation. "We Irish people," he explained, "claim to be Americans of the Americans, we were present in large numbers at the birth of this nation, . . . and when the blood of other Nationalities was needed . . . to cement and hold forever together the wavering states of the Union in the great War of the Rebellion we gave our share." A German Day orator in Richmond expressed a similar sentiment in explaining the immigrants' view of their relationship to their homeland and adopted land. "Germany is our mother," he told the governor, the mayor, and the German American crowd, "the United States of America is the wife of our choice. We . . . are prepared to defend her against one and all, even, if it should be needed, against our own mother, for the wife has the first claim on her husband's protection."[59]

Devotion to their homeland, ethnic Americans believed, did not lessen their loyalty to their adopted home. Indeed, some contended that the former made them better American citizens. The head of the women's auxiliary of Richmond's Ancient Order of Hibernians, for example, informed banquetgoers on St. Patrick's Day in 1910 that "the love for Ireland made the Irish better citizens of the United States, for all are loyal Irish-Americans." Similarly, at Seventeenth of May exercises in 1915, Oscar Haugen told his fellow Norwegians that "the man who remembers the home of his forefathers makes a better citizen in his adopted country because of his loyalty and his love for the land of his ancestors."[60]

If loyalty to one's homeland made one a better citizen, then perpetuating the traditions and culture of the homeland became an imperative of good American citizenship. Thus, the minister who spoke at the 1911 children's celebration of Norwegian Independence Day in Chicago explained that "the whole purpose of this beautiful demonstration is to stimulate in ourselves and our children the principles of true liberty and patriotism as American citizens." And the Chicago Hebrew Institute asserted that its Hebrew school, which taught Hebrew, Jewish history, and Judaism, produced "a most desirable type of the Jewish-American boy. Conscious of the great past of his nation, of the glorious contribution of his people to civilization, he makes a proud Jew and a good American citizen."[61]

Middle-class immigrants could assert that ethnic loyalty made one a better American precisely because they had constructed their ethnicity as compatible with, and even prototypical of, American liberal principles. At exercises for the 1894 centennial of Kosciuszko's insurrection, the leader of the Polish National Alliance, T. M. Helinski, explained to Americans why Poles were "celebrating on American soil the achievements of a foreign hero." They did so, he declared, "as American citizens, and to demonstrate thereby our understanding, our appreciation, and our love of the principles of American liberty." The actions of Kosciuszko, warrior for both America's and Poland's independence, revealed, according to Polish nationalists, the inborn dedication of Poles to the principles on which the United States had been founded. Other immigrant groups made similar claims. Freethinkers traced Czech dedication to the principles of free thought and speech back half a millennium to their hero Jan Hus. Mexican Americans found the roots of their devotion to liberty in their Aztec ancestors. A Sixteenth of September orator in 1885 Tucson asserted that neither the Spanish nor the French, nor any tyrant, could uproot "the phrygian cap of liberty" that covered the Mexican people.[62]

Immigrant nationalists pointed out what they described as the striking parallels between America and their homeland. Mexican Americans repeatedly referred to "las dos repúblicas," for example. Orators linked Fathers Hidalgo and Morelos and George Washington, the "fathers" of those nations, and liberal hero Benito Juárez and Abraham Lincoln, their saviors. Poles compared the May constitution of 1791 to its American counterpart, while

Norwegians asserted that the Norwegian constitution was "an instrument recognized, with the American Constitution, as one of the world's great bulwarks of liberty."[63]

This insistence on the ideals immigrants shared with Americans suggests that this was no simple assimilation to American culture. Indeed, ethnic constructions of nationalism that traced liberal principles to the homeland may be interpreted as deeply subversive of the American contention that its revolution and national principles were unique in the world. Moreover, as Rivka Lissak has argued in her study of Hull House, while middle-class ethnic leaders advocated assimilation, they did not mean by that the same thing as native-born Americans. Rather, ethnic Americans interpreted being American as "being committed to the idea of democracy and having the freedom and right of self-expression."[64] To the extent that immigrants claimed already and inherently to possess American principles, they could without guile assert that they came to the United States already Americans.

Americanization thus did not entail discarding ethnicity, but having the freedom to express it. Oscar Haugen noted in 1915 that "the Norwegians have become thoroughly Americanized while still retaining the love for the old land across the sea." If middle-class immigrants viewed the commemoration of ethnic holidays as stimulating American citizenship as well as nationalism, it is not surprising that they also celebrated American holidays, which they saw as their civic duty to their adopted land. "The Norwegians as good citizens celebrated the Fourth of July at Chicago Avenue Park," reported *Skandinaven* in 1878. Some immigrants even pointed to their own celebrations to argue that they were better Americans than the native born. In 1908, for instance, Polish Chicagoans participated in a GAR-sponsored celebration of Flag Day in Humboldt Park. "Although a strictly American celebration," *Dziennik Zwiazkowy* noted, "yet it became prominently Polish, because of the noticeable absence of Yankees." The paper castigated "native born Americans lying on the lawn, unmindful of the near-by celebration," and asserted that "[o]ur forefathers had a more profound respect for the flag, and spared not their lives in its defense."[65]

Like the Poles, other ethnic Chicagoans made American holidays their own. German, Irish, and Polish Chicagoans, along with predominantly German socialists, held the only public celebrations of the national centennial in Chicago in 1876. The *Sunday Jewish Courier* echoed its Polish counterpart by explaining in 1914 that immigrants had taken over the celebration of American holidays because of the apathy and lack of patriotism of native-born Americans. "Washington's Birthday," the paper concluded, "like every other holiday that reminds us of lofty ideals, is . . . chiefly a holiday for the immigrants, who still believe in those ideals and are ready to fight for them."[66] The liberal principles celebrated on American holidays were the same ones that, according to ethnic nationalists, immigrants had carried with them from their homelands.

Immigrant enthusiasm for American holidays, therefore, should not fool us into interpreting these as purely assimilative occasions. While they celebrated their Americanism, immigrants did not eschew ethnicity. American holidays, like ethnic holidays, provided occasions to construct and to celebrate ethnic Americanism. In this sense they subverted the assimilationist vision of middle-class native-born Americans. "To those who bemoan the lack of Italianism in our colony," *L'Italia* wrote in 1920, "we will demonstrate the fallacy of their assertion when innumerable Italians will meet to celebrate July Fourth." After this rather shocking opening statement, the paper explained that Italians would combine the celebration of the Fourth with that of Garibaldi's birthday. The sponsor of the celebration promised a "program of Italianism and sincere Americanism."[67]

Like the Italians, immigrants often paired celebrations. Poles jointly commemorated Lincoln and Kosciuszko's birthdays, and the Society of Danish Veterans in Chicago annually celebrated the anniversary of driving the Prussians out of Denmark on the Fourth of July.[68] Immigrant celebrations also paired symbols of American and ethnic identity. The American flag flew next to the homeland's banner, the "Star-Spangled Banner" joined the homeland's anthem on holiday programs, and banquet-goers toasted America and the president along with the homeland and its heroes. Holiday orators littered their speeches with references to ethnic contributions to America's history and progress. Norwegians reminded their countrymen that it was Leif Eriksson, not Christopher Columbus, who had "discovered" America, while Italians took pride in Columbus's voyage. Poles remembered Kosciuszko and Pulaski's contributions to the American Revolution, while the Irish, Germans, Czechs, Jews, Scots, and Norwegians all commemorated on Memorial Day the sacrifices made by their young men in the Civil War.

Volunteer fire department float, Mexican Independence Day in Tucson, 1905. The brilliantly attired volunteer firefighters and their floats were a common sight in holiday processions. They show their patriotism to both their homeland and their adopted land by carrying the flags of Mexico and the United States. (Courtesy of the Arizona Historical Society/Tucson, accession number 44623)

The pairings of ethnic and American symbols and the lists of contributions accomplished ethnic leaders' goals of showing the complementary nature of ethnic and American ideals. But, as April Schultz has demonstrated in her study of the Norwegian American immigration centennial, this does not necessarily mean that such celebrations served a primarily assimilative function. Indeed, ethnic symbols may be read as competing with American symbols. At the least, the very presence of ethnic symbols, music, dance, history, and language suggests a definition of Americanism that had ample room for ethnicity and thus undercut native-born Americans' definitions of assimilation.[69]

At the "prominently Polish" Flag Day celebration, for example, Kosciuszko and Polish nationalism took pride of place. Polish Chicagoans laid two wreaths at the Kosciuszko monument and "then they proceeded to the flagstaff where they did homage to our emblem." The leaders of the drive to build that monument had earlier designated 4 July 1896 "as the date for the great summer festival for the benefit of the Tadeusz Kosciuszko monument," in the hopes that sufficient money could be raised to begin construction.

In this case the American holiday served as a convenient occasion for fund-raising activities. Such activities in the service of ethnic causes were common at ethnic celebrations of American holidays. Chicago's Clan na Gael, for instance, planned to raise $2,000 for the Irish Republican Brotherhood at its 1890 Fourth of July picnic.[70]

The Memorial Day exercises held at the Bohemian National Cemetery by freethinking Czechs in 1915 illustrate just how closely ethnic and American identities intertwined at such celebrations. Czech American veterans of the Civil and Spanish-American Wars, as well as other military organizations, paraded to the cemetery and drilled in front of the monument to the Czechs who fell in the Civil War, after which they decorated the graves with flowers and American flags. The exercises that followed included recitations by children, the singing of the Czech and American national anthems, and speeches in Czech and English. The orators lauded the Czech contribution to the United States but also advised Czechs to remember their homeland. The speaker of the Illinois House of Representatives, whose wife was Czech, recited the text of the Czech anthem in English. A cemetery representative informed the crowd that they could purchase picture postcards of the crematorium, to benefit the Free Thought schools. The exercises concluded with the dual national anthems and Bohemian folk songs.[71]

Such celebrations reveal the extent to which ethnicity shaped immigrants' American identity, as well as the converse. The efforts of bourgeois Mexican Americans to maintain good relations between *las dos repúblicas*, for example, led them to rewrite their homeland's history on national holidays to omit the war between the United States and Mexico in the 1840s. Dredging up such an ugly bit of history would not have helped the cause of good commercial relations between Mexico and the United States. Nor would it serve the cause of Mexican American ethnicity, which emphasized what the two republics shared—their struggles for liberty and their moral and material progress in the late nineteenth century. A European American orator at the 1887 exercises went so far as to assert that once the Spanish had left in 1821, "[n]o foreign influence ever disturbed the quiet of [Mexico's] peaceful domain" until the French invasion of the 1860s.[72]

Perhaps the clearest evidence that immigrant celebrations of American holidays did not serve the sole function of assimilation to the dominant culture is the very fact that they celebrated these holidays as ethnic groups. As a general rule, each group held its own celebration rather than combining with other ethnic groups and native-born Americans in pan-ethnic exercises. This voluntary segregation was at one level just another indication of the fragmented nature of American holiday celebrations. Nonetheless the separation was significant because it allowed immigrants to invoke ethnic sentiment and to construct ethnicity as well as Americanism on such occasions. Pan-ethnic celebrations would have subordinated ethnic identity to American identity, and immigrants did not view that as desirable. At their own celebrations they could intertwine their history and heroes with those of America and construct an American identity that had room for ethnicity. They could, that is, create ethnic Americanism.

The efforts of immigrant leaders to construct an ethnic identity rather than simply assimilate to American culture drew mixed reactions from native-born Americans. Some, such as a speaker at the Kosciuszko centennial, looked approvingly on this process. "The Pole who would be unmindful of the glorious record of Kosciuszko," he told revelers, "has neither the sentiment nor the patriotism to remember the glorious services of Washington, Jefferson, or Lincoln." Others were much less sanguine. An orator at the American League's "Old-Fashioned" Fourth in 1889 castigated the Clan na Gael for promoting Irish nationalism on this holiday, noting that "on the flaming poster of that band of midnight assassins . . . the Stars and Stripes modestly peeps forth from under the green flag."[73] While few native-born Americans were so openly nativist, by the late nineteenth century many were beginning to wonder whether immigrants could be properly patriotic to two nations. The surge in immigration intensified these worries and led to new efforts by a variety of Americans to strengthen American national identity and to Americanize immigrants.

5

PATRIOTIC HOLIDAYS AND CIVIC EDUCATION

*O*N MEMORIAL DAY 1889 Chicagoans gathered at the scene of the 1886 Haymarket Square bombing to witness the dedication of a monument to the police officers slain there. In keeping with the Memorial Day tradition of employing orphans to maximum effect, the son of Mathias Degan, the first officer killed in the bombing, unveiled the statue of a policeman, arm raised to keep order. The monument bore the inscription "Dedicated by Chicago ... to her Defenders in the Riot of May 4, 1886." In his version of the events at Haymarket, the orator of the day, Franklin W. Head, a Republican activist and businessman, conflated the police with the heroes of the Civil War. He informed his audience that "a gallant officer, who had served with distinction through the War of the Rebellion," had praised the bravery of the police, noting that "he had never known or heard of an instance where so large a proportion of an attack-

ing force had been disabled without resulting in its demoralization and re-
treat." After the explosion, Head exclaimed, "the voices of Bonfield and Fitz-
patrick rang out like a clarion, rallying their men to the unequal combat." He
narrated the "battle" that ensued in terms that might have been lifted from a
more traditional Memorial Day speech. "Under the constant fire of the mob
the lines were formed, the charge was made upon ten times their number,
and the crowd was dispersed. Every policeman who was in the affray was a
hero," Head concluded, completing the apotheosis of the Haymarket police
officers, "every man had in him the material of which are made martyrs in the
cause of duty."[1]

If the size of the crowd was any indication, many Chicagoans disagreed
with Head's conclusions. Only about two thousand people attended the ceremonies, despite the deliberate juxtaposition of the police with "the nation's
heroes." The Haymarket monument was actually conceived by the *Chicago
Tribune*'s notoriously antilabor publisher, Joseph Medill, and erected through
the efforts of local business leaders, who had also provided funds to assist the
families of the slain and to aid the police department's hunt for subversives.
It was not surprising that working-class Chicagoans, whether or not they
agreed with the principles of the Haymarket defendants, showed little interest in a monument to the police, who were notorious for their willingness to
break heads as they broke up strikes and demonstrations. Haymarket was
but one example of this treatment. After the bomb exploded, the police, in
contrast to Head's account, panicked and began firing indiscriminately into
the mostly unarmed crowd. According to historians of the incident, most of
the officers killed by gunfire received their wounds from their own compatriots. Despite Head's tribute, the police of Haymarket were not all paragons
of virtue, either. Capt. John Bonfield, whom Head lionized for leading the
charge, had been fired from the force for corruption several months before
the monument dedication.[2] It was small wonder that so few Chicagoans
turned out to memorialize such heroes.

If the police remembered their martyrs to law and order on Memorial
Day, the anarchists had their own sacred ceremonies for the other Haymarket martyrs, the men executed, not for throwing the bomb, but for the
crime of preaching anarchy and radical socialism. In June 1893 the Pioneer
Aid and Support Association (PASA) dedicated a monument to the mar-

tyrs at their gravesite at Waldheim Cemetery. The monument depicted an Americanized version of the French Marianne, wearing a phrygian (liberty) cap, drawing a sword with one hand, and crowning a fallen male worker with a laurel wreath with the other. In symbolic symmetry with the police monument dedication, Albert Parsons Jr. unveiled the monument honoring his father and the other executed anarchists. Some three thousand men and women marched in procession through downtown Chicago before taking trains out to the cemetery. In contrast to the sparse crowd at the police monument four years earlier, the anarchists' ceremonies attracted more than eight thousand people, perhaps augmented by visitors in town for the World's Columbian Exposition.[3]

The radicals vehemently disputed the police and capitalists' version of Haymarket. Each 11 November, the anniversary of the 1887 executions, anarchists gathered at Waldheim Cemetery and around the nation to commemorate their martyrs. In Chicago they decorated the graves of their slain comrades and lauded their heroism, just as the veterans did on Memorial Day. In the anarchists' songs, speeches, editorials, and processions, they condemned the police, capital, and the government that they believed had perverted the American ideals of liberty and justice, and they reaffirmed their commitment to the fight for real liberty. If the radical workers were both victims and heroes of the anarchist story of Haymarket, the police clearly played the role of villain. Lucy Parsons, radical journalist, labor agitator, and widow of the executed Albert Parsons, asserted unequivocally that "[t]here was no riot at the Haymarket except a police riot." In a speech in New York City on the twentieth anniversary of the executions, noted anarchist writer and orator Voltairine de Cleyre scathingly rebutted the official version of the Haymarket affair, using its own text as a weapon. "The public may believe," she declared, "that the police behaved with conspicuous courage in the face of the bomb, and 'did not falter'; that 'they closed up their ranks, drew their revolvers and began to fire upon the dumbfounded people who fled in all directions.' I should not, myself, have thought it required conspicuous courage to fire upon dumbfounded and fleeing people," she concluded dryly.[4]

The commemorations of the two very different sets of Haymarket martyrs make vivid the class conflict that polarized urban Americans in the late nineteenth century, nowhere more bitterly than in Chicago. Although the

Haymarket commemorations took this combat to extremes, fragmentation rather than unity had become the norm in American cities, and American public holiday celebrations reflected this situation. Ethnic groups and African Americans commemorated their own holidays and generally observed American holidays with separate celebrations, by choice or by exclusion. Organized labor celebrated on Labor Day and socialists on May Day. Civil War veterans observed Memorial Days in the North and the South. And the Fourth of July had long since dissolved into a plethora of picnics, dinners, military parades, and bombastic oratory.

In addition, commercial excursions, amusements, and sporting events increasingly penetrated the holidays, offering attractive alternatives to what official celebrations existed. For fifty cents, Chicagoans in 1890 could attend a so-called old-fashioned Fourth of July celebration at a private park that featured music and dancing, a barbecue, balloon ascensions and parachute jumps, and fireworks. Or they could take a "grand free excursion" sponsored by a real estate company to the new suburb of Edison Park, where lots, not coincidentally, were available for purchase. Sporting events had also come to dominate the Fourth. Baseball games, regattas, horse races, tennis tournaments, and track and field contests became regular holiday features. In the cycling-crazed 1890s, African Americans in Richmond celebrated the Fourth with bicycle races, while members of the Cycle Club and costumed "bicycle horribles" paraded in Tucson. In 1895 twenty-five thousand Chicagoans attended a bicycle derby. An organization calling itself the Mystic Order of Broncho Busters inaugurated a holiday rodeo in Tucson in 1905. Even Memorial Day was not immune, to the dismay of veterans, as a bicycle road race in Chicago almost overshadowed grave-decorating ceremonies.[5]

Civic-minded business and professional men such as those responsible for the police monument viewed the fragmented and commercialized celebrations of the late nineteenth century as symptomatic of the anarchy gripping the cities. Beginning in the late 1880s, they determined to address this problem by organizing centralized celebrations in an effort to transform patriotic holidays into vehicles for the creation of urban order and unity. Blaming the chaos they perceived all around them on the lack of self-discipline, at best, or disloyalty, at worst, these self-proclaimed civic leaders found the solution in law-and-order patriotism. Public celebrations of patriotic holidays, they discovered, provided ideal occasions for the civic and patriotic education that would turn the ignorant masses into good citizens and good Americans. Moreover, as the organizers of such occasions, they could script the holiday celebrations so as to construct a transcendent national identity that overrode the ethnic, racial, sectional, and class loyalties that they thought were destroying the nation. As Carl Smith points out, although these men certainly acted in their own interest, they cannot simply be written off as hypocrites or rationalizers, for they believed sincerely that disorder threatened the health of the cities and the republic and that they could offer a solution to it.[6]

One of the first salvos in the civic elites' crusade was a proposal in *Century* magazine, in the wake of the centennial of the Constitution, to make Constitution Day an annual holiday. Unlike the nascent class holiday of Labor Day, the magazine held, Constitution Day would exert a "direct patriotic influence" on Americans. The potential such a holiday held for calming the troubled American social waters was immense. "It has been wisely said," the *Century* noted, "that the quickest way to cure the quarrelsome tendencies of children is to provide them with some common ground of interest, even the simplest, such as marching together; and the rule is not without value for the children of a larger growth." The Constitution holiday could provide quarreling Americans with such a common ground. "Merely to group about a national idea . . . is an incalculable influence in making our people homogeneous and sympathetic. We cannot but think," the magazine concluded, "that this influence would be broadened and perpetuated by a formal recognition of the day as a national holiday."[7]

Given the climate of the mid-1880s, the choice of the Constitution for a new holiday is not surprising. Since its ratification, the Constitution had symbolized two primary concepts, national union and liberty under law, which perfectly meshed with the goals of this self-proclaimed civic elite. "The use of such a holiday" as Constitution Day, *Century* magazine wrote in its plea, "would be to aid in supplying from year to year that strength of intelligent sentiment which in national emergencies is the most practical support of all law." The movement to establish a Constitution Day, however, met with resounding indifference on the part of most Americans. Reverenced it may well have been, but as the focal point of public celebration the Constitution did not work in the late nineteenth century. As Eric Hobsbawm has noted, invented traditions lacking "genuine popular resonance" rarely succeed.[8] The appeal of the Constitution was to the intellect, which may have suited the men leading this crusade, but did little to spark the popular imagination, increasingly weaned on visually oriented commercial popular culture. Moreover, while the good citizenship the civic leaders wished to produce required a thoughtful and educated populace, the patriotism that they also sought to evoke was visceral and required blind and unhesitating allegiance. To resolve this paradox, they turned to more tangible and visual symbols, which could marry the intellectual citizenship and the emotional patriotism. They found these symbols in George Washington, Abraham Lincoln, the American flag, and, to a lesser extent, Christopher Columbus.

In Chicago a cohort of civic-minded financiers, heads of merchandising and manufacturing concerns, and corporate lawyers sponsored massive public celebrations for the 1889 centennial of Washington's inauguration, the 1892 quadricentennial of Columbus's first voyage to America, and the 1909 centennial of Lincoln's birth. In these celebrations they reconstructed Americanism to emphasize law and order, citizenship, and ostentatious patriotism. The American identity they espoused was firmly Anglo-American and rooted in the early republic. It had no room for ethnic, racial, sectional, or class consciousness or loyalties. This vision of American identity was static; it had been created in the past and endured in the present. The duty of those whom the celebrations targeted was to accept and to assimilate to this America; those who refused were branded unpatriotic or, literally, un-American.

The men who dominated the committees that organized these anniversary celebrations in Chicago were among the most prominent in the city. Most were white, native born, and Protestant, although there was a smattering of immigrants, Catholics, and Jews. Contemporaries hailed them as self-made men and representative citizens, the very embodiment of the American Dream. They were financiers and attorneys, investors in real estate, traders in commodities, and presidents of banks and merchandising and manufacturing concerns. Although most considered themselves Republicans, a reformist orientation was more important than party affiliation. They belonged to social and civic clubs, especially the Union League Club, which had been founded in 1879, spurred by political corruption and the railroad strike of 1877, "to encourage and promote by moral, social and political influence, unconditioned loyalty to the Federal Government, and . . . to inculcate a higher appreciation of the value and sacred obligations of American citizenship." The cost of belonging to the club provides one indication of the wealth of its members. The initiation fee was $200 and annual dues were $80. Only the exclusive Chicago Club, a social organization, was more expensive.[9]

Most important, members of this self-professed civic elite took an active interest in the development of their city through their civic and philanthropic work; they held directorships not only of banks but also of asylums and cultural institutions. Many served on school and parks boards. Charles L. Hutchinson illustrates the marriage of civic, business, and philanthropic concerns that characterized these men. President of the Corn Exchange Bank and a member of the Union League Club, he sat on the board of directors of another bank, an insurance company, and the University of Chicago; was superintendent of St. Paul's Universalist Sunday School and a trustee of the Chicago Orphans' Asylum; and served as president of both the Art Institute and the Chicago Board of Trade. Elbridge Keith, another bank president, also held the presidency of the Union League Club, the Young Men's Christian Association (YMCA), and the Chicago Orphans' Asylum. A Chicago biographical dictionary's description of Keith could have applied to these men in general: "always prominent in benevolent work, and actively interested in everything tending to the benefit of Chicago and of good citizenship generally."[10]

Both Hutchinson and Keith also served on committees that arranged the Washington centennial and the World's Columbian Exposition. These self-conscious civic leaders not surprisingly considered themselves to be not only well qualified but also duty bound to educate other Americans in patriotic Americanism and good citizenship. In this mission they enlisted the support of the native-born, ethnic, and black business and professional middle classes, who generally shared the elites' concerns about citizenship and public order. The civic leaders invited businessmen, journalists, clergymen, lawyers, clerks, and educators to serve as speakers and as members of the numerous committees set up to organize these three ambitious undertakings in 1889, 1892, and 1909.[11]

Each of the anniversary celebrations prominently featured school exercises as well, signaling a new direction for the educational mission of public holidays. In the late nineteenth century, veterans' organizations, hereditary societies, and educators began their own ventures in patriotic and civic education, directed particularly at schoolchildren. The expansion of education and the increasingly immigrant student population made the schools a natural venue for the civic education and Americanizing functions of public holidays. Rather than simply including children in public celebrations, civic elites, veterans, professional patriots, and educators began to bring holidays into the schools. By the turn of the century, school holidays were well on their way to institutionalization as arenas of Americanization and citizenship training.

Although schoolchildren provided a captive audience, the hearts and minds of their parents proved more difficult to win. Immigrants and African Americans were eager to pledge their patriotism, but they did so on their own terms, asserting their rights to full citizenship without necessarily subscribing to the restrictive definition of Americanism articulated on these holidays. Neither they nor native-born Americans were invited to participate in these celebrations as workers. They were welcome as members of ethnic groups, military and fraternal organizations, and even religious associations, but not as members of unions. Even when invited to participate, organized labor generally chose to remain outside these celebrations and, on occasion, publicly criticized them and the America that the elites and their middle-class allies sought to create.

"LIBERTY REGULATED BY LAW": THE WASHINGTON INAUGURAL CENTENNIAL

On 22 February 1887, the Union League Club instituted annual public exercises for Washington's Birthday in the first salvo of a campaign of civic and patriotic education aimed at Chicagoans, particularly immigrants and the working class in general. In George Washington, the exemplar of patriotic citizenship, the Union League Club found a perfect vehicle for patriotic education and unity. As club members heard at their 1887 banquet, the first president "had been selected by the world as a supreme civic representative of virtue" and was thus "an ideal public man." The men of the Union League Club believed that their financial success and their concern with the public good, as demonstrated by their cultural and civic philanthropy, justified their claim to the mantle of Washington. They were not the first to turn to the first president for assistance in addressing the problems of their age. The Law and Order League, which had originated in Chicago after the 1877 railroad strike, had adopted Washington's Birthday as its annual Law and Order Day. Even earlier Washington had been proffered as a patriotic balm to heal sectional tensions. In 1857 the *North American Review* had suggested that Washington's Birthday be made a "common shrine, a national feast" in which "sectional animosity is awed into universal reverence." Although the Civil War intervened, civic leaders resurrected the holiday amid the new civil wars wracking America in the 1880s.[12]

The Washington celebrations planned by the Union League Club featured public lectures on citizenship by men prominent in business, finance, government, and letters. Writer and former abolitionist James Russell Lowell, for instance, spoke at the initial gathering. By 1889 the club was congratulating itself on the fruit borne by these exercises, which were, proclaimed president George Bissell, "more and more becoming the instrumentalities out from which the best thoughts of our public men flow into our political and social currents, and thus become creators of public opinion, and encouragements to higher citizenship."[13]

For the men of the Union League Club, citizenship and law and order went hand in hand. The timing of their first celebration, just ten months after the Haymarket Square bombing, was no coincidence. They had been outraged by the Haymarket affair, which they saw as representative of the anarchy that resulted from unrestrained liberty. The murder of police officers, the premier symbols of an orderly society, provided proof to club members of the lawlessness and anarchy of the labor movement, as well as the ignorance and potential threat of unassimilated immigrants. It was the Union League Club that directed the fund-raising effort in 1888 for the monument to the police martyrs of Haymarket, and a club man, Franklin W. Head, spoke at the dedicatory Memorial Day exercises sponsored by the club in 1889.[14]

Just a month before those exercises, the club had organized a massive citywide celebration for the centennial of Washington's inauguration. If annual celebrations of Washington's Birthday were a good way to educate the public, the centennial provided the opportunity for a veritable feast of civic education uniting Washington and the Constitution. At a meeting in February 1889, the Union League Club resolved to celebrate the centennial on 30 April "by organizing as many gatherings as can be arranged for satisfactorily, of Americans, whether native or foreign born, who are devoted to the Constitution of the United States and to Republican institutions—to liberty regulated by law." The executive committee of the celebration heralded the inauguration of the new government under the Constitution as "the real birth of the United States, as a nation." Although the Declaration of Independence had been a great milestone in national history, the Union League Club claimed that "it was surpassed by the affirmative act which made us a constitutional government and united people."[15]

It was not surprising that the men of the Union League Club, fearful of revolt from their employees and the lower classes, focused on the establishment of the government of laws under the Constitution and the first president, rather than on the act of revolt embodied in the Declaration of Independence and celebrated on Independence Day. The secretary of the committee even proposed that the inaugural celebration would provide a badly needed corrective to the excessive liberties of the Fourth of July. The Fourth, he explained, "is a day calculated to arouse enthusiasm for independence . . . a day for the removing of barriers, a day that is understood too much by the children . . . as a day for license, freedom from law and restriction." Constitution Day may have failed to spark public interest, but he suggested that the anniversary of Washington's inauguration might serve the same end, "to give emphasis to our Constitution, to creation rather than destruction, to the distinct national idea, to rejoice not that we have thrown off the yoke of England, but that we are a nation with national ideas and a history."[16]

At the instigation of the Union League Club, the inaugural centennial became a masterpiece of civic instruction. The club directed that "speakers should not only unfold the Constitution before their hearers, but that *patriotism* itself be *defined*, as a comprehensive term embracing most of the duties incident to our relation to society as well as to government." This instruction began, as on many American holidays, in the churches. In Chicago some thirty churches held special services replete with patriotic songs and sermons that complemented the pictures of Washington and the U.S. flags gracing the church walls. After the church services, however, the Union

League Club added a new wrinkle to holiday rituals by dispersing to the city's public and private schools. The club had directly targeted the city's largely immigrant schoolchildren by establishing a committee on school celebrations, which had arranged the morning exercises. After flag-raising ceremonies, students and their parents gathered for programs of student recitations, original essays, patriotic songs, and exercises. After the student portion of the program, the older children heard addresses by business and professional men on Washington's life and patriotism. Before heading home, each student in the city received a souvenir medal of the occasion, the better "to fix in their memories the lessons contained in the school exercises."[17]

These exercises taught students the gendered nature of patriotism. Girls dressed in red, white, and blue formed silent tableaux of "Columbia and the Original 13 States" and "Martha Washington's Tea Party," while boys enacted dialogues between "Uncle Sam and His Supporters" and "The Thirteen States." Boys learned they had the active civic role, while girls learned that theirs was the supporting part. Boys could grow up to become George Washington; girls, if they were lucky, could grow up to marry him. Girls at one school presented a "comedietta entitled 'Old Maids,'" in which thirty little girls went in search of husbands, wanting none better than Washington." At another school an orator warned boys, "[D]o not fail to cast a conscientious vote." Although women could not vote, he told the girls, they could "at least teach some one to vote right."[18]

Children were not the only targets of the Union League Club's civic instruction. An estimated one hundred thousand adults attended nine mass meetings organized by the club in the afternoon. The meeting places had been decorated profusely with flags and bunting, flowers, wreaths, and portraits of Washington to provide the proper patriotic atmosphere. Although Chicago's population was too large to permit one celebration, the club did its best to ensure that all participants had the same experience. The program at each meeting was the same, the simultaneity of the exercises replicating the goal of national unity. At three o'clock each chairman called his meeting to order with a brief address, then turned the floor over to the chaplain, who led the audience in a prayer of thanksgiving. A band then played national airs and a volunteer chorus led the audience in song. The chairman next read regrets from "prominent men," presumably to impress upon the audience the importance of the occasion. After this he read a series of resolutions prepared for the day, which the crowd approved by acclamation. Finally, two orators at each meeting delivered speeches on the history of American liberty, Washington's patriotism, and the wisdom of the Constitution. To close the exercises, the chorus and audience sang "America," to which its author had added a special centennial stanza.[19]

In the evening the Union League Club hosted a banquet for the orators and distinguished guests, while the populace attended three fireworks displays, which gave final imprint, in visually spectacular form, to the patriotic lessons of the day. Some four hundred thousand Chicagoans exclaimed at set pieces that included the U.S. Capitol, "its dome a scintillating ball of white flame"; the word "America," in every shade of the rainbow; Washington's head, "as large as the sphinx"; the first president taking the oath of office; and "cameo busts" of Thomas Jefferson, John Adams, and Martha Washington. The elites, sated with good food and wine, and the people, sated with gunpowder and pyrotechnics, finally called a halt to the centennial festivities near midnight.[20]

Members of the Union League Club roundly congratulated themselves on the triumph of their celebration. Member Joseph Medill's *Chicago Tribune* proclaimed that the event demonstrated "the deep patriotic sentiment of [Chicagoans], . . . their devotion to the National Union."[21] With only three months of planning, the men of the club had managed to concoct a celebration that spread their version of patriotism, in one form or another, to a large portion of Chicago's population. They did this in part by applying the managerial efficiency of the new corporation, but their master stroke was to involve the public, especially the middle class, in their scheme.

The original committee of seventeen that had conceived the celebration contained a cross section of the city's elite, including the mayor, three attorneys, two judges, two bank presidents, and four heads of manufacturing or merchandising concerns. To organize the centennial, however, they enlisted the support of a broad spectrum of middle- and upper-class Chicagoans by inviting them to serve on a larger general executive committee and fourteen additional committees and to give speeches at the schools. Occupational data for 386 of the 476 committee members indicate that small businessmen, newspapermen, attorneys, clergymen, bankers, and school officials (including the only three women members) dominated the planning, aided by a sprinkling of clerks and salesmen. Laborers and even skilled workers were conspicuous by their absence.[22]

A number of ethnic businessmen and journalists sat on the committees, enlisted in the goal of Americanization. Indeed, the committee of seventeen had purposefully enlarged the executive committee so as to secure "the co-operation of representative citizens of foreign birth or extraction," the better to reach Chicago's large immigrant population. At a meeting on 11 February, Samuel Allerton, chairman of the executive committee, told these men that the Union League Club hoped "that there may be awakened in you . . . that patriotic sentiment which will move you to go to your own people and say to them: 'It is time for us to become Americans,' which will inspire you to teach your children the American patriot's love for the Stars and Stripes, the emblem of liberty."[23] It was time, that is, for immigrants to cease their cele-brations of ethnic holidays and to assimilate to American culture.

Involving the entrepreneurs and intelligentsia of both the native- and foreign-born population was only the first step in assuring the celebration's popularity. The Union League Club resolved early in the planning stages to secure the "participation of all, young and old, native and foreign-born, in commemorations and exercises which would tend to develop interest in na-tional life and quicken patriotic impulses." Rather than rely on the largesse of wealthy men, for example, the executive committee decided to raise the $25,000 necessary for the celebration in small subscriptions from the popu-lace, "thereby cementing their interest in the celebration" by making every subscriber a "shareholder" in the enterprise. Despite this rhetoric, most of the money probably came from the middle and upper classes, and particularly from businessmen. The finance committee had subcommittees for virtually every type of business in the city, from laundries, candy makers, and meat markets to the Board of Trade, bankers, and capitalists.[24]

To reach the city's religious believers, the organizers enlisted clergymen to conduct the morning services and to serve as orators at the schools and meeting halls. They appealed to working-class Chicagoans by encouraging employers to give workers a holiday; there was even a forty-four-man "com-mittee on suspension of business." The school celebration committee re-cruited teachers to teach their students patriotic songs, quotations, and recitations; to assign patriotic essays; and to give "daily lessons in the constitutional and political history of our country," so that the children might participate actively in the celebration. The committee on decorations encouraged people to decorate their homes and businesses. The committee on speakers invited ethnic and African American leaders to speak at schools, and among the orators at the mass meetings were Rabbi Dr. Emil G. Hirsch and Virginia congressman John Mercer Langston. The program committees involved the populace in the mass meetings by offering them resolutions to approve, by recruiting volunteers rather than professionals for the choruses, and by picking popular patriotic tunes that the crowd could sing. Finally, the Union League Club appealed to the popular love of spectacle with the grandiose fireworks displays.[25]

There was one segment of the city's population whose cooperation the Union League Club did not solicit, and that was the labor unions. No labor representatives sat on the celebration committees, and the program included no trades procession. Indeed, labor strife weighed heavily on the men who organized the celebration, and their holiday instruction proclaimed their view that such conflict was not only unpatriotic but also un-American. Workers had no cause for discontent, J. M. Thurston told the audience at one of the meetings, for America was "the only country where labor is fairly paid; where the industrious working man, out of the accumulated savings of his daily toil, can pay for the pleasant home in which he lives and send his children to the public schools." Thurston warned that anarchists and other dissenters were not welcome in America. "The government of the people," he thundered, "must never be endangered by the dissemination of those monstrous theories which would overturn all government for anarchy and subvert all society to the dominion of unbridled passion and brute force."[26] One could never learn this lesson too young. Thomas Cratty instructed the students of Scammon School in their duty to root out such dissent. "Revere our flag, love it," he exhorted them. "If any little one should see anyone disrespectful to our flag, place your little fist under his nose and say 'stop.' . . . [I]f you see the flag of anarchy, socialism, or communism, stamp on it, tear it down and trample it in the dust."[27]

It was particularly important to teach these lessons to immigrants, who had not been reared in the ordered liberty of the United States. Immigrants willing to Americanize were welcome; those who were not could go back to

Europe. L. D. Thoman cautioned that citizenship must be granted more discriminatingly than was currently practiced: "The American republic should no longer confer citizenship without some evidence that the honor is being worthily bestowed." This evidence, Thoman believed, should include an understanding of the Declaration of Independence and the Constitution as well as "obedience to law." Rev. David Utter went even further. After acknowledging the "mingling of seed" that had produced the nation, he bluntly informed the students of Harrison School that it was time to close the doors: "We do not need any more people now from foreign lands. Let us mould into one union now, if we can, what we have already got." For the most part, however, the civic elite remained optimistic about immigrants' capacity to assimilate, given the proper civic instruction. "Our nation is an empire of emigrants," Judge Richard Prendergast proclaimed at a mass meeting. "The republic was founded . . . for every man who was born upon this continent or who would come to these shores willing to assume and to discharge the duties of citizenship."[28]

The most important duty of citizenship, according to the men of the Union League Club, was obedience to the law. "Liberty regulated by law" was the mantra of the day. Unregulated liberty led to license and anarchy; regulated liberty brought progress and prosperity. Rabbi Dr. Emil G. Hirsch found the difference between French and American liberty to be instructive. Whereas the French constitution did nothing to control public passions, he explained, "liberty according to the American idea is always wedded to law and to responsibility." Significantly, most of the orators at Chicago's mass meetings were representatives of law and order, either governmental or religious. The eighteen speakers included a former mayor, Carter H. Harrison, two judges, six clergymen, two congressmen, the county superintendent of schools, a professor, and an attorney.[29]

The orators made sure that Chicagoans understood the prominent role of commerce and industry in the progress of the nation in its first century of liberty under law. Peter Hendrickson argued that if the Constitution was the central pillar of the nation, the invention of the steam engine was the second: "The Federal Constitution and the steam engine are the great twin products of Anglo-Saxon intelligence and enterprise." The morning addresses at the schools were made "by men who had won distinction in professional and commercial life," whom the Union League Club considered to be particularly appropriate to demonstrate to the city's youth "the beauties of a government of the people, for the people, and by the people."[30]

Despite the large attendance at the meetings and other events, it is difficult to assess the overall success of the celebration in implanting the messages of the Union League Club. Certainly its patriotic lessons did not end labor strife or socialism in Chicago. Neither did they convince many immigrants that assimilation should proceed on elite terms. One of the invited speakers even dissented from the club's vision. The African American congressman John Mercer Langston, while acknowledging the importance of the Constitution, stubbornly cast his vote for the Declaration of Independence as the preeminent document in American history. "The animating principle of our government," he thundered in the midst of the paeans to law and order, "is defined in the immortal words of the Declaration: 'We hold these truths to be self-evident; that all men are created equal.'"[31]

Although the attendance at the mass meetings was higher than for most Chicago celebrations, it still was only about 15 percent of the city's adult population, which meant that many Chicagoans had found other things to do on their holiday. It is noteworthy that by far the largest attendance of the day came at the fireworks displays. While those may have been intended as visual reinforcement of the day's civic lessons, most of the spectators probably came for the sheer spectacle and entertainment value. A German-language socialist paper reported that "[m]any American workers undisturbed tended their business" rather than attend the meetings, perhaps because their employers, unmoved by the committee appeals, refused to give them a holiday. The only people celebrating, according to the paper, were "the native rowdies, who were lacking enthusiasm because the wealthy failed to fill them up with brandy," and "the newly immigrated, who wandered around . . . and vainly looked for something which would appear to them more beautiful and grand than similar things in their respective home-country." A few took the occasion to protest the message of the day. A defiant wood turner reportedly harassed a group of firemen putting up the American flag, then countered by displaying the red socialist banner. The firemen tore down the socialist emblem, and when the wood turner protested, they patriotically beat him up.[32]

The existing records unfortunately leave few clues as to the composition of the crowds at the mass meetings, making it almost impossible to ascertain how many workers and immigrants actually took part. The Union League Club did report that the ethnic members of the executive committee had decisively vetoed a proposal to have separate meetings for immigrants, but some school exercises were apparently conducted in foreign languages. At the Polk Street School, for instance, Italian children listened to speeches in their native tongue, while a private German-English school featured exercises in both languages. Some immigrants also chose to celebrate in their own neighborhoods, where they might retain a modicum of control over the day's lessons. The city's Czech community sponsored exercises that followed the club's program but gave all the leading roles to Czechs, undermining the club's Americanization message by suggesting that they could be good Americans while remaining loyal Czechs. German military and fraternal organizations, apparently dismayed by the lack of a procession, staged their own through the downtown streets before attending the mass meetings. As on the Fourth of July, many ethnic groups preferred to demonstrate their patriotism in exercises they controlled, rather than simply accommodating themselves to the civic elite's vision of America.[33]

"THE PEOPLE'S CELEBRATION":
THE COLUMBIAN QUADRICENTENNIAL

Perhaps in response to an unsatisfactory immigrant turnout, Chicago's civic leaders incorporated the city's ethnic and racial groups more fully into their next anniversary celebration by staging a massive civic procession. The Washington extravaganza of 1889 proved to be only a dry run for the celebration of the nation's biggest anniversary to date, the quadricentennial of Christopher Columbus's "discovery" of America. Chicago capitalists had won the honor of hosting the World's Columbian Exposition by outspending New York City capitalists, and the directors of the fair determined to observe the Columbian anniversary on 21 October by dedicating the fairgrounds.[34]

Like the Washington centennial, the dedication ceremonies were organized by representatives of Chicago's civic elite. Although the exercises centered on the dedication of the exposition, the public highlight of the cele-

Parade at dedicatory ceremonies, 22 October 1892, World's Columbian Exposition. The police officers who aided capitalists in controlling striking workers became a prominent feature of late nineteenth-century processions. Here they ride the latest in wheeled technology. (From Ellsworth-Arnold Photo Albums; courtesy of the Chicago Public Library, Special Collections and Preservation Division)

bration was a procession that showcased the first fruits of the plan of civic and patriotic education. The eighty thousand marchers displayed to spectators both the rich diversity and the patriotism of Chicago's population. Although the parade included carriages bearing the city's political leaders and the nation's governors, police officers on bicycles, and forty-four posts of the Grand Army of the Republic (GAR), the vast majority of the marchers came from the city's myriad ethnic groups. Italian military companies, bands, and fraternal and political organizations in smart uniforms demonstrated both their patriotism for their adopted country and their pride in their native land by carrying the red, white, and blue alongside the green, white, and red. Garbed in the military uniform of independent eighteenth-century Poland, the members of the Polish National Alliance were sentimental favorites with the crowd. German, Polish, Swedish, Danish, Norwegian, and Czech turners all marched and performed for spectators. A huge division consisted solely of the city's Catholic organizations, and Jewish societies participated as well. Benevolent and fraternal associations representing virtually every ethnic group in the city joined the procession, as did African American organizations and the black Ninth Battalion of the U.S. Army. Although the city no longer had a significant Native American population, the procession's organizers had brought in three companies of boys from the Government Indian Industrial School in Carlisle, Pennsylvania, to demonstrate that even the nation's Indian population could, with the proper civic education, become loyal Americans. Clad in their school uniforms and led by their own brass band, the Native American students, whom the *Chicago Tribune* called "the real genuine American feature of the parade," paused at the reviewing stand to execute several drills for the officials and dignitaries seated there.[35]

The *Chicago Tribune*, an ardent backer of the parade and exposition, pronounced the procession a resounding success in a postparade editorial. "[T]he people's celebration," the paper concluded, "will long be remembered as a grand exhibition of all the arts of peace and toil, of national forces blending into one, of people from all countries coming together to celebrate the accomplishment of the great Italian navigator." The civic procession was indeed "the people's celebration" of the quadricentennial. The line of march included representatives of virtually every race, nationality, and creed in Chicago, but the civic elites who had planned the parade and other dedicatory exercises were not among the marchers. The parade was, in fact, the only part of the festivities in which "the people" could participate actively. They played no role in the dedication exercises; the exposition grounds were closed to the public on the day of the dedication, and admittance to the ceremonies was by invitation only. Various receptions and dinners welcoming distinguished visitors were likewise off limits to most Chicagoans. Other than marching in the civic parade, ordinary citizens could only participate passively in the Columbian celebration as spectators of the procession and the fireworks displays held after the dedication.[36]

Although the civic parade was supposed to be their celebration, the people also had little control over its form or content. Members of the committee on ceremonies headed manufacturing concerns, banks and brokerage firms, railroads and utilities, and law firms; the committee contained no representatives of ordinary people. The committee carefully orchestrated the parade to present its message of Americanization, as one reporter suggested: "Chicago was seen to be assimilating its mighty new elements with the ease which comes from the strong solution of liberty and employment." In the Chicago depicted in the civic parade, immigrants were in the process of exchanging their native cultures for an American one that united all Americans, whether native or foreign born, under the culture symbolized by the nation's flag, music, and founding fathers (who now included Columbus). Poles in military dress and Scots in tartans pinned American flags to their breasts, and ethnic bands followed Italian and Swedish airs with the "Star Spangled Banner." Similarly, the Native Americans who participated were model Indians from what one reporter called "the only place in America where good Indians are really turned out." They marched in platoons representing the various industries taught at their school and thereby enacted the limited roles open to Indians if they chose to become "civilized." Above the dizzying array of ethnic colors and costumes, the red, white, and blue reigned supreme. A highlight of the procession was a "living flag" composed of schoolchildren.[37]

But assimilation into some version of the melting pot is only one way to read the procession. Marching in ethnic costume can also be read as subverting the civic elite's concept of assimilation and a homogeneous American identity. The participation of immigrant groups may well have signified assimilation to both the immigrants and the committee on ceremonies, but the immigrants' perceptions of what constituted that assimilation differed vastly. Similarly, the participation of African Americans in Chicago's procession was a way of asserting their centrality to American identity. This became more evident in the subsequent protests of black leaders such as Frederick Douglass and Ida B. Wells-Barnett against the lack of representation of African Americans in the planning and exhibits of the World's Columbian Exposition.[38]

Immigrants and African Americans were not the only ones to present countermessages to the elites' carefully staged portrait of America. The procession, composed as it was of fraternal, benevolent, and patriotic societies, embodied the organizers' ideal of an America free from class and ideological conflict, but this facade barely concealed the festering divisions between Chicago's employing and laboring classes, as well as among workers. The parade was in fact free of class tension because Chicago's organized workers had declined to play their designated role in the nation defined by the parade. Unlike the Washington celebration committee, the committee on ceremonies in 1892 had invited the members of the Trades and Labor Assembly to march in the procession. After a vehement debate over the board of directors' deafness to demands for fair wages and the eight-hour day for the laborers building the exposition, however, the assembly voted by a substantial margin to "decline absolutely" the invitation to march, much to the chagrin of its more conservative members. Socialists in the assembly, on the other hand, were delighted by the vote and added that the workers should refuse to parade "as slaves before the plutocrats and capitalists."[39]

Chicago's procession revealed the potential danger of pluralism to the project of civic education. Despite its attempts, the committee on ceremonies could not conceal entirely the ideological, class, and ethnic conflicts that wracked Chicago in the late nineteenth century. Nor could civic elites unilaterally impose their notion of Americanism on the city's diverse populations, who had their own reasons for marching in the parade and their own visions of America.

"THE SPONTANEOUS TRIBUTE OF THE NATION":
THE LINCOLN CENTENNIAL

The difficulty of imposing the elite vision of America across the broad spectrum of Americans became even clearer seventeen years later during celebrations of the centennial of Abraham Lincoln's birth. Chicago's civic elites again took a leading role in the local and national commemoration of this third anniversary. Lincoln, like Washington, exemplified their notion of a patriotic hero, but although sponsors of the celebrations proclaimed the universality of the nation's homage to Lincoln, the day's exercises revealed the sectional, racial, and class tensions that still permeated the city and the nation.

Republican organizations and the GAR had begun holding Lincoln dinners and exercises in Chicago in the late 1880s. Along with promoting Republican ideology through the party's martyred hero, the celebrations had much the same genesis in political reform and patriotic education as the Washington exercises of the Union League Club. The Lincoln Council of the National Union sponsored a public lecture and program in 1888, for example, which was "intended to revive in this materialistic age the old spirit of patriotism," and the Marquette Club, a Republican organization, began holding dinners on Lincoln's Birthday in the 1880s. White ambivalence toward the beneficiaries of emancipation pervaded these exercises. While orators praised emancipation and abolitionists such as Charles Sumner, William Lloyd Garrison, and even John Brown, either they omitted mention of African Americans or they referred to them condescendingly as less than civilized and certainly not full participants in the American republic. In a sermon about Lincoln in 1900, for instance, Rev. J. H. O. Smith commented that the "earth's greatest heroes seem in strangest company. Christian and the thief, the missionary and the cannibal, Lincoln and the black man." Rev. Frank Gunsaulus suggested that white elites had a duty to uplift African Americans. "The four million negroes of the South," emancipated from slavery, "are yet beseeching emancipation," he explained, "from their worst self—clamoring for recreation and freedom from their passions and ignorance." Not surprisingly, in light of such treatment, African American organizations held separate exercises to honor the author of the Emancipation Proclamation. In 1900, for instance, the *Chicago Tribune* reported that "[t]he colored people of the West Side held a meeting at St. Stephen's African Methodist Episcopal Church" to mark Lincoln's Birthday.[40]

In late 1908 Illinois governor Charles S. Deneen issued a proclamation calling upon the citizens of Illinois to unite to make the centennial of Lincoln's birth "an incentive to patriotism in our schools and among our citizens" by arranging "appropriate exercises by the schools of the State and by all municipal, civic, social and religious organizations." As with the Washington centennial, Lincoln was to become an object lesson in citizenship. Leading Republicans and civic elites in Chicago formed a Lincoln Centennial Memorial Committee of One Hundred, which organized a weeklong celebration in February 1909. Like the Washington exercises, the Lincoln celebration, its sponsors explained, "was planned to be educational in its scope." They arranged public exercises in the city's schools on the eve of the holiday and placed a bronze tablet containing the Gettysburg Address in each public and parochial school. As in 1889, they held giant public meetings around the city on 12 February. They controlled the message of the celebration by thoughtfully supplying speakers for the meetings and for the exercises at schools, libraries, and other sites. The entire Committee of One Hundred, joined by city, county, and state officials, the GAR and Women's Relief Corps, patriotic societies, and army and navy officers, attended the most prestigious meeting at the Auditorium Theater, where they heard Woodrow Wilson, then president of Princeton University, speak on Lincoln's legacy.[41]

Nathan MacChesney, a professor of law at the University of Illinois who served as secretary of the committee, reported that the centennial celebration had not been restricted to Lincoln's home state but had become a national fête, encompassing even ex-Confederates. He reported that "the Mason and Dixon line . . . was forgotten, . . . while Lincoln was lauded in the South," noting that Union and Confederate veterans in Atlanta had held a joint memorial service. In Tucson Confederate and Union veterans sat side by side on the dignitaries' platform at the Lincoln exercises at the high school. "Never before did a whole people approach the centenary of the birth of a man with such interest and unanimity, or carry out its celebration with such enthusiasm," MacChesney concluded. "It was the spontaneous tribute of the nation."[42]

If the extensive planning of the Chicago committee belied MacChesney's description of the celebration as "spontaneous," the centennial was also not quite the unifying force he depicted. Sectional and racial animosities intruded on the celebration. Former Confederates had begun in the 1890s to commemorate the birthdays of Robert E. Lee, Stonewall Jackson, and Jefferson Davis, and most southern states had no more intention of adding a Lincoln holiday to their calendar than of incorporating the federal Memorial Day. Many southern cities refused to honor Lincoln on his centennial, and most celebrations there were probably sponsored by the GAR or by black organizations. In Norfolk, Virginia, for example, the African American post of the GAR and the Lincoln Emancipation Association held centennial exercises, and in Richmond the [Paul] Dunbar Literary and Historical Society celebrated. The *Richmond Times-Dispatch* reported that businesses remained open in the former Confederate capital and that there was neither a general celebration nor exercises in the schools to mark the day.[43]

The *Confederate Veteran* further revealed that many ex-Confederates were not ready to join in the apotheosis of Lincoln by publishing a series of post-holiday commentaries purporting to "express the truth concerning Mr. Lincoln." Writers accused Lincoln of starting the Civil War, of devastating the South, of allowing "brutal atrocities" against Confederate prisoners to go unchecked, and even of giving African Americans the vote (apparently posthumously). One writer suggested that Southerners would honor Lincoln's birthday as soon as Northerners were ready to celebrate Jefferson Davis's birthday. The best the *Confederate Veteran* had to offer was the editor's summation that Lincoln "was an eminently kind man; but his mold was not great." One woman would not grant him even that. "He was a hypocrite in religion," she claimed, "a vulgar buffoon, indecent in his anecdotes, and cruel in his instincts." She accused Lincoln of not only emancipating the slaves but also "exciting them to insurrection" by "placing guns in the hands of negroes to murder their former masters."[44]

Although Northerners were much more unanimous in their celebration of Lincoln, there were clear indications that the racial fault lines of the South, exacerbated by disfranchisement and Jim Crow, extended their tentacles even into the heart of the Land of Lincoln. A Richmond newspaper noted pointedly that whites in Lincoln's long-time hometown of Springfield, Illinois, excluded African Americans from their centennial banquet, leading blacks there, like their southern brethren, to sponsor a "separate-but-equal" banquet. In Chicago, as well, African Americans attended a separate meeting sponsored by the black Eighth Infantry of the Illinois National Guard and a Colored Citizens Committee. "The meeting was a most unusual one," noted MacChesney condescendingly, "and perhaps nowhere in the limits of the city was the Lincoln Centennial observed with such feeling, such enthusiasm, such exaltation and homage."[45]

Along with a reverence for the author of emancipation, however, the speakers at the black celebration focused on the contemporary struggle to hold on to the benefits of freedom. As they did at Emancipation Day exercises, black orators adamantly refuted the notion that American identity was monoracial. Rev. J. W. E. Bowen, for example, repudiated disfranchisement by calling for "a complete amalgamation into the body politic" for African Americans. Although he, like Booker T. Washington, cautioned that legislation was not a panacea, he clearly asserted that African Americans should have full political rights. Deliberately using the term that struck fear into every white supremacist's heart, Bowen claimed that "Lincoln's idea . . . was that the liberated slave should ultimately become amalgamated with the American Republic and become a member of this great nation." He made clear, however, that by amalgamation he meant that America should become a nation "not homogeneous in its blood but homogeneous in its Nationalism." African Americans should accept nothing less than full citizenship in the nation, Bowen told his audience, and they must seize control of their own destiny. "[Y]ou must liberate yourselves," he urged them in conclusion.[46]

The chairman of the Committee of One Hundred, Judge William J. Calhoun, followed Bowen to the rostrum. Calhoun demonstrated no such belief in the inevitability of an equal role for African Americans in American public life. Instead, he expressed the civic elites' conviction that they knew best and must paternalistically educate the rest of Americans on proper patriotism and citizenship. He claimed that it had been a mistake to grant the vote to African Americans after the war because in their ignorance they "became the unwilling tool of an unscrupulous class of politicians called 'carpet baggers.'" He lectured black Chicagoans, who still had the ballot, on their poor use of it. Although he stopped short of endorsing disfranchisement before an audience of African Americans, he did advise them, "Do not trouble yourselves too much about politics. Don't be discouraged if you are not allowed to hold office." Instead, he told them to heed the example of Booker T. Washington, embraced by white industrialists across America, and "[l]et honesty, industry, and economy be your watchwords." If they did so, he held out hope that they could follow the path of the white race "from barbarism to civilization."[47]

In addition to condemning black voting habits, Calhoun lectured his audience on the alleged mistakes made by the freedpeople since emancipation. Before an audience of urbanites, he rather curiously claimed that their most "serious mistake" had been to move to cities, where many had succumbed to "the corrupting influence of poverty" and "the white man's vices." To add insult to injury, Calhoun praised those slaves who had tended to their wounded masters and their homes during the war. He recounted an anecdote told him by a "Southern gentleman, an ex-Confederate soldier" about one of his slaves who had remained so loyal to his master that he had buried and guarded his gold, rather than fleeing to freedom with the Union Army and the money.[48]

This story was too much for Rev. A. J. Carey, who made an impromptu speech in response. "I could not help feeling as I listened to the burning words of eloquence as they fell from the lips of Judge Calhoun," he began tartly, "that if all the negroes in the Civil War had been the one, described by the Judge, who made his way to his wounded master and brought him back to home and slavery, we would have been unworthy a part in the celebration." Instead, looking at the platform where sat African Americans who had "answered to the call of Father Abraham," he avowed, "we have just right to be here." To the claim that granting the black man the ballot had been a mistake, he replied that it was "his only weapon of defense, his only means of protection against injustice and oppression."[49]

Carey and the other African American orators and celebrants made clear that they had no use for the condescension of whites such as Calhoun, who sought to elevate them, like immigrants, to a properly docile and decidedly second-class citizenship. They used the Lincoln anniversary, like Emancipation Day, to demand (however cautiously) full incorporation into America.

While African Americans worked from within to reconstruct America as biracial, socialists rejected the official celebration out of hand. Contending that "[t]he only compact organized body of men that is today standing for the things for which Lincoln stood in the '60s is the Socialists," the *Chicago Daily Socialist* published a special Lincoln centennial edition, in which socialist writers interpreted Lincoln as a champion of labor and asserted that the spirit of the martyred president could best be served by supporting socialism. Socialists suggested that, were Lincoln to return, he would complete emancipation by freeing workers from wage slavery. The paper quoted Lincoln's statements that "[l]abor is the superior of capital" and that "[t]o secure to each laborer the whole product of his labor, or as nearly as possible, is a worthy object of any good government." An editorial cartoon depicted Lincoln comforting a worker, while capitalists looked on angrily. The caption noted, "He would probably be an 'undesirable citizen.'" Lincoln, socialists claimed, would have abhorred the capitalists who celebrated him and would surely condemn his party for "allow[ing] capital to use the militia to drive miners from their homes" and for doing nothing while "hundreds of thousands of blacks and WHITES in the south [were] shorn of their only peaceable weapon against despotism—the right to vote."[50]

Socialists celebrated the centennial and raised funds for the ever-broke *Chicago Daily Socialist* with a four-day bazaar sponsored by the Young People's Socialist League. On the actual anniversary, the bazaar hosted a "foreign night" to welcome immigrant socialists. Afternoon exercises included a lecture on Lincoln by A. M. Simons, editor of the *Chicago Daily Socialist*, and a visit from Freedom, personified by a veteran of the 1905 Russian Revolution. Black minister George W. Slater proclaimed that the best way for African Americans to thank Lincoln for emancipation was by "assisting in the great battle to free all men from industrial slavery." Not surprisingly, socialists concluded that their celebration was the most appropriate one held in Chicago. "Freedom had heard that it was Lincoln day," the *Chicago Daily Socialist* explained, "and after looking over the list of places where celebrations in honor of Lincoln were being held selected the Socialist bazaar as most expressive of what Lincoln stood for."[51]

The socialist dissent from the holiday's official message, the African American revision of it, and the white southern rejection of the holiday and Lincoln reveal that the efforts to unite the nation around the symbol of the Great Emancipator fell short of the mark. Substantial pockets of dissent from the civic elites' vision of law-and-order Americanism remained. But if those elites had failed to reach many adult Americans, they did not despair. Indeed, they had already developed a new weapon of civic education and assimilation and had aimed it straight at the heart of the nation's schoolchildren.

SCHOOL HOLIDAYS AS "AN EDUCATIONAL FORCE"

The Lincoln centennial, like the Washington and Columbian anniversaries, extended patriotic education to schoolchildren as well as their parents. The day before adult Chicagoans gathered for Lincoln exercises, children had participated in school exercises honoring Lincoln. In a letter addressed to Illinois teachers, Francis G. Blair, the state superintendent of public schools, explained the importance of the Lincoln centennial "as an educational force" for American children. The study of the lives of great men such as Lincoln, Blair contended, provided "a unifying, nationalizing force," particularly for immigrants. "How can we engender common ideals of conduct and life?" Blair asked. "How beget and fix a feeling of kinship, a love of country, a national spirit?" Beyond learning English, he answered himself, "nothing goes further towards creating a spiritual unity and a common love of country than the story of the lives of great men." To harness this nationalizing force, Blair issued a book of recitation materials to be used in school celebrations of the centennial.[52]

The school celebrations of the Washington and Lincoln centennials heralded a new direction for America's public holidays. This development had reached full fruition in 1892, when the directors of the World's Columbian Exposition enlisted educators and the *Youth's Companion*, a children's magazine, in a plan to create a national school celebration for the Columbian quadricentennial. The executive committee for the school celebration was composed of state education officials, but the real work was done by chairman Francis Bellamy, a writer for the *Youth's Companion*, who proved to be a patriotic dynamo. He secured a presidential proclamation endorsing the school celebration and asking that "the exercises be such as shall impress upon our youth the patriotic duties of American citizenship."[53]

Bellamy scripted the official program for the celebration and forwarded it to school districts and newspapers across the country. In an unprecedented act of national unity, schoolchildren across the nation were simultaneously to listen to the president's proclamation, watch as veterans raised the flag, salute the flag, acknowledge God, sing a "Song of Columbus Day," and listen to an official ode and address. At the end of the program, Bellamy generously allowed for "whatever additional Exercises, Patriotic Recitations, Historic Representations, or Chorals may be desired." The *Youth's Companion* asserted that the Columbian celebration was, above all, a civic lesson for the nation's youth. "The boys and girls are going to learn from their Columbus Day rites a lesson in intelligent patriotism worth a year's study of text books," the magazine claimed. The most lasting contribution of the school celebration to the history of patriotic education was the twenty-two-word flag salute that Bellamy composed for the occasion, which would become the centerpiece of patriotic

Children saluting the flag. It was never too early to learn the proper way to salute the flag on Flag Day and other patriotic holidays. The Pledge of Allegiance was composed for the Columbian school celebration in 1892. (Courtesy of the Chicago Park District Special Collections)

school ritual: "I pledge allegiance to my Flag and the Republic for which it stands; one Nation indivisible, with Liberty and Justice for all." The *Youth's Companion* commented after the celebration that "the flag over the schoolhouses . . . impressed powerfully upon the youth that we are a nation."[54]

The school exercises for the three anniversary celebrations were not isolated incidents but served as springboards for the emergence of the school holiday celebration. The success of the Washington celebration had taught members of the Union League Club that schools were fertile ground for holiday lessons in patriotism. While it was difficult to reshape the behavior of adults, children were much more malleable. The Union League Club justified its school celebration in 1889 by explaining that "[i]n the warmth and enthusiasm of youth are found the best soil for planting the seeds of patriotism." In the aftermath of the anniversary, the club increasingly focused its holiday efforts on the future workers who populated the public schools. In 1890 it added a children's program to its annual Washington's Birthday exercises, in accordance with its centennial resolution to establish "a course of education in our public schools."[55]

At the first annual exercises, some nine thousand children at two halls listened to declamations on Washington's greatness and sang patriotic songs, including a special ode to Washington, to the tune of "America," which had been written for the occasion by the superintendent of schools. The lessons of Washington's life, as in the previous year's celebration, lay in his patriotism and his sense of civic duty, which the boys in the audience were urged to emulate in their future careers as voters. The message of liberty under law was not neglected either. The fledgling Society of Patriotic Knowledge, which "taught a boy to say 'I will be obedient to the laws of the school and the laws of the state,'" also sent a representative to the exercises. Rev. Martin L. Williston, secretary of the society, used the stereopticon to impress visually upon the children the lessons of the day, with scenes of Washington's career and the American Revolution. By 1895 the Union League Club had moved the Washington exercises into the schools, the better to reach all of the city's schoolchildren. The club retained sponsorship of the celebrations and control of their messages by distributing song sheets and recitations and by supplying orators. As a further stimulus to the club's efforts, member Joseph Medill's *Chicago Tribune* established a holiday essay contest, offering cash prizes and publication of the ten best essays on Washington by students.[56]

In the 1890s school holidays grew rapidly as venues of patriotic education. In Chicago and across the nation, schools introduced exercises for Lincoln's Birthday, Memorial Day, and the new holiday of Flag Day, and the public school emerged as one of the most important arenas for the celebration of patriotic holidays. The main purpose of these exercises was, a Tucson newspaper explained in 1889, "to inculcate into the minds of the boys and girls the correct spirit of patriotism."[57]

Civic elites and their middle-class allies gained new partners in this campaign to instruct the nation's youth in patriotism and nationalism. As Cecilia O'Leary argues, a variety of organizations contended for the power to define American patriotism at the turn of the century. The Union veterans of the GAR had long believed that their service had made them the supreme exemplars of patriotism and disinterested virtue and therefore that they were the best qualified to teach true patriotism. The 1890s also saw the explosion of hereditary societies whose members took upon themselves to preserve Anglo-American culture from the perceived threat of immigrants and working-class upstarts. Like the men of the GAR and the Union League Club, members of the hereditary societies considered themselves to be uniquely qualified for patriotic instruction, based on their ancestry. Finally, education schools were transforming the curriculum and professionalizing teaching, and the teachers they turned out maintained that they had the best background to teach civics and patriotism.[58]

The stimulation of a patriotism that emphasized law and order appealed to each of these constituencies as the key to addressing the class conflict, urban disorder, political corruption, and ethnic diversity that accompanied industrialization. Schoolchildren provided an impressionable and malleable audience for patriotic instruction. Indeed, as the *Youth's Companion* claimed in 1889, the nation's children were "already very patriotic." What was needed was to direct that patriotism to its proper end. "What they now need," the magazine explained, "is to be taught the duties we all owe to such a country as ours—to keep it pure and good."[59] Holiday celebrations became the centerpiece of this program of patriotic education because their rituals provided children with sensory stimuli to national loyalty, as well as patriotic models to emulate. Best of all, schools provided an essentially captive audience for the prophets of patriotism, and they rushed to take advantage of it in the 1890s.

The holiday of most concern to the GAR was Memorial Day, and it began in the 1890s to enlist the participation of children in its Memorial Day exercises by having veterans visit schools before the holiday to talk to students about its meaning. In Chicago in 1890, following the example of the Union League Club, the GAR instituted school-based Memorial Day exercises, consisting of essays, recitations, and songs by students and speeches by veterans. An orator in 1894 explained that because the schools did not teach children about the war, veterans had to fill the gap on Memorial Day, which had "done much to inculcate American patriotism in the hearts of the young." The *Chicago Tribune* praised the addition of school celebrations, arguing that "[t]he impulses of patriotism stirred in eager young minds by these exercises are worth more for securing the future safety and perpetuity of the union than a great standing army."[60]

Although Memorial Day remained veterans' most important holiday, it was not their only vehicle of patriotic instruction. The GAR spearheaded a schoolhouse flag movement in the late 1880s that added the flag to the rank of patriotic symbols of American identity. GAR posts presented flags to schools on Memorial Day and other patriotic holidays and petitioned states to make school flags mandatory. In Tucson, for example, the local GAR post gave a flag to the public school at Washington's Birthday exercises in 1890. The *Youth's Companion* promoted the movement in its pages, asking, in an 1890 advertisement, "Have You Raised a Flag over Your School-house?" To entice schools, the magazine offered to all schools that complied a free illustrated souvenir edition, "suitable for framing," of its Fourth of July poem, "Raising the School-house Flag."[61]

Whether swayed by such inducements or not, school administrators and many teachers rushed to embrace the patriotic crusade. One of the first was Col. George T. Balch, a New York City school official and a pioneer in patriotic education, who introduced his modestly titled "general plan for the patriotic education of the youth of this nation" to the Children's Aid Society in 1889. The plan, which he sought to implement first in the society's industrial schools, focused primarily on the flag, which was to become both a reward for good citizenship and a symbol and "object lesson" of patriotism. Balch's definition of patriotic citizenship underscored the Union League Club's call for law and order; small flag badges and individual "scholar's flags" were to go to students demonstrating "good conduct," and the classroom flag was a weekly reward for the class that was "pre-eminent for punctuality and attendance." Balch specified that students should assemble to salute the flag, in military fashion, every morning. Thus the flag, like George Washington, became a symbol of liberty under law. In a telling comment, one New York City teacher observed in 1891, "I notice it is easier to govern the children since the flag was raised."[62]

The new hereditary patriotic societies, particularly the Daughters of the American Revolution (DAR) and Sons of the American Revolution (SAR), joined the school flag campaign as well. In 1890 the SAR proposed that the anniversary of the flag's adoption be celebrated as a new holiday, and educators took up the cry, including Chicagoan Bernard J. Cigrand, a second-generation Luxemburg American schoolteacher, who also edited the *American Standard*, a magazine founded in the late 1880s to "inculcate reverence for the American emblem." In 1893 a Chicago musician named LeRoy Van Horn founded the American Flag Day Association "for the purpose of fostering patriotism among the school children by the holding of patriotic exercises in the parks on the third Saturday in June, in commemoration of the adoption of the national flag." That year Van Horn, in conjunction with the GAR, inaugurated Flag Day with a celebration in a west-side park. The program included a salute to the flag, a children's procession, addresses on the origins of the flag and American nationality, patriotic songs, and a gun drill by a boys' cadet corps.[63]

Following the success of the celebration, the American Flag Day Association incorporated to push for a national holiday. The next year the organization staged the first citywide celebration, with exercises targeting children at five city parks. The exercises resembled those of the prior year, with additional patriotic performances by schoolchildren. At Washington Park, for example, sixty young women of the Armour Institute Drill Corps, patriotically garbed in red sailor caps, blue flannel blouses, and short skirts, executed an exhibition drill, while the boys of the Chicago *Turngemeinde* performed gymnastic exercises at Lincoln Park. Former governor John M. Hamilton, perhaps thinking of the Pullman boycott then raging, warned the children at Lincoln Park that "[i]n these turbulent and trying times we need to have all the fires of patriotism rekindled." That patriotism, he assured them, "is aptly measured by the love of [the nation's] people for its flag." A speaker at another park suggested that the flag should be an object of veneration. "Of all things that be or exist," he told the students, "the flag is the sublimest."[64]

INSTITUTIONALIZING CIVIC EDUCATION

In the early twentieth century, holiday celebrations became a schoolhouse institution, as a veritable industry emerged to produce holiday exercises and supplies. Teachers and holiday experts shared program ideas in journals such as the *Normal Instructor* and the *Journal of Education*, and state education departments published holiday manuals that provided recitation materials and

Washington souvenirs. This hatchet and cherry sprig
were part of the growing industry of school holiday
celebrations. Teachers could order these items from
trade catalogs as props and souvenirs for their students.
(From March Brothers, *A Catalogue of Thanksgiving
Exercises, Christmas Goods, and Requisites for the February
Holidays*, 1902; courtesy of the Winterthur Library:
Printed Book and Periodical Collection)

exercises. School supply companies jumped on the bandwagon, offering holiday decorations, props, and souvenirs. March Brothers, for instance, published a catalog of holiday goods "specially selected for teachers," such as a
hatchet and sprig of cherries for Washington's Birthday exercises.[65]

In an article in the journal *Education* in 1911, Horace G. Brown, a historian
at the Worcester Normal School, set up guiding principles for school celebrations. The exercises, he declared, should provide activities for students,
who learned best by doing. Children could cut out decorations such as Lincoln's ax or Washington's hatchet. Programs might include such physical activities as marching, dramatic pantomimes, tableaux, pageants, and even
dances. Older students, Brown said, should be encouraged to write compo-
sitions on the lives of the presidents and to compose illustrated acrostics of

Girls perform a flag drill on Washington's Birthday. Drills and exercises became common features of school holiday celebrations, as well as at other celebrations, such as this one at a Chicago neighborhood park in the early twentieth century. (Courtesy of the Chicago Park District Special Collections)

their names. Another advocate of school celebrations, pageant director Constance D'Arcy MacKay, promoted the use of holiday plays, explaining that they made "[h]istoric personages become actual, vivid figures" to the students. Portraying America's history, rather than simply reading about it, she argued, impressed it more firmly upon the children. In an effort to make the lives of American patriots more compelling to students, she depicted scenes from the youth of American heroes, "so that the lad who plays George Washington or Benjamin Franklin will be in touch with the emotions of a patriot of his own years, instead of incongruously portraying an adult."[66]

It was important, Brown emphasized, to use a variety of exercises to stimulate student patriotism and to avoid boring the teacher. The holiday programs presented in the various journals and manuals amply demonstrated the variety and activities Brown sought. One program for Washington's Birthday, for example, included a flag salute and drill, nine songs, five recitations, three tableaux, and a ceremonial garlanding of a bust of the president.[67]

February, which March Brothers dubbed "the month of school celebrations," contained two of the most significant holidays for patriotic instruction. Exercises for school celebrations of Washington and Lincoln's Birthdays positioned the two presidents as models of patriotic virtue for schoolchildren. Obedience was a cardinal virtue in a society that equated patriotic citizenship with obedience to law, and children learned the importance of obedience through Parson Weems's cherry tree myth. One exercise featured boys who sang and performed a "Little Hatchet Drill," perhaps using hatchets ordered from March Brothers. The cherry tree myth also taught children the virtue of honesty. A didactic poem urged children to imitate Washington's honesty and obedience in their own lives.

> When Washington was little
> He never told a lie;
> Now to resemble him in that,
> We all can surely try.
> And even when a great big boy
> He minded well his mother;
> We all can copy him in this
> As well as in the other.[68]

Lincoln exercises similarly suggested the intertwining of character and civic education. On Lincoln's Birthday children heard variations on his stock honesty story, the lengths he went to as a storekeeper to deal honestly with his customers. Like the cherry tree myth, "Lincoln Cabin Scene," a holiday play by MacKay, intimated that Lincoln had been known for his honesty even as a boy. When a group of Native Americans arrives to trade skins and furs, the chief defers to the fourteen-year-old Lincoln to determine fair trades, reciting in ludicrous pidgin, "Red Plume know Lincoln. Lincoln heap square. Lincoln heap just. Honest Abe decide." Lincoln exercises also focused on his role in ending slavery. "Lincoln Cabin Scene" not surprisingly suggested that even as an adolescent Lincoln abhorred slavery. When a friend tells him about catching a squirrel, the young Lincoln, "looking straight before him to something far beyond the narrow world of Little Creek," replies presciently, "I don't like to see things in cages; I like to see 'em free. I believe in freedom for everything living!"[69]

While teaching the lessons of patriotic virtues and deeds, the presidential holiday exercises reinforced the gendered nature of patriotism. One Washington's Birthday program featured a dramatization of the song "When George Goes Marching Off to War, Martha Stays at Home," and a holiday reading lesson encouraged boys to be "a brave soldier" like Washington. Another song, sung to the tune of "Yankee Doodle," suggested what women could do to serve their country while their men were dumping tea in Boston Harbor. Girls in kerchiefs and frilled caps sang:

> We're only dames! We can but do
> Our best—or what we think it;
> The tea is taxed. We here do vow
> That we'll refuse to drink it![70]

Memorial Day exercises taught similar lessons of patriotic virtues, deeds, and gender roles and also provided history lessons on the Civil War. The best way to do this, according to New York's *Manual of Patriotism*, was to invite a veteran, preferably a GAR man, to speak at school exercises. In this way, students would learn that "it is always the mission of Right and Duty to declare and carry on war, whenever the Union is in peril, or the cause of Freedom demands the sacrifice." The Memorial Day programs revealed the touch of the GAR in their emphasis on the soldiers' valor and sacrifices in the cause of liberty and union. A recitation piece asserted that "[t]he soldiers of the Republic were not seekers after vulgar glory." Rather, "[t]hey were the defenders of humanity, the destroyers of prejudice, the breakers of chains." Other than such references to emancipation, African Americans were virtually invisible in the programs published in education journals and manuals. In keeping with the reconciliation embraced by their elders, children recited Francis Miles Finch's famous poem "The Blue and the Gray." Another poem urged students of the North and the South to "[c]lasp hands forever and ever—/ There are no sections now."[71]

Such displays of conciliation, however, were not always matched in the South. Echoing their counterparts in the GAR, Confederate veterans concerned about the lessons of the war southern children were learning took steps to shape their patriotic education. The Virginia Department of Public Instruction, in response to a request by the Confederate Memorial Literary Society, published a *Memorial Day Annual* in 1912 to set the record straight.

My name is Fred.
I am a little soldier boy.
I like to play soldier.
I have a drum and
a gun. I have my
flag now. I can tell
the story about the flag.
Shall I tell you about it?
The flag is red white and blue.
It has thirteen stripes.
Seven are red. Six are white.
It has a star for each state.
The stars are on a blue field.
George Washington loved the flag.
I love it too. I want to be a brave
soldier.

Washington exercise. Journals aimed at teachers contributed
to the proliferation of school holidays by publishing holiday
exercises. This reading lesson instructed young children on
the American flag and their duty to venerate it.
(From *Normal Instructor*, February 1908)

Whereas the programs in education journals praised Union soldiers for freeing the slaves, Virginia's manual featured songs nostalgic for slavery, including "Old Black Joe" and "Suwanee [*sic*] River." A piece on the origins of
Memorial Day redefined Americanism to encompass the Confederate cause,
asserting that "the children of Virginia should learn to know Lee's soldiers,
and to understand the great cause for which they fought as the world has already learned to estimate Washington. . . . Both men were called rebels. . . .
Both were patriots who fought to defend their native land. Virginia children

must honor them equally." The suggested centerpiece of the holiday program was an allegorical recreation of Virginia's decision to secede, in which Virginia resists the seduction of "Centralized Government, Victory, Wealth and Worldly Honors," proclaiming that "I do not believe in centralized government and dearer to me than success and worldly honors and wealth is TRUE HONOR." Thus, the state casts its lot with the South and secedes, whereupon "True Honor" and Robert E. Lee join Virginia on stage. Although the program closed with the students singing "America," the lesson students were to draw from the exercises was clearly sectional.[72]

Although Memorial Day exposed the sectional tensions that still smoldered, northern and southern educators could agree that the flag was the central symbol of American nationality. While children were reminded of the importance of the Stars and Stripes on Memorial Day and Washington and Lincoln's Birthdays, on Flag Day the national banner was the sole focus. Exercises began with the raising of the flag and a flag salute, either the *Youth's Companion's* Pledge of Allegiance or another salute, such as one embracing law-and-order patriotism: "I pledge myself to stand by the Flag that stands for Loyalty, Liberty and Law!" The flag salute of the Women's Christian Temperance Union (WCTU) emphasized the need for a homogeneous national identity: "I give my head, my heart and this right hand, for God and home and native land. One country! One language! One flag! One God!"[73]

Flag Day exercises generally reflected the WCTU's view and the motto of the American Flag Day Association, "One Country, One Flag." Children learned that the red flag of socialism and the national flags of immigrant homelands had no place in America. At Flag Day exercises in Chicago in 1895, for example, one speaker "disparaged the practice of the unfurling in this country of foreign flags by the side of the Stars and Stripes." A Flag Day exercise taught schoolchildren to recite:

> This is our flag, and may it wave
> Wide over land and sea!
> Though others love a different flag,
> This is the flag for me.

Other exercises had children perform flag drills and physically represent the American flag. In one skit girls playing Columbia and Freedom explained the symbolism and history of the flag, while forty-six children representing the states pinned on stars and announced the date of their admission to the union. Even more impressive was to have children dressed in red, white, and blue create a "living flag."[74]

On Flag Day as on the other patriotic holidays, children learned that obedience to law was the truest form of patriotism. One program suggested that the teacher quote Henry Ward Beecher on the flag: "Every color means liberty; . . . not lawlessness, not license, but organized, institutional liberty— liberty through laws and laws for liberty." To pound the lesson home, the teacher was to catechize students, asking them, "What is the office of the flag?" The correct response was, "It typifies the nation; it stands for our country; it is the symbol of liberty and the emblem of lawful authority."[75]

Those who wrote and sponsored school exercises for patriotic holidays claimed that these celebrations stimulated patriotism and good citizenship. After the Washington centennial, the Union League Club asserted that the school celebrations revealed that children "fully appreciate the sentiments of patriotism and realize their full import."[76] What went unsaid was the coercive nature of the patriotism engendered by school celebrations. The mass participation of children in such exercises revealed little more than their forced attendance at school and the fact that they had undergone weeks of rehearsals. Although it is indeed possible, even likely, that most children participated enthusiastically and even that such celebrations helped to develop patriotic sentiments, the children's participation alone is not sufficient evidence of that.

On at least one occasion, schoolchildren rebelled against their teachers' holiday plans. In 1900 boys from a Chicago high school petitioned the board of education for the day off in honor of Lincoln's Birthday. When refused, they staged a strike and prevented the girls from entering the school, telling them to "go home or join the 'strikers.'" The students then paraded through the city streets, blowing horns, throwing beans and pebbles at other schools, and recruiting other schoolchildren to join their demonstration.[77] If asked, most children would doubtless have agreed with the strikers that a holiday from school was the best way to celebrate.

Although it is almost impossible to document the reactions of schoolchildren to holiday exercises, the programs published in journals, manuals, and newspapers provided few figures with whom immigrant and minority children were likely to identify. Patriotic celebrations portrayed an American history in which they and their ancestors had played no significant part. Immigrants, African Americans, and Native Americans rarely appeared in the exercises, and when they did, it was as condescending stereotypes, such as the Indians in MacKay's play about Lincoln. Her play about George Washington similarly demeaned African Americans by depicting them in a state of childlike dependence on and adoration of Washington. In the play happy "plantation hands" sing an "African" song. "Uncle Ned," who would likely have been known to children and their parents as a stock minstrel character, further reinforces racial stereotypes by saying "I certainly do love music" and playing the fiddle while the children dance.[78] There were virtually no other Native American or African American characters in suggested holiday plays and tableaux.

Nor were there recognizably immigrant characters. The school holidays, like the three anniversary celebrations, constructed an American identity frozen at some date before the current waves of immigration. The American cultural symbols were those of the nation created in 1787, not the nation being continually remade by immigration in the late nineteenth century. The lessons that the school holidays taught were of an America that had no room for the dual loyalties and identities of immigrants. Indeed, educators touted the school holiday as a springboard to the Americanization of the immigrants crowding urban schools. "To take these children and make of them Americans is no small task," wrote Lee F. Hanmer of the Russell Sage Foundation in 1912, "and the influence of our great American holidays rightly celebrated will help mightily in this undertaking."[79]

Private and parochial ethnic schools, and probably black-run public schools in the South, countered homogeneous representations of America with their own celebrations of both American and ethnic holidays. For the Washington centennial, for example, a private German-English school in Chicago offered exercises in both languages in a hall decorated with intertwined German and American flags that symbolized the interconnectedness of the students' ethnic and national identities. Henry Fick, one of the school's proprietors, countered the implication that immigrant cultures had contributed little to American identity by speaking on "the virtue of patriotism as inherent in the German Character." He pointed to Revolutionary War heroes T. P. G. Muhlenberg, Baron Friedrich von Steuben, and Baron Johann de Kalb as evidence of the role played by Germans in the establishment of the American government.[80]

In addition to putting their own spin on American holidays, immigrants continued to educate their children in their own heritage. If the public schools did not countenance the observance of ethnic holidays, private schools and after-school programs did. In October 1912, for example, Chicago's Federation of Bohemian Free Thought Schools organized exercises for the anniversary of Karel Havlíček's death. The students of the city's more than twenty Free Thought schools paraded to the Havlíček monument at Douglas Park, where they sang the American and Czech anthems and listened to addresses on the Czech patriot. Chicago's Greek schools annually celebrated the feast of the three hierarchs or holy commanders of the schools. Programs featured the Greek and American anthems, as well as national dances and patriotic songs, recitations, dialogues, and speeches that fostered the acquisition of ethnic identity and taught the students loyalty to their Greek homeland.[81]

Although immigrants and racial minorities broadened the Americanism offered in the official school holidays, most did not question the basic premise of patriotic education. Only political radicals dared to protest this. The socialist *Chicagoer Arbeiter-Zeitung*, for example, was scathing in its condemnation of the school exercises for the Washington centennial. "Special stress was laid yesterday on stuffing the brains of our dear youth with patent-patriotism," the paper scorned. "The teachers and other speakers lacked the feelings which could have been transmitted to the little ones only directly, and by that the celebrations became ceremonious and stiff."[82]

The *Chicago Daily Socialist* had perhaps the most caustic commentary on school holidays and the hypocrisy of the civic elites who promoted and sponsored them. In honor of Flag Day in 1905, the paper printed a fictional story titled "Little Abe's Flag Day," which featured a new Abraham Lincoln, sent to save the country from destruction again. Unfortunately, little Abe has to quit school at age twelve and goes to work in a glass factory to replace his landlord's thirteen-year-old daughter, who has killed herself by eating match heads. Abe sickens because of the hard work and unhealthy conditions in the factory. He dies under the doorstep of his old school, where he is discovered by his former schoolmates as they arrive to celebrate Flag Day. The moral of the tale comes from "the Shining One," a godlike figure who appears to little Abe as he is dying. The boy's "murder" by the capitalist system that forced his family into poverty and him into the factory, "the Shining One" tells him, has doomed America to destruction because it has killed its savior.[83]

In a variety of ways, then, immigrants, African Americans, and radical workers worked to modify or to counter the law-and-order patriotism and civic education propounded by civic elites and their middle-class allies. They used their participation (or lack thereof) in the exercises to subvert the portrait of homogeneity scripted on patriotic holidays. They also continued to attend commercial and sporting events rather than official celebrations, choosing to spend their limited holidays in amusement instead of edification. Although the three anniversary celebrations attracted large audiences, none drew even close to a majority of the population, and they probably did little to educate and to assimilate working-class Americans to law-and-order patriotism. The problem did not lie entirely in the message, however, but in its presentation also. Aside from the Columbian procession, the celebrations relied primarily on oratory to provide civic education. But oratory was a disappearing art and certainly was no longer the most effective way of reaching a mass, ethnically diverse audience, many of whom did not speak English. The concurrent rise of more visual forms of commercial entertainment, such as baseball, vaudeville, and the new movies, suggested that patriotic educators, rather than ignoring commercial culture, might profit by imitating its presentational style.[84] School holiday exercises, by incorporating skits, dances, tableaux, popular music, and such new technological wonders as the stereopticon, illustrated a way to borrow elements of popular entertainment and to refashion them into wholesome educational vehicles. In the first two decades of the twentieth century, progressive educators and reformers extended and expanded the elements of the school celebration into the community, borrowing freely from commercial entertainment in an effort to attract and to educate a popular audience.

6

HOLIDAYS AND THE PROGRESSIVE
SEARCH FOR COMMUNITY

*I*N 1909 Dr. Julia Barnett Rice took aim at American holidays in the pages of the progressive magazine *Forum*. In contrast to "civilized nations," which observed their holidays "sanely and merrily, or reverently and with beautiful patriotic fervor," Americans, she charged, celebrated with a "frenzied, hysterical abandonment to license which disgraces our country." On New Year's Eve, revelers used every variety of noisemaker to create a fearful din, crowds turned into riotous mobs, and guns and fireworks caused injuries and property damage. The Fourth of July was even worse. Rice noted that between 1903 and 1908 more than 1,300 Americans had been killed and almost 28,000 had been injured in accidents resulting from holiday play with guns, firecrackers, and bombs. Most of the victims, she claimed, were children. To those who called this insanity patriotism, she replied that it was "only craving for noise and excitement and

danger." Rice closed with an appeal to Americans to find a better way to celebrate their national holiday. She urged them to replace the "Day of Carnage"
with "a celebration where thankfulness and gratitude and a wholesome sense
of universal brotherhood will enhance the merry sports and commemorative
exercises in honor of our National Birthday."[1]

In the early twentieth century, progressive reformers and educators such
as Rice entered the contest for control of American public holidays. Like the
civic elites and professional patriots, Progressives viewed urban chaos with
alarm, but rather than placing the blame on individual disregard for law and
order, they viewed disorder as the product of the social structure, and they
took a more environmentalist approach to the problem. By changing the environment of the city, they hoped to create good citizens. Like their late-
nineteenth-century predecessors, they seized on public holiday celebrations
as a vital component in this civic education. Progressives shared their concerns with Americanization, patriotism, and the eradication of class and ethnic conflict. But while civic elites and their allies sought to instill law-and-
order patriotism and a homogeneous national identity, Progressives focused
on developing citizenship, building community spirit, and creating a more
pluralist Americanism.[2]

Drawing on contemporary sociology, progressive reformers believed that
the creation of a unified nation must begin at the community level. Looking
to European peasant villages and the small towns in which they had grown
up, they sought to create local and national communities that encompassed
the diversity of America while emphasizing the elements all Americans had
in common. Accordingly, Progressives developed and sponsored community-based celebrations for a variety of holidays, ranging from Arbor Day
and Columbus Day to Christmas and New Year's Eve. Progressives deplored
the passivity of American celebrations, their lack of artistic merit, and their
overreliance on bombastic oratory, which the big anniversary celebrations
had done little to alter. They sought to restore citizen participation and
artistry to American holidays by creating celebrations that blended both into
a sort of participatory spectacle. Their biggest concern, as Rice's critique suggests, was the Fourth of July, which Progressives sought to transform into a
wholesome and pluralistic celebration of American history, culture, and community. Although Progressives celebrated ethnic diversity (within limits),

they, like the elites, generally did not envision a role for organized labor or the celebration of class in American identity. A few reformers suggested ways to make Labor Day a community celebration rather than a class celebration, but most ignored the holiday.

The Progressives' vision of a more pluralist America was put to the test by World War I, as resurgent ethnicity and the drive for national unity led them to intensify Americanization at the expense of pluralism. The peak of the drive for holiday-based Americanization came on the Fourth of July in 1918, a day of precisely orchestrated, mammoth demonstrations of patriotism by the nation's ethnic groups. But the very form that these celebrations took, wherein individual immigrant groups pledged their loyalty as ethnic groups, undermined the drive for 100 percent Americanism, as immigrants paired symbols of ethnic and American identity in tribute to their continuing construction of an Americanism roomy enough for ethnic diversity and loyalties.

THE SCHOOL AND THE COMMUNITY ON ARBOR AND BIRD DAYS

The first holiday embraced by progressive reformers and educators was one that predated both the Progressive movement and the inception of the patriotic school holiday. Arbor Day had been established in 1872 by Nebraskan J. Sterling Morton for the purpose of foresting the treeless plains. It was subsequently taken up by both the village beautification movement and the fledgling conservation movement. "There is scarcely a village . . . which could not greatly increase its value," observed the *Youth's Companion* in 1890, "by carefully investing a moderate sum every year in removing ugliness and developing beauty. Arbor Day is a good time to organize movements in this direction."[3]

One of the most important spots for beautification was the schoolyard, where trees might serve an educational as well as a practical purpose. In 1883 Birdsey G. Northrup, an early advocate of planting trees for beautification and chairman of the American Forestry Association, proposed at its annual meeting that the day become part of the nation's school calendar. Ohio was the first state to introduce Arbor Day to its public schools, and states across the country followed suit in the next decade. Promoted by the National Education Association, the GAR, the Grange (a farmers' association), women's clubs, and the forestry association, the holiday spread, and by 1906 more than forty states and territories celebrated Arbor Day. Because of the nature of the day, its date varied with planting seasons, from February in southern states to March and April in more northern ones.[4]

A related holiday, Bird Day, was also introduced in the 1890s for the purpose of preserving the bird population from slaughter for women's hats and boys' sport. Advocates contended that by teaching children about birds, educators could help stem the destruction of birds and their habitats. Morton, now secretary of agriculture, endorsed the day in 1894, expressing his belief that the celebration of Bird Day would make "a respectable woman . . . ashamed to be seen with the wing of a wild bird on her bonnet, and an honest boy . . . ashamed to own that he ever robbed a nest or wantonly took the life of a bird." Two years later Morton's Department of Agriculture published a pamphlet extolling the benefits of Bird Day as a school holiday. "A powerful influence for good can be exerted by the schools if the teachers will only interest themselves in the movement," the pamphlet concluded, suggesting that "if it may seem too much to devote one day in the year to the study of birds, the exercises of Bird Day might be combined with those of Arbor Day." Many schools followed this course, while others celebrated Bird Day on 4 May, the birthday of John James Audubon. Aside from their common conservation purpose, the two holidays were intimately connected, as one promoter pointed out: "in order that [birds] may have a harbor and a nesting place for their young, let us plant a tree."[5]

In the schools Arbor Day took on a broader significance than its original pragmatic purpose. The holiday, according to its promoters, not only taught children the value of trees but also awakened "the aesthetic sense," stimulated a "love for nature," and taught "the lesson of economy and unselfish foresight" by providing for future generations. "Plant trees, plant trees, on Arbor Day," began one holiday poem, "Who plants a tree shall surely be / A blessing to humanity." Beyond conservation and aesthetics, Arbor Day, proponents claimed, fostered the development of community spirit by instilling in children a "high regard for public property." Finally, the holiday provided citizenship training for students. "In awakening an interest in the life of tree and plant," wrote one advocate, Arbor Day "gives a larger love of home and familiar scenes and a deep interest in men and things, which is at the heart of good citizenship."[6]

In his Arbor Day proclamation in 1892, the governor of Illinois "especially enjoin[ed] the teachers and scholars in our public and private schools . . . to celebrate the day" by planting trees, "whereby our homes, highways and public places will be beautified, and a lasting benefit conferred upon the people of our commonwealth." To encourage school celebrations, state school superintendents subsequently began to publish annual pamphlets containing the history of Arbor and Bird Days and suggested recitations and holiday programs. In 1906 the state school superintendent noted that 1,722 Illinois schools still had not so much as a single tree on their grounds. Arbor Day, however, provided teachers and students with the means of rectifying this. If the schools observed the holiday properly, he explained, "the children will not only learn something about trees, but also . . . get valuable training in community spirit, which is the beginning of the larger thing we call patriotism."[7]

The equation of community spirit and patriotism signaled a subtle shift in the definition of patriotism at the turn of the century. The promoters of Arbor and Bird Days in the schools envisioned the holidays as stepping stones in the development of the community spirit they found lacking in modern America. And community spirit would beget patriotism. "Arbor Day," Northrup contended, "has fostered love of country" through the planting of memorial trees to honor American patriots and the presence of the flag and patriotic songs at holiday exercises. He claimed that the day had a patriotic effect even on southern schoolchildren, who combined the celebration with Washington's Birthday. Indeed, Arbor Day was so important an influence on the nation's youth that Northrup approvingly cited the educator who proclaimed, "Any teacher who has no taste for trees, shrubs or flowers is unfit to be placed in charge of children."[8]

To reap the community benefits of Arbor and Bird Days, teachers had first to interest students in the subjects of these holidays. One way of doing so was to anthropomorphize trees and birds. Some promoters advocated using the pet relationship already familiar to children to evoke their love for trees and birds. Noting that "[t]he interest of children in pet animals . . . springs largely from their life and their dependence upon human care," George Curtis suggested that students name the trees they planted. "When the young tree also is regarded as living and equally dependent upon intelligent attention, when it is named by votes of the scholars, and planted by them with music and a pretty ceremony, it will also become a pet and a human relation will be established." Similarly, the school superintendent in Oil City, Pennsylvania, claimed that because of Bird Day "[o]ur children generally know most of our bird residents, they also love them, and feel like protecting them." Holiday promoters even extended natural rights theory to trees and birds. "Somebody must teach our people," wrote one advocate, "the rights and the dignity of a tree." The secretary of the Illinois Audubon Society wrote a letter to teachers suggesting that they tell students that organizations such as hers were working to protect birds by "giving them rights under the law, like other citizens."[9]

Northrup and others had also introduced the concept of planting memorial trees on Arbor Day. At Tucson's first Arbor Day exercises in 1889, students and citizens planted groves of trees dedicated to presidents, pioneers, soldiers, American authors, the public schools, and the American flag. For the latter, "the trees were planted in the form of an American flag." The value of memorial trees, like pet trees, lay in the personalized relationship this fostered between children and the trees they planted. "Watching to see how Bryant and Longfellow are growing," wrote Curtis, "whether Abraham Lincoln wants water, or George Washington promises to flower early, . . . the pupil will find that a tree may be as interesting as the squirrel that skims along its trunk."[10]

To instruct students in the value of trees and birds, holiday exercises included didactic catechisms to be memorized and recited. In one such exercise, the teacher was to ask, "Of what use is Arbor Day?" to which one student responded that "Arbor Day will make the country visibly more beautiful every year," and another that it would "prevent the ruthless destruction of the forests." Once students had ingested the lessons of Arbor and Bird Days, they could pass them on to their parents. Farmers were particularly singled out as needing education on the significance of birds and trees. A humorous dialogue had fourteen boys teaching an old farmer about Arbor Day, with poems on trees and patriotic songs interspersed with information about the holiday and trees. The skit equated conservation with patriotism. One boy explained to "Uncle Jim" that "men who waste the timber . . . are just as unpatriotic and as much traitors as if they gave the government over to some foreign enemy." By the end of the dialogue, the boys have convinced the farmer, who began by viewing the only good tree as the one cut down, to go out and plant a tree. Similarly, children in a Bird Day play based on Longfellow's poem "The Birds

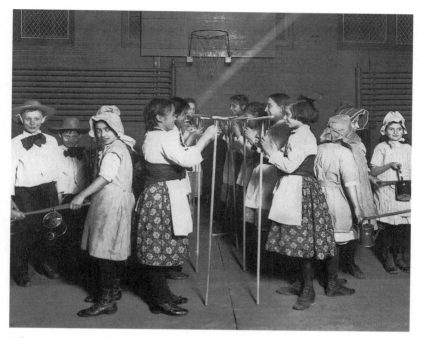

Arbor Day exercise, Chicago, early twentieth century. The children, clad in a Progressive's vision of rural attire, perform a planting drill with hoes and watering cans. (Courtesy of the Chicago Park District Special Collections)

of Killingworth" condemned farmers for killing all the town's birds "for the gain / Of a scant handful more or less of wheat." Like the boys in the Arbor Day dialogue, the children sought to convince the farmers of birds' service to the farm. "They are the winged wardens of your farms," one child proclaimed, "[w]ho from the cornfields drive the insidious foe," insects and slugs.[11]

In addition to catechizing children on the value of trees and birds, the holiday exercises enlisted their active participation in the service of beautification and conservation. George P. Morris's "Woodman, Spare that Tree" was a popular recitation piece, as was "Don't Kill the Birds" for Bird Day. One program featured children wearing smocks and straw hats, carrying gardening implements, and singing a song about planting trees. In another, the entrance of Flora, "the Queen of Arbor Day," signaled that the planting should begin. Flora, "dressed in white, crowned with flowers and bearing a branch of willow as a scepter," was followed by eight boys in green who served as her attendants. After Flora ceremoniously threw "a handful of dirt" on the tree's roots, her attendants finished planting it.[12]

The various skits, dialogues, songs, and recitations were only prefatory to the main event of the day. They primed students for the actual planting process, which was the centerpiece and climax of Arbor Day. The 1889 New York State program had students sing a marching song while walking to the planting site, where the tree and planting tools waited. The program suggested that students make a sign for the tree with the name of the person to whom it was dedicated and advised that each student should participate in the actual planting by "deposit[ing] a spadeful of earth." The ceremonies at the site were to include songs, a statement about the dedicatee, and recitations from the person's writings, if applicable. Suggested musical selections to accompany the planting included "Planting the Tree," sung to the tune of "America," and the "Arbor Day March," sung to the tune of "Marching through Georgia."[13]

Although it is unclear to what extent Arbor and Bird Days developed citizenship, they undeniably raised student (and public) awareness of the threats to trees and birds. Bird Day probably stopped some boys from taking aim at songbirds, and Arbor Day certainly achieved in large measure its advocates' practical goals of forestation. The holiday was responsible for the planting of thousands of trees across the nation at the turn of the century. Northrup reported that at one ceremony he attended at Carlisle Indian School some one hundred trees were planted, including an American white ash in his honor. Not surprisingly, Arbor Day was particularly popular in the tree-scarce Great Plains and Southwest. Tucsonans adopted the day with special enthusiasm, attempting on Arbor Days to turn the Sonora Desert into a forested Eden. On Arbor Day in 1891, some three hundred trees were planted at the city's public school, and in 1909 one hundred trees were planted on the grounds of the high school. The state's Arbor Day pamphlet in 1916 included a "Record of Arbor Day Exercises" to be filled in by each teacher, which noted the length of the literary and planting exercises, the number of visitors and speakers, and the numbers of trees, shrubs, and vines planted.[14]

The holiday was not limited to the schools; all Tucsonans were urged to participate. "Every home in Tucson should have more or less trees and shrubs,"

Arbor Day tree planting, Chicago, early twentieth century. The climax to Arbor Day exercises was the ceremonial tree planting. One promoter of the holiday suggested children name the trees they planted and make them into pets to develop a bond of attachment to them. (Courtesy of the Chicago Park District Special Collections)

proclaimed the *Tucson Arizona Daily Star* in 1905, because "these ornaments of the home are a constant educator; a continuous influence upon the children who are growing and carving characters into manhood and womanhood for future influence in their communities." On a practical note, the paper added that trees could reduce the summer heat. Thus, it concluded, "Plant trees and benefit yourself and the community." Another advocate of Arbor Day suggested that planting trees would inspire "a kindred feeling to that experienced on the Fourth of July," making Americans "one people engaged in something to do good to mankind."[15]

HOLIDAYS AND THE PROGRESSIVE LONGING FOR COMMUNITY

Arbor and Bird Days heralded a broadening of the definition of patriotism and national identity, from the narrow focus on liberty under law to citizenship as community spirit. Law and order were still important elements of patriotism, but Progressives believed that these would follow naturally if children learned the lesson of community spirit. In his 1908 Memorial Day address, education professor William Burnham conceded that "[s]aluting the flag and instruction in patriotism are important," but he argued that "more important is the actual training in patriotism when a pupil gives up his own personal interest for the sake of the school." Burnham contended that this community spirit was the essence of patriotism. Horace G. Brown concurred. "[M]ore than the individual spirit," he wrote in an article on school holidays published in 1911, "we desire to emphasize the group spirit, or team play, of the pupils, and *the joint celebration of schools with the community*." The school, Brown contended, should be "the best social center of civic influence" in the community.[16]

The changing emphasis of school holidays paralleled and reinforced the changing conception of civic education after 1890, from a focus on learning the Constitution and the structure of national government to preparing children to be active citizens of their community as well as their nation. To this end, students were to study the family, the school, and the community and thus gradually work their way up to the study of the national government. Above all, the purpose of the new civic education was to inculcate the spirit of cooperation that Progressives saw as necessary to the harmonious community. Constance D'Arcy MacKay suggested that the properly conducted patriotic play contained "the very essence of democracy—*efficient team-work, a striving together for the good of the whole*."[17]

School holiday advocates such as Percival Chubb, festival director at New York City's Ethical Culture School, recognized that incorporating a full annual slate of celebrations would take considerable time away from other schoolwork, but Progressives believed that what these holidays taught was just as important to children's education. The head of costuming at the school asserted that "[i]t has come to be regarded as a matter of course that work for a festival is a legitimate and profitable interruption of the regularly prescribed course of study." Celebrations formed an integral part of the curriculum at the Ethical Culture School, which held annual festivals for All Souls' Day, Thanksgiving, Christmas, Patriots' Day (which combined Lincoln and Washington's Birthdays), and May Day.[18]

The pedagogical benefits of festivals, according to Chubb, were many. They restored the "art of recreative play," provided moral education, and promoted "a deeper civic and national patriotism." Above all, Chubb argued, festivals, by utilizing "the fundamental dramatic instincts proper to childhood," would awaken in children a "delighted interest in school life and school work" and thus enhance learning. The *Journal of Education* concurred, noting in an editorial that "[i]nstead of being a hindrance to regular school work, [holiday celebrations] are its noblest inspiration."[19]

Drawing on sociologist Charles Horton Cooley's theory of primary groups, which he argued gave "the individual his earliest and completest experience of social unity," progressive reformers sought to create such groups in the schools, on the playgrounds, and in city neighborhoods. The ideal primary group, according to Cooley, was "a moral whole or community wherein individual minds are merged and the higher capacities of the members find total and adequate expression." He defined the key principles of moral unity as "loyalty, lawfulness, and freedom." The loyalty developed in the primary group was essential to national unity. In Cooley's ever-widening concentric circles of loyalty, the nation was simply a much larger version of the primary group. "Reduced to its lowest terms," explained Rev. William N. Hutchins, "patriotism signifies loyalty, with the nation as the group." The problem was how to create such groups. The ideal primary group in the minds of many Progressives was the mythicized community of the small towns of their youth, the towns that, not coincidentally, they had escaped as quickly as possible. But absence made their hearts grow fonder of their hometowns, and Progressives set out to reproduce the community they remembered, however romanticized, in the cities to which they had moved.[20]

The school, according to philosopher of education John Dewey, was one place where such a community might begin to be constructed. The school could become "an embryonic community life, active with types of occupations that reflect the life of the larger society," by implementing the vocationally oriented curriculum Dewey favored. The school, he explained, must be made into "a genuine form of active community life, instead of a place set apart in which to learn lessons." The rewards of making the school a true community, Dewey believed, went beyond simply improving education.

"When the school introduces and trains each child . . . into membership within such a little community," he claimed, "we shall have the deepest and best guarantee of a larger society which is worthy, lovely, and harmonious."[21]

The school's impact on the larger society did not even have to await the students' graduation. If the school was such a valuable source of community spirit for children, might it not prove just as valuable to their parents after hours, with the added benefit of making more efficient use of the school plant? Community spirit, according to Cooley, was "the basis at once of citizenship, of morals, and of religion." To aid in building community, he declared that each community should have "a centre of social culture connected with the public schools." In an article published in *Century* magazine in 1916, progressive journalist and reformer George Creel used Cooley's primary groups model to justify making the school a community center. "The neighborhood is the group unit next in importance to the family itself," he wrote, "and the school building is the center of the neighborhood. What reaches every child in the United States can reach every parent."[22]

In addition to building the elusive spirit of community, progressive educators and reformers believed that transforming the school into an after-hours community center could help them combat the evils of commercial recreation. Creel made clear just how conscious Progressives were of the allure of commercial recreation and its impact on their plans for the school community centers. "In competition with the reckless greeds of commercialized amusements," he explained, "the social center offers amateur theatricals, debates, dancing parties, moving picture shows, receptions, gymnasium games, all in a clean, inspiring environment, subjected to the wholesome restraints of the family group and neighborly friendship." Finally, just as the school served its students as a force for Americanization, so it could serve the neighborhood after hours. "To watch an interracial pageant in a New York school building, shared in by twenty nationalities," Creel proclaimed, "is [a] complete answer to the question of assimilation."[23]

Although immigrants were the primary targets of progressive community building in the school and the neighborhood, immigrant communities also inspired Progressives as models. Sociologist Robert Park, for example, found a real community life in the ethnic neighborhoods of Chicago. At the same time that Progressives endeavored to Americanize immigrants in behavior and culture, they sought in immigrant life the key to the mystery of community. Some Progressives found this key in ethnic folk culture. Creel suggested tapping immigrants for "their rich store of folk songs, games, and traditional customs." Activists in the playground movement agreed that American celebrations needed an infusion of ethnic cultural forms. Dr. Luther Halsey Gulick, president of the Playground Association of America, suggested that Americans lacked appropriate celebrations for the Fourth of July because they had let "the great folk-dances and folk festivals" slip away. "These folk dances and games in which many individuals can participate afford one of the few avenues that exist for the expression of mass feeling," he explained. The Playground Association of America and city parks sponsored folk festivals in the early twentieth century, in which immigrants demonstrated their folk and national dances. "The social value of encouraging the beautiful dances of the people who come to America cannot be overestimated," Gulick wrote in 1908. Americans needed folk dance, he argued, because it provided a spur to local and national unity. It constituted "a positive moral force, a social agency" that served the function of "welding [diverse Americans] into a unified whole."[24]

Forces that threatened that unified whole had to be neutralized. The development of community, Progressives believed, required that class, racial, and ethnic divisions be downplayed because they disrupted community harmony. True community spirit would transcend such differences. The historical pageants created for holidays and anniversaries presented the past as a time of true community, marked by harmonious social relations and freedom from racial, ethnic, or class conflict, and suggested that contemporary citizens could learn from this past how to re-create community in the present. Many pageants ended with a woman dressed to represent the Spirit of the Community welcoming recently arrived immigrants. But transcendence of differences, to Progressives, meant acquiescence to a decidedly Anglo-American, middle-class conception of America. They glossed over divisions in American society in their celebration fare. The festival, according to Percival Chubb, was a means of "emphasizing and idealizing . . . the common life" of Americans, rising "above class spirit, race, color, denomination." His Patriots' Day festival for the Ethical Culture School presented racial conflict as a part of America's past, not its present. Although he acknowledged that students must learn the history of "the aboriginal Indian" and "the unfortunate imported negro," he advised that "any dramatization of this racial struggle is brought to its conclusion by the representation of the idea of reconciliation and friendly intermingling." Nevertheless, the historical scenes of one of his Patriots' Day programs concluded with the French surrender to England in 1763, skipping any mention of slavery.[25]

As Chubb's omission of African Americans suggests, Progressives had a difficult time incorporating America's racial history into their vision of the past as a model for contemporary community. Moreover, most Progressives shared the prevailing racism of white Americans and were ambivalent about how far African Americans should be integrated into their envisioned communities. Although they believed that immigrants could be assimilated, they were less sure about African Americans. Cooley, for example, claimed that "[t]he presence of the Negro in large numbers creates a race problem, because assimilation is generally held undesirable, and does not, in fact, take place." Because of this problem, he argued that there were "excellent grounds of national policy for preventing [people of different races] mingling in large numbers," as racial antagonisms weakened the "common spirit" requisite to a healthy national life. Thus, Cooley endorsed segregation as a reasonable and wise social policy, implying that true communities must be racially homogeneous.[26]

School holiday celebrations seemed to bear him out, as they taught children that America was a white nation, by the omission of visibly ethnic or nonwhite characters. On the few occasions when African Americans were represented, it was in a demeaning fashion. The humorous Arbor Day dialogue, for example, contained a black character, dubbed "Snowball," but the exercise specified that he be played by a boy "blacked up." Snowball's lines were to be spoken in exaggerated black dialect. Apparently the author of the dialogue did not conceive of it being performed by black children, despite the vast numbers of African American farmers and sharecroppers. Rather, the skit depicted African Americans in minstrel fashion in the role of comic relief and entertainment for white Americans.[27]

Progressives were almost as uncomfortable with class as with race. For the most part, they ignored organized labor and labor holidays in their community-building efforts. Robert Haven Schauffler's series of books on American holidays did not include a volume on Labor Day. Only a few reformers even considered it to be a potential community holiday, and then only if removed from the hands of organized labor. Lee Hanmer, for instance, suggested making Labor Day an occasion to celebrate "the dignity of labor" while helping Americans to understand "that the labor problem is not a class problem, but one in which the whole community is concerned." A properly conducted Labor Day celebration that focused on the progress of industry in the community, Hanmer claimed, would work wonders in "clearing up much of the misunderstanding that now exists between employer and employee" and allow the achievement of true community. A Labor Day pageant in a Chicago park in 1913 followed Hanmer's blueprint by depicting Labor and Capital symbolically joining hands to work together for progress.[28]

Holiday celebrations, Progressives believed, provided perfect opportunities for building community spirit, patriotism, and Americanism. They decried the lack of imagination of contemporary celebrations, with their military parades, bombastic oratory, and fireworks, and called for a return to pageantry. Constance D'Arcy MacKay charged that contemporary parades were "from an art and civic point of view utterly worthless." They must be transformed into pageant-processions and joined by pageants, plays, pantomimes, masques, and folk celebrations. A proper procession, according to Barr Ferree, was "a work of art" carefully arranged "with the object of producing an effect on the minds of the spectators." A scholar of pageantry described the pageant-procession as "a procession with floats or images" depicting "symbolic, or historical, allegorical, or mythological personages." Although, given their expense, large-scale community pageants could only feasibly be done on an occasional basis, pageant-processions could be made part of annual celebrations. Mary Porter Beegle and Jack Crawford, who taught summer courses in pageantry at Dartmouth College, suggested that through holiday festivals pageantry could be made "a permanent element in modern life." They claimed that patriotic holidays in particular provided "opportunities for the creation of an American festival tradition" and proposed festivals for the Fourth of July, Lincoln and Washington's Birthdays, and Labor Day.[29]

The participatory spectacles that Progressives had in mind required the services of experts, from pageant and festival directors to artists, architects, choreographers, costumers, and musicians. Promoters such as MacKay, Chubb, and Ferree believed, somewhat self-servingly, that celebrations must be artistic to be most effective in accomplishing their purposes, and Progressives were happy to supply their expertise and to create careers for themselves. Just as playground and pageant directors were in the process of creating new careers for themselves, festival and holiday advocates sought to do the same. Ferree even suggested that the procession required a colorist to direct it, claiming that "the chief reason for the success of processions in older times was because the use of color was better understood than with us." The colorist's job was not only to choose proper colors for the procession but also to arrange and to harmonize them. Chubb provided a guide to the symbolism of color for those who could not hire a professional colorist to help them. The wrong colors apparently could be disastrous, even if they were patriotic. Another festival writer suggested that George Washington and Betsy Ross had been color challenged. The American flag, he asserted, was "not the most successful piece of decoration," because "the equal proportion of red to blue is not a fortunate color-combination."[30]

Not coincidentally, the visually oriented progressive celebrations were tailor-made to appeal not only to children and non-English-speaking immigrants but also to Americans enamored of popular commercial culture. In addition to building community and patriotic spirit, proper celebrations, MacKay suggested, would develop Americans' artistic sensibility and overcome the excessive commercialism of American society. Properly conducted holiday celebrations, Progressives argued, could provide a wholesome and moral alternative to the commercial popular culture that they abhorred. "[T]he chaste simplicity and good taste" of celebrations at the Ethical Culture School, Percival Chubb argued, refined the tastes of his students, who spread these lessons to their homes, thereby providing for the community as a whole "a way out of this muddy stream of vulgar popular culture."[31]

Holidays and festivals thus played a vital role in the progressive conception of community. "It is by these commemorations," explained Chubb, "that we can develop—unconsciously, of course—that underlying consciousness of kind, of human solidarity, of co-operative unity, which may offset the crude and narrow individualism that everywhere menaces us." Unfortunately, according to Progressives, Americans no longer knew how to celebrate properly, which meant that they could not reap the benefits of festivals. "We all need to acquire the spirit and to learn the methods of celebration," Gulick asserted.[32] And Progressives were more than willing to step into the breach. Playground and park activists, pageant promoters, educators, women's clubs, and sympathetic philanthropists worked in the years before World War I to teach Americans the art of celebration, which they deemed absolutely necessary to building community spirit and patriotism.

"A CONSTRUCTIVE TYPE OF CELEBRATION":
THE SAFE AND SANE FOURTH OF JULY

Luther Gulick declared in 1909 that "the vacant national holiday needs to be utilized as much as the vacant lot," and the progressive coalition began its campaign to change the way Americans celebrated their holidays by overhauling the nation's original public holiday, the Fourth of July. The Safe and Sane Fourth of July movement was active from about 1908 to 1916. Although its roots lay in the threat to persons and property posed by traditional methods of celebration with guns and firecrackers, at its heart the movement sought to create new forms of celebration that would inspire community spirit and patriotism.[33]

As early as 1864 a British visitor to New York City had complained of the Fourth of July, "It has come to mean this: simply crackers." George Sala deplored the fires and injuries that resulted. "Is it absolutely necessary," he asked caustically, "for the anniversary of American independence to be celebrated by burning down houses and mutilating and slaying human beings?" Not only did the licentious Fourth produce mayhem, as Sala suggested, it also violated the property rights held so dear by Americans, as Samuel Canby Rumford made clear in his recollection of the Fourth of his youth in late nineteenth-century Wilmington, Delaware: "The day was a very noisy one because of the habit of young men of setting off large firecrackers and other explosives all over town, not caring upon whose property the explosion took place, and as a result there were many serious fires." In response to mounting criticism, merchandisers did introduce safety features. The Safety Cannon Company advertised in 1890 "the Home-Guard Safety Cannon" for firing firecrackers, which the company claimed was "perfectly safe." It "satisfies the child's longing for a cannon and makes his firecrackers harmless," the advertisement promised.[34]

Fourth of July scene on Boston Common. This illustration depicts the "insane" Fourth of pistols, firecrackers, and public disorder condemned by the American Medical Association and progressive reformers in the early twentieth century. (From *Ballou's*, 1859; courtesy of the Library of Congress)

By the turn of the century, however, reformers wanted more than safer firecrackers. Along with the American Medical Association, they called for an end to the carnage resulting from the traditional celebration of the Fourth when, according to Dr. Julia Barnett Rice, "freedom shrieks and Patriotism goes mad." The *Chicago Tribune* began to publish an annual holiday casualty list in 1899, and the *Journal of the American Medical Association* followed suit in 1903. Newspapers and magazines also published stories of children hurt and killed on the Fourth. The *Ladies' Home Journal*, for instance, presented a story from a mother whose son had been blinded and daughter killed by an exploding firecracker. The girl's clothing had caught fire, the mother explained, and "our darling was burnt beyond recognition . . . her face was absolutely cooked. She lived four hours." When even such horror stories had little impact on the problem, reformers stepped up the campaign by organizing Sane Fourth Associations across the country, beginning in 1908.[35]

The Sane Fourth Associations united the American Medical Association, reformers, journalists, play activists, pageant directors, women's clubs, and educators in a coalition to end the "insane" Fourth. They adopted two strategies. First they sought legislation restricting or banning the sale of guns and fireworks. By 1911, 161 cities and towns had adopted either prohibitory or restrictive legislation. "But the prohibition and restriction are only half the problem," cautioned the *Journal of Education*. "We take away the noise and the fireworks, and we must supply diversions equally attractive to Young America." Reformers thus endeavored to create an alternative type of celebration that conformed to progressive ideas about community festivals; Lee Hanmer called this "doing the positive progressive thing rather than that which is negative and prohibitory." The safe and sane Fourth of July celebration, he explained, should be "an inspiration to patriotism" while offering a wholesome and attractive substitution for the "old barbarous Fourth." Reformers offered various alternative celebrations, including pageants, sporting competitions, folk and playground festivals, processions, and city-sponsored fireworks displays to assuage some of the popular longing for noise and fire.[36]

Percy MacKaye, a dramatist and pageant master, suggested that pageantry was the way to go. In 1910 he planned an ambitious Fourth of July pageant for Pittsburgh. This extravaganza was to feature balladeers, arts and crafts vendors, and puppeteers dispersed around the city, a children's parade, "pantomime-pageants" on wheeled stages, a vendors' fair, a historical military parade, evening illuminations and fireworks displays, and a "folk-pageant symboliz[ing] the fusion of many nationalities in the American nation." At the folk festival, immigrants "in their national costumes, singing their national anthems and led by their national heroes," would be reviewed "symbolically by Washington and the Signers of the Declaration of Independence from a raised stage representing the interior of Independence Hall." After performing their national dances, all participants were to unite for "a national 'Liberty Dance' expressive of America." Oratory, a staple of traditional celebrations, was to be revived but "subordinated to pageantry purposes." Unfortunately, MacKaye's vision of the Fourth went unrealized when city officials canceled the pageant in the wake of a political scandal.[37]

MacKaye's plan revealed the progressive conviction that industrial America, having forgotten how to celebrate, must look to the past and to immigrants for proper festal forms. The strolling singers and puppeteers harked back to the Renaissance, the arts and crafts vendors to the preindustrial era of craftsmanship. Although the immigrant participants were ultimately to celebrate their Americanism, MacKaye intended the inclusion of their national songs, dances, and costumes to be instructive for Americans. He cautioned those cities that wished to start their own holiday pageants to "[u]se only American material," yet he added that they should also "conserve all the riches which other countries have brought to us," including "the folk-lore, music, costumes, pantomimes, puppet-shows, histrionic gifts, and above all, the *temperament*, which are inherent in our immigrant population."[38]

MacKaye was not alone in suggesting that immigrants knew better how to celebrate and had a stronger sense of community than native-born Americans. One of the most common forms used by the organizers of urban Sane Fourth celebrations was a variation of the pageant-procession, which presented historical floats but featured most prominently the city's ethnic groups, in national costume and with floats depicting their national heroes, historic scenes, or their contributions to America. Such processions were not exactly novel, having appeared occasionally in the nineteenth century, such as Chicago's Columbian procession in 1892. The first place to adapt the "Parade of Nations" to the Sane Fourth, however, was Springfield, Massachusetts, in 1908, with a procession of historical floats and thirteen ethnic groups.[39]

Pageant-processions were less expensive to produce than an extravaganza like that envisioned by MacKaye, as ethnic groups and other participants could generally be induced to pay for their own floats and costumes. These processions also reflected the progressive ambivalence toward ethnic culture, which they saw as both model and historical artifact to be swept away eventually by Americanization. In such celebrations, reformers sought to harness certain elements of ethnic cultures to the end of a more unified community, which would require the ultimate dissolution of the very ethnic communities that had produced these cultures.

The Sane Fourth movement in Chicago exemplified the strategies, philosophy, and trajectory of the movement. The city's Sane Fourth Association began its life with a successful campaign for restrictive ordinances, by distributing literature to churches, Sunday schools, fraternal organizations, and the police and fire departments. In response the city adopted ordinances in 1909 restricting the sale of fireworks, the type of fireworks available, and the places where they could be lit. Other regulations prohibited the discharge of cannons and toy pistols (but not of real guns), the building of bonfires on public property, and the discharge of approved fireworks on any day other than the holiday.[40]

The next year Marquis Eaton, the president of Chicago's Sane Fourth Association, announced that while the organization took pride in the success of its campaign against the "DESTRUCTIVE type of celebration, . . . [w]e may, I feel, take equal satisfaction in the success of the campaign for a CONSTRUCTIVE type of celebration." For the Fourth the organization planned a historical pageant that Eaton modestly termed "the most important thing of its kind ever presented in this country." The pageant was to feature a "Peace" float and floats contributed by the city's ethnic groups and organizations such as the California Club. The association was short on funds, however, its appeal for subscriptions from the community having fallen on mostly deaf ears. Apparently not all Chicagoans agreed that the Fourth needed fixing; at the very least, they did not wish to pay for it. Eaton wrote to the secretary of the American Peace Society asking the society to bear the expense of the "Peace" float, which, he claimed in a fit of marketing hyperbole, would be "by far the most beautiful and elaborate float shown in the pageant." The immigrant groups, he explained, had "generously assumed the entire expense of their floats," reinforcing the progressive notion that they, unlike Americans, understood the concept of community.[41]

In the end, the main feature of the 1910 Sane Fourth celebration was, ironically, not a peace float but a demonstration of military prowess. Soldiers from nearby Fort Sheridan staged a ten-day tournament at the lakefront beginning on the Fourth. They performed drills, maneuvers, and demonstrations of such new war technology as the machine gun, all before a delighted crowd. The *Chicago Daily Socialist* looked on in disgust at this so-called sane celebration that "glorif[ied] wholesale murder in uniform" and served as a recruiting tool for the army by teaching schoolchildren "to look upon and admire the glitter and gilt of war." A piercing preholiday editorial attacked the wholesale hypocrisy of this allegedly sane alternative to the insane Fourth. On the new holiday, the editor observed, "[b]oys will not be permitted to kill and wound themselves accidentally." Rather, "[t]hey will be taught how to kill and wound their brothers intentionally." The *Chicago Daily Socialist* did not oppose the move to stop the accidental destruction of the Fourth, but it condemned the alternative celebration embraced by the Sane Fourth Association. "The discharge of explosives was doubtless a very insane way to show patriotism," the paper conceded, "[b]ut the substitution of military display, the importation of hired butchers from Fort Sheridan, the hysteria of militarism is far more crazy and idiotic and criminal."[42]

Ignoring socialist criticisms, the Sane Fourth Association deemed the 1910 celebration a success. It did not, however, repeat the military demonstration in 1911. Rather, the association moved to expand its celebration with a morning procession featuring "a greater number of nationalities than has ever before co-operated in this country in a patriotic demonstration," followed by afternoon exercises in the city's parks and playgrounds. Despite the larger scale, Eaton noted that the celebration cost several thousand dollars less than that of the previous year, no doubt by placing even more of the burden of cost on the participants themselves. The organization raised more than $6,000, primarily from women's clubs and businesses, including the Industrial and Historical Pageant Corporation, which contributed $50 and received more than $2,000 from the association for floats and equipment. The rest of the money went to pay for bands, salaries, and advertising and for supplies and bands for the park celebrations.[43]

The parade's floats included scenes from both national and local history, such as "Washington Crossing the Delaware" and "Father Marquette's Chicago Camp." Suffragists sponsored a float depicting "Woman's Service to the State," featuring a tableau of women from St. Bridget to Carrie Nation. The most popular floats, however, were those of the city's ethnic groups. Croatians in peasant dress promoted a united Croatia, and German turners drilled on a moving gymnasium; Greeks presented the Parthenon, Swedes the "Entrance of King Oscar the Great," and Norwegians a snowy hill with skiers. After the procession, immigrants dispersed to city parks for exercises. In addition to the official celebration staged by the Sane Fourth Association, the city's Playground Association sponsored a Sane Fourth play festival, as did the Chicago Hebrew Institute. The United Irish Societies offered a night pageant with tableaux of Columbia on the throne and various historical figures and events. As if this was not enough, Chicagoans could pay to see a reenactment of the "Battle of Fort Dearborn" presented by the Pain Fireworks Display Company at White Sox Park. Although this presentation was not part of the association's celebration, it did indicate the trend toward substituting professional fireworks displays for the more dangerous thrills of crackers and guns.[44]

Fourth of July pageant, Lincoln Park, 1911. The Safe and Sane Fourth of July movement substituted community-centered exercises for the guns and fireworks of the "insane" Fourth. Progressives believed that ethnic folk dances could teach Americans the mysteries of community. (Courtesy of the Chicago Historical Society, negative number ICHi-30176)

The Sane Fourth Association and the mainstream press proclaimed the celebration a triumph and a wholesome alternative to the "insane" celebrations of years past. One newspaper praised the festival as "dignified and instructive and altogether enjoyable. The Fourth can be devoted to no better uses than in pictorially reviewing the history of this country . . . and bringing together in one grand conclave all the elements of citizenship, native born and contributed by foreign lands, that have developed one united and patriotic nation." The *Chicago Tribune* seconded this melting pot theme with a paean to the "nations of different races, creeds, and attainments, paying their respect to the country into which they have been welded."[45]

The message of the Sane Fourth procession, however, like that of other ethnic celebrations of American holidays, was not quite so simple. The immigrants who participated did indeed desire to demonstrate their loyalty to their adopted country, but, as in the Columbian procession, they did so as ethnic Americans, not "welded" Americans. They marched separately, clad in national, folk, or historical costumes. Polish Americans demonstrated the close connection between their two nations with a float depicting Polonia, the Spirit of the Nation, and America, with the latter represented by George Washington, Casimir Pulaski, and Tadeusz Kosciuszko. Each ethnic group held separate afternoon exercises, the better to present and to preserve their dual identities. The Scottish societies' program included Highland dancing, bagpipe music, and Highland games, while the Czech exercises featured Sokol drills and folk dances. In between their tableaux of American history, the Irish societies performed Irish dances.[46] In other words, although the intent of progressive celebrations was to unite the community and to break down ethnic barriers, the very form that those celebrations took contributed to maintaining the vitality of ethnic identity. The celebration may well have inspired community feeling, but that sense of community was primarily within immigrant groups. Progressive efforts to contain ethnicity and thereby render it harmless against Americanization, thus, ironically ended up reinforcing ethnicity.

Although the Sane Fourth Association encouraged the active participation of immigrants, it followed the lead of late nineteenth-century elites and provided no role for organized labor on the Sane Fourth. As in 1892, working-class Chicagoans were welcome to participate as individuals, as members of ethnic groups, and as members of clubs and organizations, but not as members of unions. The progressive celebration was as adamant in denying the existence of class conflict as were the celebrations of the civic elites. For their part, Chicago socialists did not bother to criticize the 1911 celebration. The *Chicago Daily Socialist* pointedly ignored it, lecturing its readers instead on the real lesson of the Fourth:"The war of Independence was fought at the will of the American capitalist class. The American workers were simply the pawns in the game." The newspaper urged the worker to stop "commemorating a revolution in whose program he was an unconsidered trifle" and instead "give his attention to the coming social revolution, . . . wherein he will enact the leading role."[47]

Despite socialist disregard and ethnic persistence, the 1911 procession constituted a substantial redefinition of the Fourth, from an anarchic celebration of freedom to an orderly celebration of the community. The success of the celebration, however, did not mean that it would continue. In Eaton's report to the trustees of the Sane Fourth Association after the celebration, he suggested that the members were wearying of their organizing efforts and the constant struggle for funds and asked "whether the purpose of the Association has been so far served as to justify the Trustees in excusing themselves from the degree of responsibility they have for four years exercised in the interests of the community." Building community spirit was expensive and time-consuming work, and the trustees had already tired of it. The expense of the Sane Fourth festivals, as well as the work involved, including soliciting funds, drove the association to search for a cheaper alternative. In 1912 the organization decided to devote its "entire efforts and resources . . . to programs in the parks and playgrounds." Eaton noted that the benefit of such a celebration was that it was inexpensive and yet would still reach the entire city. The entertainment at each park and playground consisted of a band concert, a program of patriotic songs, and a stereopticon lecture with historical slides. The program committee assigned association trustees to present the lectures. They also received leaflets with the words to "America" and the "Star-Spangled Banner" to distribute so that the audience could participate in the singing. The Sane Fourth Association thus incorporated technology and showmanship to provide a so-called sane celebration that was cheaper but that still provided visual and aural stimulation. If less participatory than the 1911 celebration, the exercises nevertheless took place in the neighborhoods, the better to reach more Chicagoans and to work on creating community spirit.[48]

The Sane Fourth Association used this less expensive and less labor-intensive form of celebration again in 1913 and 1914, but by 1914 its trustees had completely lost their enthusiasm for the project. Eaton wrote to the Chicago Association of Commerce in November to inform it that the association wished to withdraw from its responsibilities for the next Fourth. In justification of this position, Eaton noted both the expense in time and money to the trustees because of the lack of any municipal appropriations and the success of the association in reducing holiday casualties. The city parks apparently continued to sponsor celebrations for the Fourth, despite the withdrawal of the association. The annual report of the West Chicago park commissioners in 1915, for instance, featured a photograph of the children's celebration of the Fourth at Dvorak Park that year.[49]

Once their enthusiasm and funding dried up, other Sane Fourth Associations around the country disbanded as well. In some ways these associations could well afford to abandon their efforts by 1915. The parks took over the celebrations in Chicago, as did parks, playgrounds, and other community groups in other cities. Moreover, the movement had proven an unqualified success in reducing injuries, fatalities, and property damage, which, after all, was its founding purpose. Eaton claimed in 1913, for example, that as a result of the efforts of Chicago's Sane Fourth Association, accidents had been reduced by more than 95 percent, and fire losses had decreased comparably. Depending upon how strictly regulations were enforced and their proximity to districts without restrictions, many individuals still had access to fireworks. But the movement did succeed in drastically cutting back the supply. And holiday casualty lists no longer resembled battle figures.[50]

The Sane Fourth movement was less successful in establishing permanent new traditions of celebration. Despite the efforts of Sane Fourth Associations around the nation, a new celebratory tradition for the Fourth had not taken hold. In 1916 Mary Porter Beegle and Jack Crawford were still calling for "a definite ceremonial tradition which will become associated in the popular mind with the Fourth of July and thus emphasize the meaning of the day." Some observers even criticized the movement for ruining a perfectly good, if boisterous, holiday. The *Independent*, for example, complained in 1914 that the movement to control "an unwholesome custom" was sadly also "denaturing . . . another picturesque holiday." Whereas the Fourth had been unique, "[n]ow it has joined the tame procession, with its pageants and sports and speech-making and lemonade and generally an air of enjoyment-as-per-program by a few and unspecialized relaxation by the many." The magazine's solution, oddly, resembled that of the Sane Fourth promoters. Although America was losing its old holiday customs, "the folkways of the races who are coming to us, conserved by a wise hospitality in the city playgrounds . . . ought to endow our cosmopolitan holidays with a new picturesqueness."[51]

Finally, the movement failed to create any permanent sense of community. The immigrants who came together for the Sane Fourth celebrations celebrated as ethnic groups and then retreated to their ethnic communities. The very structure of the celebrations, with their focus on immigrants, tended to reinforce the sense of community that many ethnic groups already had, rather than to construct an overarching bond with other members of the community. Despite the efforts of the movement and of parks workers, play activists, and settlement house workers, the achievement of any kind of transcendent community identity remained elusive.

"PICTORIALIZED PREACHING OF PATRIOTISM": EXTENDING THE COMMUNITY CELEBRATION

This failure to create true community spirit did not mean that Progressives gave up trying. At the high point of the Sane Fourth movement, reformers blazed with enthusiasm at the possibilities for reforming the entire holiday calendar and experimented with various community celebrations. Lee Hanmer suggested that the lessons of the Sane Fourth could fruitfully be applied to community celebrations of virtually every holiday in the American calendar. Municipal governments, he argued, should take charge of Memorial Day and Labor Day, in addition to the Fourth. Schools could arrange celebrations for Washington and Lincoln's Birthdays, Arbor Day, May Day, and Flag Day. He held religious organizations responsible for the observance of Christmas, Easter, and Thanksgiving.[52]

In New York City, Progressives took aim in 1913 at a holiday that had almost as bad a reputation as the Fourth of July. That year a committee led by Jacob Riis sponsored a "Sane New Year's Eve" celebration. The Salvation Army and the People's Choral Union presented concerts of patriotic and religious songs in two city parks from 11:00 P.M. until just after midnight. Although thousands of people jammed the parks, the celebration was less than a success. As midnight approached, revelers flocked to Times Square, ignoring the Riis committee's program. Those who remained in the parks also failed to cooperate. "Bravely the songsters did their part," the *New York Times* noted, "but ten times as many could not have made themselves heard above the noise that was raised by the irresponsible rattle and horn users." The paper concluded sadly that in the race for control of the holiday, "'safe and sane' comes out second best with 'horn and rattle' leading by at least a full length."[53]

Christmas was another holiday that reformers attempted to remake in the community mode. New York City, Chicago, and other cities established community Christmas celebrations featuring municipal trees, lighting ceremonies, and carol singing. Constance D'Arcy MacKay, who advocated drama and pageantry as methods for Americanization and community building, suggested merging patriotism with the Christian holiday to make it an Americanization day. The "Tree of Light," she advised, should remain "dark until Liberty appears with her uplifted torch," and afterward Liberty should lead the revelers in patriotic carols such as "America the Beautiful." In other years, she proposed, the community celebration could focus on the melting pot by including "Christmas carols of the different nations which sent colonizers to America" or on American traditions by featuring American music performed by community bands and choruses.[54]

Chicago civic leaders and reformers, inspired by New York City's successful celebration in 1912, organized the Municipal Christmas Festival Association to sponsor a community Christmas celebration in Grant Park in 1913. The president of the association was Charles L. Hutchinson, the banker and civic leader who had earlier helped to organize the Union League Club's Washington centennial and the Columbian quadricentennial. In preparation for the celebration, workers constructed a 75-foot "tree" by arranging 75 donated trees around a 40-foot pole. Commonwealth Edison donated the electricity and lighting equipment for "the wonder tree," and the Illinois Central Railroad promised to furnish "a bank of steam" as background. A decoration committee, which included an artist and an architect, oversaw the construction and decoration of the site. In addition to a tree-lighting ceremony, the festival featured carols performed by a mixture of community and professional choruses and professional vocalists, including the Paulist Choir, the Swedish Singing Society, and six opera stars. The crowd was invited to join in the singing of "Auld Lang Syne" and the "Star-Spangled Banner."[55]

While some Progressives attempted to make Christmas and New Year's Eve into community affairs, reformers in Boston applied the multiethnic celebrations of the Sane Fourth movement to a holiday that was less widely celebrated and thus less likely to have inappropriate traditional festivities. The city of Boston was unusual because it funded holiday celebrations and even had a director of public celebrations, appointed by the mayor, and a Citizens' Public Celebration Association. In 1912 the celebration association chose Columbus Day, which many states had made a legal holiday in the wake of the quadricentennial, to be the city's premier community celebration. Whereas the Fourth in Boston was "distinctly a children's day" with park- and playground-

Municipal Christmas tree, Lakefront, Chicago, 1913. Progressives attempted to make a variety of holidays, including Christmas, into occasions for building community spirit. The municipal tree, composed of seventy-five individual trees, appears to be on fire, owing to its many lights. The steam in the background was provided by the Illinois Central Railroad. (Courtesy of the Chicago Historical Society, negative number DN-61915)

based sane celebrations, Columbus Day was to become "a grown-ups' day," according to Everett B. Mero, secretary of the association. Mero contended that "Columbus Day is really the one great holiday of all Americans." The association envisioned the day celebrating the alleged discoverer of America as the holiday par excellence of Americanization. Mero explained that the holiday was "part of a big plan for using holidays as a means of promoting nationalism among all the peoples who come hither from every corner of the earth."[56]

The highlight of the inaugural festivities in 1912 was a pageant-parade similar to Chicago's Sane Fourth procession in 1911. As in that celebration, the ethnic sections dominated the procession, with floats and marchers from twenty-six groups. Mero proudly asserted that Boston, in contrast to other cities, had made "a conscious effort to invoke the interest of the whole community, including every nationality, race and color." The purpose of the ethnic divisions was, Mero explained, to show "their respective contributions to American citizenship." The floats and marchers, however, like those in the Sane Fourth celebrations, focused more on the homeland. Armenians made rugs on their float, Scots wore Highland dress and danced on theirs, and Italians marched in "the costume of Garibaldi's soldiers." The Chinese, still celebrating their homeland's 1911 revolution, won the prize for best feature with four floats, including one depicting "Old China and New" and another bearing women and children in native dress. "The applause that greeted [the Chinese]," Mero asserted, "was evidence of the immediate value of the celebration in removing race prejudice." Apparently there were limits to the celebration's ability to dispel prejudice, however. African Americans were notably absent from Mero's account of the celebration, as was organized labor.[57]

The paradox of demonstrating American citizenship by presenting elements of ethnic heritage illustrated Progressives' ambivalence toward immigrants' culture and the tension between ethnicity and assimilation. Mero praised the pageant-procession "of real moving pictures that tell history and point to ideals of the future" for relieving "the tiresomeness of long marching bodies monotonously arranged." Immigrants and their cultures thus furnished the celebration with the artistic pageantry that Progressives found lacking in American culture. But those immigrants did more than lend an artistic touch to the day. Even as Progressives called for Americanization, they idealized a pluralistic American identity. "The day becomes much more signi-

ficant," Mero argued, "if the descendants of each of the nationalities compos-
ing the community . . . display scenes or incidents connected with their own
history and traditions." Such an array, he claimed, "tells the whole story of the
making of the American nation." The celebration, Mero concluded, constituted "pictorialized preaching of patriotism" and an "inspiration toward good
citizenship."[58] This definition of patriotism and citizenship was assuredly one
that the Union League Club would have had a hard time recognizing.

In addition to these large celebrations intended to bring together the citywide community, Progressives sponsored more intimate neighborhood celebrations. They viewed neighborhood parks, an offshoot of the urban parks
movement, as particularly important venues for child-centered celebrations
that would promote neighborliness and community spirit. In Chicago, which
developed an extensive network of neighborhood parks in the early twentieth
century, park organizations not only held Fourth of July exercises but also
sponsored celebrations for Arbor Day and Washington's Birthday. At the 1911
exercises celebrating the first anniversary of West Park No. 2, the West Park
commissioners announced that the park had in its first year held the largest
Arbor Day celebration ever in Chicago. Fifty-one thousand people had gathered to listen to band concerts and to watch as children performed skits and
planted trees. The anniversary exercises themselves coincided with Washington's Birthday, and the park commissioners sponsored a weeklong gala that
reflected the influence of playground and school holiday activists. Afternoon
exercises on the eve of the holiday featured children from neighborhood
schools. That evening women's gymnastics classes performed Hungarian and
Swedish folk dances. On the afternoon of the holiday, after a ceremonial flag
raising, the children's clubs at the park provided the entertainment, including
a tableau of "A Washington Birthday Party" by the Girls' Domestic Science
Club and a play, "Honesty Is the Best Policy," presented by the Youths' Sporting Club. That evening the park held its official anniversary exercises, which
featured performances by the men's and women's gymnastics classes and other
clubs. That the park commissioners envisioned a significant role for the
neighborhood parks in building community was evident in the titles of the
speeches they gave at the various exercises. These included "The Park and the
School Children," "The Parks and Patriotism," "The Parks and the People,"
and "The Park and the Neighborhood."[59]

Above: Washington's Birthday celebration at West Park No. 2, Chicago, 1912. The development of a system of neighborhood parks in Chicago provided Progressives with a new venue for creating community on holidays. In the grand finale, children waving American flags fill the stage while their parents watch from the audience. (Courtesy of the Chicago Park District Special Collections) *Below:* Washington's Birthday celebration at West Park No. 2, Chicago, 1912. Immigrant girls pose after their holiday performance. Progressives hoped that such exercises would serve an assimilative function for immigrants. (Courtesy of the Chicago Park District Special Collections)

Of all the progressive ventures into community-building holiday celebrations, the local celebrations were probably the most successful because they drew on some semblance of a preexisting community, often dominated by a single ethnic group. The citywide community celebrations, while grand, suffered from the same constraints as the Sane Fourth celebrations. It was expensive to mount such spectacles. Unlike Boston, most cities did not consider public celebrations important enough to provide regular funding. Philanthropists and businesses might be induced to contribute to special commemorations but balked at annual requests for money. It was also expensive for the participants in parades; the cost of costumes and uniforms, as well as the materials and labor for building floats, was hard for many Americans to meet. In the absence of government funding, large-scale celebrations could simply never become annual events in the United States.

THE FOURTH OF JULY AS "AMERICANIZATION DAY," 1915

Just as reformers' enthusiasm began to wane and philanthropists' pocketbooks to close, the outbreak of World War I lent renewed vigor and urgency to the effort to transform American holidays. Progressives turned their attention from creating local community bonds to translating those bonds into a sense of national community. The drive for 100 percent Americanism intensified the Americanizing aspects of their celebrations and even revitalized the flagging Sane Fourth movement.

In 1914 Cleveland's Sane Fourth Committee organized a "citizenship reception" on the Fourth of July to welcome the city's new citizens. The Committee for Immigrants in America, a national Americanization group, thought this reception was a splendid idea and established a National Americanization Day Committee to push for a nationwide celebration in 1915. The committee enlisted the support of Frederick C. Howe, U.S. commissioner of immigration, who sent a letter to the mayors of some one thousand cities, asking them to follow Cleveland's example and to make 4 July 1915 "Americanization Day." Dr. Philander P. Claxton, the national commissioner of education, added his endorsement, explaining that "'Americanization Day' is a patriotic call to all citizens, American-born and foreign-born alike, adults and children, to rally to American ideals, purposes and common interests of

many people united into one nation." Government and naturalization officials, educators, women's clubs, patriotic societies, and ethnic organizations
all sent representatives to local celebration committees. The National Americanization Day Committee recommended that cities hold receptions for
new citizens on the Fourth, treating them and their families as guests of
honor by allowing them to sit on the raised platform customarily reserved
for dignitaries. The holiday program, Claxton advised, should feature patriotic songs and the Pledge of Allegiance and might also include pageants,
tableaux of American history, or films such as "Uncle Sam at Work." Missing
this time were the melting pot pageant-processions. Oratory, on the other
hand, was back, resurrected because of the perceived Americanization crisis.
Claxton even spelled out what themes the orators should emphasize. Chief
among these themes were the admonitions that "every foreign-speaking person in America should learn English by attending the public schools" and
that "adults and children, native and foreign-born, [should] be given civic
training in both evening and day schools." Schoolchildren, he continued,
would be instructed to ask their parents to take them to the celebration. The
committee promoted the celebrations by sending out explanatory literature
and program suggestions and by blanketing the country with more than fifty
thousand advertising posters.[60]

Survey magazine reported that Americanization Day had been a resounding success, celebrated in 150 communities around the nation. In Pittsburgh
a thousand schoolchildren sang patriotic songs and formed a huge American
flag. Foreign-born citizens of Jackson, Michigan, presented a flag pageant.
And in Indianapolis "new Americans" gave speeches in eleven languages "on
the duties of American citizenship." The celebrations, the magazine concluded, personified the progressive ideal of community, showing that "while
European nations were locked in deadly combat, the sons of these same nations in America through common interests and loyalties could live in peaceful neighborliness."[61]

If New York City was any indication, however, some Americanization
Day celebrations fell a bit short of their organizers' expectations. The desire
to indoctrinate immigrants there meant that pageantry and art took a back
seat to bombastic oratory. The Mayor's Fourth of July Committee organized
two public meetings and promised "[t]he safest and sanest Fourth on

record." More than twenty thousand new citizens were welcomed at exercises at City College, but the oratory was less about Americanization than about preparedness. Speakers focused on "America's mission to the nations and . . . President Wilson's role in consummating Columbia's destiny." At the second meeting at City Hall, the city controller spoke out for preparedness, asserting that "[it] must be understood that there may come times when boys will have to shoulder muskets to protect their own honor and their nation's honor." The only artistic note came at City College when "two dancers, Uncle Sam and Columbia, . . . went through the mazes of the tango, and then dashed off in a gayly decorated automobile."[62]

The League of Foreign Born Citizens, founded "to help make good citizens out of immigrants," offered a celebration more in keeping with the Americanization theme. At the league's headquarters, immigrants stood in a drizzling rain and watched as "[a] series of motion pictures vividly depicting the history of this nation, the birth of the flag and the natural resources of the country were shown on a screen stretched across the front of the building." Orators reportedly attempted to speak on "the glories of American citizenship," but the crowd preferred the visual excitement of the moving pictures to the oratory, and the speakers eventually gave up. Jewish New Yorkers, in conjunction with the Henry Street Settlement, eschewed the mass meetings for a neighborhood celebration of the Fourth, which featured "exercises in the Neighborhood Playhouse," a speech by Lillian Wald, historical movies, and "a great neighborhood dance." Wald proclaimed that the holiday was particularly significant to Jewish immigrants "because there are so many among us who have known persecution and wrong, who have made great sacrifices for ideals, who have come to America believing that here could be realized our highest ideals."[63]

Although the Jewish celebration came close to the progressive ideal of community and Americanization, the two meetings sponsored by the city came in for harsh criticism from Progressives. Writing in the *New Republic*, Louis Weinberg condemned New York's celebration as "an incongruous inartistic blend of up-to-date advertising and publicity methods with old New England sentiment." It completely abandoned progressive ideals of celebration, according to Weinberg. He blasted the oratory as "differing very slightly from the good old spread-eagle variety" and decried the lack of any artistic features in the celebration other than the "two vaudeville performers" dressed up as Uncle Sam and Columbia.[64]

New York's poor excuse for a celebration was the product, according to Weinberg, of the seeming inability of Progressives to inspire community spirit. "What is there about this wonderful democracy," he asked, "which makes our community sense so starved and our attempts at community play so nearly ludicrous or positively pathetic?" Despite some efforts at pageantry and festivals, in most American cities, Weinberg lamented, "our group celebrations are deficient in imagination." He blamed this deficiency on the "successful men" who "arrange the old things in the old way" and on the cities that made only "niggardly appropriations" for celebrations, both of which favored inexpensive oratory over artistic celebration. But he also blamed Progressives for not doing enough to develop community celebrations at the neighborhood level. Oratory and large-scale celebrations, he contended, would never inspire community feeling. Instead, Weinberg advocated more intimate celebrations centered around schools and playgrounds. "Contrast the emotion of a crowd sitting through several hours of speech," he commanded, "with the mood of the same group gathered as a family party to watch brothers, sisters and children in tableaux, pageants, and dancing." To Weinberg the difference was obvious; the latter group, through the magic of art, was transformed into a community, while the former remained a collection of individuals with no common bond.[65]

WAR AND THE RESURGENCE OF ETHNIC IDENTITY

New York City's celebration revealed once again that the progressive vision of community had not taken root in the unfavorable soil of urban America. At the same time, the war posed a new threat to that vision by amplifying ethnic loyalties. While progressive reformers and educators sought ever more vigorous methods of Americanizing immigrants, ethnic Americans stubbornly continued to believe that ethnicity and Americanism were compatible. The advent of war in Europe intensified this conviction, despite the best efforts of Americanizers. African Americans, for their part, viewed the war as yet another opportunity to realize their own dream of an America that recognized the contributions of the one-tenth of its citizens who were of African descent.

German Americans, who believed the early events of the war increased the prestige of their homeland, proudly celebrated their heritage. At a 1914 celebration of German Day in Chicago, the head of the University of Wisconsin's German department explained that German Americans were "justified and duty-bound to espouse the German cause," which did not in any way conflict with the interest of their adopted land. That German loyalties were not yet overly controversial in a city with a large German population was evident in the fact that the governor of Illinois attended that evening's exercises. This lack of controversy had changed, however, by early 1915. When the Germania Club celebrated the birthday of the kaiser, "the man under whose leadership Germany is fighting against a world of enemies," Chicago's mayor "could not find the time to attend." *Abendpost* noted that his opponent in the upcoming election had attended and that he, "as a descendant of a purely German family, was more acceptable."[66] Despite German Americans' attachment to Germany, once America entered the war, the vast majority of them put loyalty to their adopted land first. This patriotism came at a high price, as other Americans forced them to discard virtually all elements of their treasured German heritage.

The war put Mexican Americans in a similarly awkward position. In 1916, with tensions running high because of Pancho Villa's border raids and the U.S. punitive expedition into Mexico, Tucson's Mexican Americans, fearful of inciting anti-Mexican sentiment, decided to forgo their annual celebration of Mexican Independence Day. Two years later the planned celebration included a tableau "to represent the two nations united and surrounded by the allies fighting on the Western front today." In the wake of border skirmishes at Nogales, however, the *junta patriótica* announced that, "to show its patriotism and loyal regard for peace, order, [and] the friendship of the two countries," it was canceling the celebration.[67]

Poles and Czechs, on the other hand, intensified their national work, optimistic about their homelands' chances of gaining independence from the war. The Polish National Alliance, aided by the Polish Women's Alliance, transformed its annual national exercises into weapons of practical patriotism in the Polish struggle. At each celebration the Polish National Alliance collected money for its independence fund, for the relief of Polish war victims, and for the Polish army sponsored by France. Speakers chided Poles for their lethargy toward the national cause. At a commemoration of the November 1830 insurrection just months after the start of the war, John Przyprawa, editor of *Dziennik Zwiazkowy*, lamented that "at mass meetings and celebrations we spout phrases and give our homeland assurances and make promises which we do not keep." The Polish National Alliance invited veterans of the January insurrection to share the stage and to provide a visible reminder of the Polish cause, the same in 1917 as in 1863. One such veteran advised Poles in 1918 to forget their differences and to unite to "crush that barbarous enemy of ours, the Prussians."[68]

Nationalists called upon their countrymen to join the Polish army, even after the United States had entered the war. They also urged Polish Americans to buy Liberty Bonds and otherwise to support their adopted land, because, *Dziennik Zwiazkowy* explained, "under its leadership and through its intervention, we will regain . . . the freedom and independence of our homeland." As in all nationalist ventures, the Polish National Alliance led the way, announcing on 3 May 1918 that it had purchased $150,000 worth of Liberty Bonds. At exercises in 1917 commemorating the May constitution, the Polish Women's Alliance staged a tableau of the "Resurrection of Poland" that couched nationalism in the language of the participants' religion and linked ethnic and American patriotism. After the crowd sang "Boze Cos Polski," three girls and one boy, dressed in Polish national costumes, removed a crown of thorns and shackles from a figure representing Poland, replacing these with a laurel wreath and a scepter. Even in this striking example of nationalism as civic religion, with Poland in the role of the crucified and resurrected Christ, Polish nationalists made certain to show that Poland's independence was in the national interest of their adopted land. The children raised an American flag over the tableau, showing that Poland would rise under the auspices of the United States.[69]

World War I also brought American Czechs together in the national cause, along with their new Slovak allies. In 1917 Czech and Slovak Catholics, Freethinkers, and socialists united in Chicago for a commemoration in memory of those Czechs and Slovaks who had lost their lives thus far in the struggle for independence. In honor of the new alliance, the musical selections featured not only "Kde Domov Muj" and the "Star-Spangled Banner" but also "the other Czech national anthem," the more inclusive "Hej Slované" ("Hail, All Ye Slavonic Peoples").[70]

For African Americans, U.S. entry into the war also provided opportunities, not for their homeland's independence, but for the improvement of their position within American society. By their patriotic support, they hoped to demonstrate again to white Americans their tradition of service to the republic and thereby to gain the demise of Jim Crow, disfranchisement, and institutionalized racism. To this end Chicago's African Americans held a mammoth procession to launch the Fourth Liberty Loan Drive in September 1918. The *Chicago Defender* urged "[e]very citizen who believes in the cause" to contribute to the drive, adding, "He who refuses to subscribe has contributed through his negligence to the unwarranted murder of some father or brother." As an inducement, the paper promised to publish the amounts subscribed by "lodges, organizations and individuals" in its Christmas edition.[71]

African Americans made it clear that they fought not only to make the world safe for democracy but also to make America safe for true racial democracy. An advertisement for Kashmir Whitener and Cleanser depicted a black woman in nurse's garb. "The colored Red Cross nurse is ready 'to do her bit' for humanity and democracy," read the copy, asking, "Will prejudice give her her chance to prove her worth?" At a 1918 Flag Day benefit for the relief of the families of black soldiers, orator Dr. John R. Hawkins, financial secretary of the national African Methodist Episcopal Church, proclaimed, "If this war is being fought for democracy, then let this democracy be the leveler of racial hatred forever." If black soldiers came home to renewed "discrimination, Jim Crowism, and humiliation," he warned presciently, "this war for democracy . . . shall have been in vain."[72]

The Flag Day exercises and a joint celebration the previous February of Abraham Lincoln and Frederick Douglass's birthdays exemplified the biracial nation that African Americans sought to construct. Although African Americans organized these affairs and were the main speakers, performers, and audience, each celebration also drew a significant white audience. Of the eighteen thousand attendees at the Lincoln-Douglass exercises, for instance, some four thousand were white. The *Chicago Defender* noted that "[c]itizens in both races mingled freely in the tremendous throng" and that "young white girls" sold Lincoln buttons outside the hall. Chicago's mayor William Hale Thompson, various other city officials, and local white businessmen such as Cyrus H. McCormick, Sears's Julius Rosenwald, William Wrigley Jr., and J. Ogden Armour joined *Chicago Defender* publisher Robert S. Abbott, Chicago alderman Maj. R. R. Jackson, and prominent black businessmen and clergy in the boxes at the Flag Day celebration.[73]

At these celebrations black leaders renewed their quest to reconstruct the white notion of American identity to recognize the integral role of African Americans. At the Flag Day exercises, a black chorus, orchestra, and soloists performed not only American patriotic music but also classical music, opera arias, and Negro spirituals, which the *Chicago Defender* called "the folk lore of the Race." The musical variety demonstrated that African Americans were patriotic, that their folk music had contributed materially to American culture, and that their singers and musicians rivaled the best that whites had to offer. The *Chicago Defender* dubbed pianist T. Theodore Taylor "the modern Paderewski" and claimed that tenor George Garner Jr. "rank[ed] with Murato and Caruso."[74]

As the war raged, African Americans focused particularly on black military contributions to the American republic. The Liberty Loan parade featured the John Brown Post of the GAR and veterans of the Spanish-American War. "From the beginning of American history the Race has had an honorable place in her annals," announced the prominent Georgia clergyman Dr. Charles T. Walker at the Lincoln-Douglass celebration. "We fought in every conflict from Bunker Hill down through San Juan hill, and the Mexican engagements—and we will help to hoist Old Glory over the ramparts of France and carry it into Berlin!" To assure whites that this was news only to them, Walker added that "the Negro man was a man long before America ever made him a citizen." Judging by the white attendance, at least some whites by 1918 accepted African Americans' vision of America, although political motivations and manpower considerations undoubtedly played a role as well. The secretary of war and the governor of Illinois both sent their regrets at being unable to attend the Lincoln-Douglass celebration, but the former praised black contributions to the war, and the governor's message declared that "the celebration of the birthday of Lincoln was never more fitting than now, because, by the hearty and patriotic participation of the Negro in the war he had more than justified Lincoln's greatest act."[75]

THE FOURTH OF JULY AS "LOYALTY DAY," 1918

As American troops—black and white, immigrant and native born—prepared to ship out in 1918, the demands of Progressives and other native-born Americans for 100 percent Americanism on the part of immigrants increased. The Chicago Association of Commerce, for example, encouraged employers to hold Flag Day ceremonies at the workplace that year, "in the interest of the Americanization of the foreign-born citizenship." The president of the association suggested that the flag raising and exercises be held at noon, undoubtedly so that they would interfere with the employees' unpaid lunch hour rather than the business day. The penalties for noncompliance could be severe; one man lost his job and was reported to federal authorities for failing to participate.[76]

In response to the pressure, immigrant leaders, in conjunction with progressive reformers, set in motion a plan to make the Fourth of July 1918 a massive demonstration of immigrants' loyalty to their adopted land. Building on the Sane Fourth and Americanization Day movements, they created one of the largest national celebrations in American history. As on other such occasions, however, the message was ultimately a mixed one. Immigrants pledged their patriotism to the United States without ceding their loyalty to their homelands; even Germans managed to find a way to maintain their dual identities.

The Committee on Public Information had established a Division of Work among the Foreign-Born, which set up foreign-language bureaus for ethnic groups, headed by immigrant leaders. These immigrant-led bureaus came up with the idea of making the Fourth an occasion for immigrants to demonstrate their loyalty, and in May 1918 their leaders asked President Woodrow Wilson to issue a proclamation to this effect. Wilson did so, requesting that the committee work with the bureaus to arrange holiday exercises. The president himself contributed a four-minute speech to be read as a part of the program.[77]

The Committee on Public Information, the foreign-language bureaus, and the Council of National Defense prepared a uniform program to be presented across the nation on the Fourth. The program was to begin with the raising of the flag, followed by the national anthem and a flag salute. The oratory was to consist of the reading of Wilson's holiday address, messages from other dignitaries, and the Declaration of Independence, followed by patriotic addresses and a welcome to the new citizens present. Exercises were to conclude with the singing of "America." In addition to the official program, local and ethnic arrangements committees organized processions and other exercises. Immigrants were acutely aware of the need to prove that they were no slackers in the matter of national loyalty. Ethnic leaders pushed for large and enthusiastic turnouts for the Fourth. "The more Jews there are marching," a Jewish leader in Chicago explained, "the better it will be for our community, and the more it will indicate Jewish loyalty." Czech leaders in the same city warned "that Czech is an enemy of this country—who will not participate in the manifestation of the Czechoslovak people to the Republic of the United States and its President."[78]

In New York City, the mayor's Committee on National Defense organized a massive pageant-procession, featuring some seventy-five thousand marchers and dozens of historical and ethnic floats, which no doubt made many a Progressive weep for joy. The first division presented "a complete picture of the activities of a nation at war," from marching soldiers and sailors and the latest in military technology, including machine guns, armored trucks, and airplanes overhead, to floats depicting life at the front and "a boatload of forlorn survivors . . . from a torpedoed ship." The Salvation Army's float, which depicted volunteers feeding doughboys doughnuts at the front, was a particular delight with the crowd, as the volunteers tossed the sweet snacks to onlookers. And what was a doughnut without coffee? The YMCA's float featured "a dugout canteen where secretaries with coffee were stimulating soldiers." The first division also included representatives of the victims of American imperialism expressing their gratitude to America, in the form of Native Americans led by "a chief in full war bonnet" and Filipino sailors preceding a float on which "a Filipino girl held out her hands to the Statue of Liberty."[79]

The much larger second division of the procession consisted of New York City's immigrant groups, who declared their loyalty to America while they reinforced their ethnic identities. Many floats promoted the war goals of immigrant homelands. Armenians, for example, featured "the Armenian Joan of Arc who led the nation's war against the Turks" in the fourteenth century, followed by representatives of the contemporary Armenian infantry engaged in a new struggle against their old oppressors. The French section included a float on which figures representing Alsace and Lorraine, in chains, looked to France and Columbia for assistance. Other floats depicted scenes from the history of immigrant homelands, such as the Jewish float portraying "Judas Maccabeus [sic] and his warriors fighting for liberty." The Poles put on a crowd-pleasing display of a series of Polish rulers and warriors who had defeated the Germans, ending with a float that showed "the Prussian ruler of 1522 giving homage to King Zigmunt of Poland." A third kind of float depicted immigrant contributions to American history. Norwegians featured models of Leif Eriksson's ship and John Ericcson's *Monitor*, while the "Friends of German Democracy" presented German heroes of the American Revolution and the Civil War.[80]

As in the earlier Sane Fourth processions, New York City's 1918 pageant did as much to reinforce ethnicity as to promote a melting pot that disgorged 100 percent Americans. In addition to the fact that immigrants paraded by ethnic group, the messages of the floats and banners made clear that immigrants had no intention of discarding their ethnic loyalties. Only a few floats and sections carried wholly American themes, and those were primarily from the nations that America was currently fighting. Hungarian Americans thus marched "as ordinary American citizens in civilian dress," carrying banners that proclaimed, "We are 100 per cent Americans," while German Americans focused solely on German contributions to American history.[81]

In Chicago the story was much the same, although the celebration had a more competitive edge than New York City's procession. Arrangement committees for each of the city's ethnic groups planned separate afternoon meetings in city parks, and many organized morning processions. There was no general procession bringing together all groups. Instead, each group strove to prove its loyalty by the intensity and the magnitude of its own celebration. Some groups strengthened their display of patriotism by passing resolutions of loyalty. More than ten thousand German Chicagoans, for example, declared their "whole-hearted and individual allegiance" to their adopted land.

"We solemnly pledge our fortunes, our lives, and our sacred honor," they resolved, "for the support of the United States and its government in the present war against the German government." The competitive nature of the patriotic displays was evident in the postholiday reports in the foreign-language
press. A Czech newspaper proclaimed that "Czechs and Slovaks, always in
the forefront in their demonstration of patriotic ardor, carried off first honors this time." The Greek press disagreed, asserting that the Greek celebration had "received by the unanimous voice of the city's press due credit for ex-
celling all others with their parade."[82]

At the same time that the format of separate exercises encouraged such
competition in the demonstration of patriotism, however, the separate exercises, even more than the separate ethnic sections in New York City's procession, had the benefit of enabling Chicago's immigrants to reinforce their
ethnic identities. The joint Czech and Slovak procession featured a float depicting "Slavonic peoples" paying tribute to Columbia. On the sidelines, in a
striking juxtaposition of ethnicity and Americanism, the women's auxiliary
of the Czech-Slovak army sold buttons with the slogan "Czech-Slovaks for
America" to raise money for the soldiers' tobacco fund. A Swedish float portrayed John Ericsson and Abraham Lincoln "clasping hands in front of the
figure of Columbia," while a Greek one featured women representing ancient
Greece and Columbia, "the ancient and modern democracies." Such pairings
of ethnic and American heroes and symbols illustrated the immigrants' belief that their heritage was not something to be Americanized out of existence but that it continued to make a vital contribution to the United States.
African Americans also put their own distinctive spin on the message of loyalty. At their exercises at Institutional Church, speakers exhorted attendees
to support their nation's war effort but also pointedly noted that the meaning of America was "that each citizen's rights should be protected and safe-
guarded against all forms of tyranny, whether at home or abroad."[83]

Despite the predominance of ethnic celebrations, the *Chicago Tribune*
noted that "there will not be wanting evidence that the crucible of America
is working, silently and effectively, in blending all the nation's constituent elements into true and dependable American metal." Progressive Americanizers had not given up on their vision of community. Hull House and other
settlement houses held neighborhood celebrations, and the Illinois State

Above: Girls form a human flag at Dvorak Park, Chicago, on the Fourth of July, ca. 1918. The human flag was a favorite feature of early twentieth-century celebrations and generally consisted of girls. (Courtesy of the Chicago Park District Special Collections) *Below:* Fourth of July exercises in Dvorak Park, Chicago, on the Fourth of July, 1918. Yugoslavs and other immigrants organized massive Loyalty Day exercises to demonstrate their patriotism to their adopted land. (Courtesy of the Chicago Park District Special Collections)

Council of Defense and the Joint Committee on Education and Naturalization sponsored "community celebrations" in parks and community centers around the city. These exercises, the *Chicago Tribune* reported, were designed to "embrace the young and old of all racial groups, fusing in their demonstrations as the elements of citizenry in the normal life of the nation."[84]

But the progressive vision of community was not to be. The ethnic celebrations overshadowed the community ones, undermining the unified American identity Progressives sought. The celebrations in New York City and Chicago did demonstrate national unity in support of America's war effort. Their organizers demanded no less. But immigrants and African Americans insisted on defining Americanism more broadly than even the most liberal Progressives. African Americans avowed their loyalty to the biracial America they constructed. Immigrants were happy, as usual, to declare sincerely their patriotism to their adoptive home, but they never forgot the lands they had left behind. Even on the day of the greatest test of their loyalty, they continued to join their ethnicity and their Americanism. The tenacity of ethnic identity perhaps revealed itself most clearly in the German-American celebration of Loyalty Day. With their culture castigated from all sides in America, German Americans nevertheless found something in their heritage in which to take pride. In New York City they focused on German contributions to American development. In Chicago a group calling itself the Friends of German Democracy resurrected and carried in procession, along with the Stars and Stripes, the flag of the 1848 revolution against autocracy, which had sent so many German exiles to America.[85]

Immigrants simply could not completely separate their ethnic and American identities and saw no compelling reason to discard the former, despite the pressures of 100 percent Americanism. They might, as German Americans did, disavow certain policies and actions of their homeland, but they could not reject their heritage as so many Americans demanded. While acknowledging that the Fourth presented Chicago Jews with "a most welcome opportunity . . . to display their patriotism for America," a Jewish newspaper revealingly maintained that they "must celebrate this occasion as Jews."[86]

Some twenty years of progressive efforts at community building and Americanization had managed to make but the barest dent in the ethnic, racial, and class divisions inhibiting community. Much of the fault lay in the

Progressives' willful conviction that such divisions were not real, as well as their own ethnocentrism, racism, and middle-class biases. Although African Americans took part in Chicago's Loyalty Day celebration, they were apparently excluded from New York City's procession and from most of the nation's other loyalty demonstrations.[87] And despite the American Federation of Labor's endorsement and support of the war effort, Chicago and New York City's exercises, like other progressive celebrations, pretended that organized labor and class conflict did not exist.

Progressives' attempts to use celebration to construct community spirit were also hampered by the unrealistic nature of their notion of community, which they based on the models of relatively homogeneous small towns and ethnic communities. Such a vision was not well suited to the heterogeneous industrial city, with its transitory populace. Moreover, the vision was at base a flawed conception of small towns and immigrant groups, which were dynamic, living communities, not the static, communal Edens of progressive dreams.

Finally, the reformers, like the elites before them, found commercial culture to be remarkably impervious to the alternatives they created. For every Sane Fourth celebration, there was a Pain fireworks demonstration. Most of those who attended progressive celebrations and other recreations probably added them to their leisure activities rather than substituting them for commercial amusements. And despite the size of the biggest progressive celebrations, they never attracted more than a small fraction of urban populations. An estimated seventy-five thousand New Yorkers marched in the 1918 Loyalty Day procession, for instance, but this number represented less than 2 percent of the more than five million New Yorkers.[88]

A 1914 editorial in the *Independent* gently criticized the progressive holiday workers, explaining that "there are two sorts of people busy with holidays. One kind is always thinking up something appropriate and touching for other people to do. . . . It is they who invent commemorative programs." The other sort, ordinary people, stubbornly resisted such efforts at civic education and community building, instead "enjoying to the full every respite from routine." The magazine predicted that "these folk, the great majority, will continue to stay away from the other people's exercises and to follow their own sweet holiday will."[89]

The progressive notion of creating community spirit and transforming recreational habits through holiday celebrations was no more unrealistic than the efforts of civic elites in the late nineteenth century to build nationalism and patriotism the same way. Both groups found the most success at the local level, whether in the neighborhood school or park. What they discovered ultimately, as had all the others who had put holidays to work constructing collective identities, was that the targets of their instruction had their own ideas about community, nationalism, and Americanism. In 1918 no less than in the 1860s, Americans, through their participation (and nonparticipation) in public holiday celebrations, continued to present divergent visions of America.

CONCLUSION

ON 11 NOVEMBER 1918 World War I ended when the combatants signed an armistice in France. Americans greeted the news with hastily organized processions and spontaneous outpourings of elation. The Sane Fourth of July was forgotten as millions of firecrackers exploded in the streets. "A delirium of joy possessed the city," reported the *Richmond Times-Dispatch*. "It was as if all the Fourth of July and Christmas celebrations in the history of the city had been rolled into one." In Tucson noise was the order of the day, the louder the better. The *Tucson Citizen* noted that "[p]istols were used to assist in the noise making," the whistles blew for a full half hour, "[a]n incredible amount of firecrackers" ruled the streets, and young men adjusted their automobiles so that they would backfire. "The most popular sport," according to the paper, "was tying a string of kerosene cans or wash-tubs behind a car and dragging it through the streets." In Newport News,

Virginia, the celebration got out of hand as "[t]housands of soldiers and sailors took possession of the city." Harking back to the insane Fourth of July, they wrecked street cars and delivery wagons, smashed windows, cut trolley ropes, and built bonfires in the streets from the debris. Officials had to call out the National Guard to restore peace, leading to the ironic spectacle of soldiers "with fixed bayonets" patrolling the streets to prevent the celebration of the peace.[1]

The *Tucson Citizen* pronounced 11 November "a new American holiday." Come what may, the paper editorialized, "it must be made a national holiday . . . by virtue of the tremendous event which transpired on this morning." Armistice Day, as the day came to be known, did indeed become a new American holiday. Just as the Grand Army of the Republic seized control of the federal Memorial Day, so the newly minted American Legion took charge of the holiday that remembered the veterans and the dead of its war. In 1920 Arizona's governor "urgently request[ed] that it be observed as a public holiday" and encouraged Arizonans to "participate in the exercises to be held by the American Legion." In Tucson the legion revived the military parade, inviting "[v]eterans from all wars" to march in its Armistice Day procession, and requesting that they wear their uniforms. Although the celebration was more controlled than the spontaneous revelry of 1918, the *Tucson Citizen* noted, nevertheless, that "firecrackers and shooting" pervaded the day. An editorial in the newspaper made clear the purpose of the day: "The American people have the saving virtue of gratitude" to the soldiers who made the world safe for democracy. The celebration of the holiday demonstrated that "[t]he American people will not forget the doughboy."[2]

But if Americans did not quite forget the doughboys, they did move on. Despite the efforts of the American Legion, Armistice Day did not long remain an occasion for massive public celebration. In 1921 Washington, D.C., marked the occasion with the solemn ceremonial interment, in Arlington National Cemetery, of an unknown soldier, which John Dos Passos savagely satirized in *1919*, contrasting the empty platitudes of the ceremony with the obscene deaths of all the "John Does" who died in Europe.[3] In 1932 President Herbert Hoover ordered the army to drive out of Washington veterans demonstrating for early payment of their federal bonuses. Douglas MacArthur complied with brutal precision.

Armistice Day was not the only new holiday to come out of World War I. Many ethnic Americans added new national holidays to their calendar as the result of the war. Czechs and Slovaks, for example, commemorated the 28 October anniversary of their independence. In a holiday editorial *Denní Hlasatel* asserted that 28 October represented "the crystallization of our revolutionary activities, in which the Czech-Slovaks of America took part not only financially and through active propaganda but also by recruiting volunteers among our people and sending them abroad to join the colors of the Czech-Slovak army." Poles as well commemorated the reestablishment of their nation. And in 1922 the Italian Chamber of Commerce in Chicago combined its celebration of Armistice Day with that of King Victor's birthday. The orators stressed the importance of the Italian victory in 1918 rather than the American victory.[4]

Despite the creation of new holidays, however, the large public celebrations of the late nineteenth and early twentieth centuries were on the wane after the war. The spread of public schooling and the rise of the mass media provided the middle class with more effective and efficient tools for inculcating American identity. It was in the schools that American holidays remained most significant as vehicles of Americanism, as generations of teachers decorated bulletin boards and taught their students that Washington could not tell a lie and that Columbus sailed the ocean blue. For the parents, the new mass media, particularly motion pictures and radio, proved much more efficient than public celebrations at inculcating American values. Whereas even the huge celebrations of the late nineteenth century drew but a fraction of urban populations, the mass media had the potential of reaching millions of Americans at once.

Although public holiday celebrations diminished, they did not disappear. Despite the continuing Americanization pressure between the wars, for instance, ethnic Americans persisted in celebrating the holidays that recalled their homelands. In 1935, for instance, Chicago's *Chinese Daily Times* recounted a celebration of Double Ten Day (for the revolution of 10 October 1911) at the On-Leong Chinese School, which included a speech in the Mandarin dialect by the Chinese consul and the singing of the anthem of independence, and concluded with "[a] loud acclamation of 'Long Live the China Republic.'" Even German Americans renewed their public celebration of their heritage.

In 1926 the *Sonntagpost* urged Chicago Germans "to be on the spot when 'The Star-Spangled Banner' and the German Song are heard" on German Day. In 1934 the celebration featured American and German flags to show that "it is possible to be a good American and yet remain a German at heart." After the American anthem, *Abendpost* recounted, there came from the revelers "in a powerful roar 'Deutschland, Deutschland ueber alles.'" Evidently this celebration of Hitler's Germany was not viewed with alarm by Chicagoans; the paper reported that Mayor Kelly and other city officials attended the exercises.[5]

In addition to the ethnic celebrations, periodic crises spurred renewed attention to public holidays. After a decline during the postwar red scare and rising antiunion sentiment, Labor Day and May Day both revived during the union-building years of the Great Depression. On these days unions again paraded to demonstrate their strength and to recruit the unorganized. The Popular Front of the war years also contributed to May Day's revitalization. World War II inspired new patriotic holidays and revived old ones. The federal government's Office of War Information sent photographers around the nation to capture Americans celebrating Memorial Day, Flag Day, and Armistice Day. Once again the advent of war led many Americans to perceive a crisis in Americanization. Instead of using the Fourth of July, this time Congress created a new holiday, given the unwieldy name of "I Am an American Day," to be celebrated on the third Sunday in May. Richard Fried notes that more than a million New Yorkers attended exercises in Central Park in 1942 and that more than a thousand towns sponsored celebrations of this new holiday in 1945. Although the holiday declined in popularity after the war, it was replaced by a Cold War counterweight to May Day dubbed Loyalty Day. The new Veterans of Foreign Wars led other veterans' groups and sympathetic organizations in rituals that constructed America as a bastion of anticommunism. The American Bar Association also joined the struggle for control of May Day, dubbing it Law Day and, echoing the civic elites of the late nineteenth century, asserting its purpose as inculcating Americans with the proper regard for law and order.[6]

Ethnic and labor celebrations, meanwhile, waned after the war. In the first case, this decline reflected the impact of wartime Americanization pressures, as well as the lack of new immigrants, which fostered the assimilation of those

Children at the Memorial Day parade, Ashland, Maine, 1943. The crisis of World War II revived patriotic holiday celebrations, and the government sent photographers to document them. Children, as usual, were particularly targeted by the organizers of these celebrations. (Photograph by John Collier for the Office of War Information; courtesy of the Library of Congress)

here. The decline of labor celebrations, on the other hand, was both the product of the Cold War repression of radicalism and the triumph of nonradical organized labor and its members' assimilation into the middle class. Emancipation celebrations, in contrast, thrived in the South throughout the twentieth century and were brought to the North by migrants. They received energizing vigor from the Civil Rights movement, until today Juneteenth has become the near-universal anniversary of independence for African Americans. And in 1983 African Americans finally won congressional recognition of a holiday that celebrated their contributions to American culture with the enactment of a statute making Martin Luther King Jr.'s birthday a federal holiday.[7] The ethnic revival of the 1960s and 1970s and the reopening of immigration after 1965 have also reinvigorated ethnic holidays in the last few decades. Ethnic and racial holidays have thus reemerged as important venues for the construction and inculcation of new visions of America.

Scarred by the excesses of the Cold War, the Vietnam War, and the Watergate generation's revulsion against conspicuous patriotism, the patriotic American holidays have never quite recovered from their decline. Americans have united for sporadic bursts of celebratory fervor, most notably for the bicentennial of American independence. Spurred on by the congressional legislation in 1968 that moved most holidays to Mondays, however, American patriotic holidays have become primarily the occasion for three-day weekends and shopping sprees for millions of Americans. A New York City social worker commented on Presidents' Day, "To be honest, I don't really care about George Washington.... What I care is, I get a day off from work." The Veterans of Foreign Wars, echoing an earlier generation of veterans, laments Memorial Day's descent into a weekend of auto racing, picnics, and sales. Nevertheless, interested groups continue to organize public commemorations, attended by small crowds. Veterans' associations sponsor programs for Memorial Day, Flag Day, and Armistice (now Veterans) Day, while labor unions in some cities still sponsor Labor Day parades.[8]

As several recent controversies attest, however, holidays still have the potential to erupt into ideological battlegrounds. In Syracuse, New York, in the 1980s, for example, Memorial Day received new vigor from a conflict over the holiday parade between veterans and peace groups, each of whom sought to adapt the symbolism of the holiday to its cause. The attempt to extend Martin Luther King Jr. Day to all the states also occasioned heated battles, most notably in Arizona, where lame-duck Governor Bruce Babbitt bypassed the legislature to create the holiday. That caused a public furor and led to the question being put on the ballot, where it went down to an ignominious defeat. The ensuing battle pitted holiday supporters against a coalition of Italian Americans who objected to a proposal to replace Columbus Day with the new holiday, conservatives who did not believe King was worthy of a holiday for various reasons, and Arizonans who believed that state workers already had more than enough holidays. After boycotts by numerous conventions and even the Super Bowl, Arizonans finally approved the holiday.[9]

Although King Jr. Day is a national holiday, it, like Juneteenth, continues to be commemorated primarily by African Americans and viewed by many white Americans as an interest-group holiday. The institutionalization of these holidays, perhaps the most symbolically charged American holidays other than the Fourth of July, has failed to unite white and black Americans in celebration of the fulfillment of American independence through emancipation and the Second Reconstruction. But in one respect King Jr. Day has become a full-fledged American holiday. Americans can now shop special Martin Luther King Jr. Day sales and clearances.

The longest-running holiday controversy today surrounds the participation of gay men and lesbians in New York City's St. Patrick's Day parade. In 1991 the Irish Lesbian and Gay Organization (ILGO) applied to march in the city's annual St. Patrick's Day procession. The Ancient Order of Hibernians (AOH), the Irish-American Catholic fraternal association that sponsored the parade, turned down the ILGO, alleging that there was a long waiting list. After the same sequence of events occurred in 1992, the ILGO sued the AOH, claiming that its denial of permission to march constituted illegal discrimination under the city's Human Rights Law. The Hibernians argued that because the event was a religious celebration, they could not welcome an organization that flouted the Catholic Church's position on homosexuality. In that they received warm support from John Cardinal O'Connor. Echoing the segregationists of a generation earlier, they also contended that the celebration was private and that the organization thus had the right to assert its First Amendment right to free assembly. The ILGO, with Mayor David Dinkins's support, countered that the parade was a public event and thus was subject to the city's Human Rights Law prohibiting discrimination against homosexuals.[10]

In 1993 the federal court ruled in favor of the AOH. The triumphant Hibernians sponsored the procession, while the ILGO and its supporters staged a protest and urged New Yorkers to boycott the celebration. On St. Patrick's Day, the police arrested 228 protesters for contempt of the court ban and marching without a parade permit. At St. Patrick's Cathedral, a happy Cardinal O'Connor reviewed the procession and told holiday worshipers that "[n]either respectability nor political correctness is worth one comma in the Apostles' Creed." Mayor Dinkins declined to participate in the procession, while his Republican challenger, Rudolph Giuliani, saw it as an opportunity to kick off his campaign. The ILGO won a victory of sorts; the *New York Times* concluded that "[t]he parade was notable for the few major politicians in sight and for the sparseness of the crowds watching along Fifth Avenue."[11]

The strength of the fight put up by both the AOH and the ILGO and the political maneuvering of Dinkins, Giuliani, and even Cardinal O'Connor indicate that the question of who was entitled to march on St. Patrick's Day bore a great deal more symbolic weight than it might first seem. Indeed, the dispute, which has spread to other cities as well, transformed the holiday into no less than another battleground of the war waged by gay men and lesbians for equal rights and acceptance in American society. The AOH's rather disingenuous claim that the parade was an essentially private and religious event not only echoed segregationists but also flew in the face of years of boisterous St. Patrick's Day revelry by Americans, whether of Irish descent or not. The ILGO's charges of bigotry also oversimplified the issue. As one woman watching the parade pointed out, "There's plenty of gays in the parade" already; they simply chose to march as members of other organizations without flaunting their sexuality. After all, she explained, "It's not a parade about sex."[12]

Those who wondered why the ILGO had to force its members' sexuality into the holiday procession, however, missed the larger point. What had become almost lost in the general hilarity of St. Patrick's Day, when "everyone is Irish," was the fact that at its core the holiday remains an expression of Irish American identity. In the late nineteenth century Irish Americans had debated fiercely whether Catholicism was a necessary component of Irish American identity. The 1993 conflict in New York City reopened the debate, only now the question was whether open homosexuality was compatible with Irish American identity. The AOH did not embark on a witch-hunt to be sure no homosexuals marched in the procession. What it objected to was the open proclamation of sexual identity. If sexuality was kept private, there would be no confrontation with the Catholic Church's position against homosexuality. By insisting upon marching openly as gay men and lesbians, the ILGO knowingly precipitated that confrontation. For the AOH, and many other Irish American Catholics, Irish Americanism could not comprehend open homosexuality. The ILGO believed otherwise. Its members wished on St. Patrick's Day to proclaim that they were not just Irish Americans but that they were gay and lesbian Irish Americans. By doing so, they asserted that their sexuality was as integral a part of their American identity as their ethnicity.

These examples suggest that public holidays still possess the power to lay bare the tensions in American society and to serve as arenas for the construction of competing visions of America. It remains to be seen whether the rise of multiculturalism and the explosion of immigration at the turn of the twenty-first century will lead middle- or upper-class Americans to emulate their late nineteenth-century counterparts in reinvigorating national holidays as a unifying force. But that seems unlikely, given the existence of mass culture's more effective means of assimilating and homogenizing Americans. Nevertheless, the growing vitality of ethnic and racial holidays, in addition to the explosion of other venues of ethnic-racial culture, reveals that Americanism at the end of the twentieth century continues to be contested terrain.

NOTES

INTRODUCTION

1. These holidays included Memorial Day and Confederate Memorial Day; Emancipation Day and various local emancipation holidays; the birthdays of Abraham Lincoln, Robert E. Lee, Stonewall Jackson, and Jefferson Davis; Labor Day, May Day, and Haymarket Martyrs' Day; myriad ethnic holidays, such as the birthdays of Robert Emmet and Tadeusz Kosciuszko, German Day, and Mexican and Norwegian Independence Days; Constitution Day and Flag Day; Arbor Day and Bird Day; Mother's Day; and Armistice Day.

2. David Waldstreicher, *In the Midst of Perpetual Fetes: The Making of American Nationalism, 1776–1820* (Chapel Hill: University of North Carolina Press for the Omohundro Institute of Early American History and Culture, 1997); Len Travers, *Celebrating the Fourth: Independence Day and the Rites of Nationalism in the Early Republic* (Amherst: University of Massachusetts Press, 1997); Simon P. Newman, *Parades and the Politics of the Street: Festive Culture in the Early American Republic* (Philadelphia: University of

Pennsylvania Press, 1997); Shane White, "'It Was a Proud Day': African Americans, Festivals, and Parades in the North, 1741–1834," *Journal of American History* 81 (June 1994): 13–50; Geneviève Fabre, "African-American Commemorative Celebrations in the Nineteenth Century," in *History and Memory in African-American Culture,* ed. Geneviève Fabre and Robert O'Meally (New York: Oxford University Press, 1994), 72–91; Elizabeth Rauh Bethel, *The Roots of African-American Identity: Memory and History in Free Antebellum Communities* (New York: St. Martin's Press, 1997); William B. Gravely, "The Dialectic of Double-Consciousness in Black American Freedom Celebrations, 1808–1863," *Journal of Negro History* 67 (Winter 1982): 302–17. In addition, Mary P. Ryan looks at civic celebrations in the antebellum and Civil War eras in *Civic Wars: Democracy and Public Life in the American City during the Nineteenth Century* (Berkeley: University of California Press, 1997).

3. John Bodnar, *Remaking America: Public Memory, Commemoration, and Patriotism in the Twentieth Century* (Princeton: Princeton University Press, 1992); Richard M. Fried, *The Russians Are Coming! The Russians Are Coming! Pageantry and Patriotism in Cold-War America* (New York: Oxford University Press, 1998).

4. April R. Schultz, *Ethnicity on Parade: Inventing the Norwegian American through Celebration* (Amherst: University of Massachusetts Press, 1994); Kathleen Neils Conzen, "Ethnicity as Festive Culture: Nineteenth-Century German America on Parade," in *The Invention of Ethnicity,* ed. Werner Sollors (New York: Oxford University Press, 1989), 44–76; Michael Kazin and Steven J. Ross, "America's Labor Day: The Dilemma of a Workers' Celebration," *Journal of American History* 78 (March 1992): 1294–323; Mitchell Kachun, "'The Faith That the Dark Past Has Taught Us': African-American Commemorations in the North and West and the Construction of a Usable Past, 1808–1915" (Ph.D. diss., Cornell University, 1997); Leigh Eric Schmidt, *Consumer Rites: The Buying and Selling of American Holidays* (Princeton: Princeton University Press, 1995). On ethnic holidays see also Ramón Gutiérrez and Geneviève Fabre, eds., *Feasts and Celebrations in North American Ethnic Communities* (Albuquerque: University of New Mexico Press, 1995).

5. Victor Turner, "Introduction," in *Celebration: Studies in Festivity and Ritual,* ed. Victor Turner (Washington, D.C.: Smithsonian Institution Press, 1982), 11–30; Jürgen Habermas, *The Structural Transformation of the Public Sphere: An Inquiry into a Category of Bourgeois Society,* trans. Thomas Burger (Cambridge, Mass.: MIT Press, 1989), 1, 22; Eric J. Hobsbawm and Terence Ranger, eds., *The Invention of Tradition* (Cambridge: Cambridge University Press, 1983); Benedict Anderson, *Imagined Communities: Reflections on the Origin and Spread of Nationalism* (London: Verso, 1983). My understanding of public ritual has also been influenced by Sally F. Moore and Barbara G. Myerhoff, "Introduction: Secular Ritual: Forms and Meanings," in *Secular Ritual,* ed. Sally F. Moore and Barbara G. Myerhoff (Assen, the Netherlands: Van Gorcum, 1977), 3–24.

6. Robert Wiebe, for instance, includes both skilled workers and local elites in his definition of the middle class (*Self-Rule: A Cultural History of American Democracy* [Chicago: University of Chicago Press, 1995], 113–20, 138–42). Tony Bennett, *The Birth of the Museum: History, Theory, Politics* (London: Routledge, 1995), 27–31.

7. Alexis de Tocqueville, *Democracy in America*, ed. and abridged by Richard D. Heffner (New York: Penguin, 1956), 198–209. On associations and the middle class, see Mary P. Ryan, *Cradle of the Middle Class: The Family in Oneida County, New York, 1790–1865* (Cambridge: Cambridge University Press, 1981), 105–44; and Ryan, *Civic Wars*, 8–9, 59–60. On the middle-class nature of the press, see Habermas, *The Structural Transformation of the Public Sphere*, 20–22; and Philip J. Ethington, *The Public City: The Political Construction of Urban Life in San Francisco, 1850–1900* (Cambridge: Cambridge University Press, 1994), 15–21.

8. John R. Gillis, "Memory and Identity: The History of a Relationship," in *Commemorations: The Politics of National Identity*, ed. John R. Gillis (Princeton: Princeton University Press, 1994), 3; Hobsbawm and Ranger, *The Invention of Tradition*, 2.

9. Ryan, *Civic Wars*, 4.

10. Jack Santino, *All Around the Year: Holidays and Celebrations in American Life* (Urbana: University of Illinois Press, 1994), xx.

11. A number of recent books have scrutinized this preoccupation with public order on the part of late nineteenth-century elites. The most helpful have been Carl Smith, *Urban Disorder and the Shape of Belief: The Great Chicago Fire, the Haymarket Bomb, and the Model Town of Pullman* (Chicago: University of Chicago Press, 1995); and Paul Boyer, *Urban Masses and Moral Order in America, 1820–1920* (Cambridge: Harvard University Press, 1978), 123–87. Also useful are Ryan, *Civic Wars*, 183–258; and Ethington, *Public City*.

12. On this point, see Boyer, *Urban Masses*, 175–90.

I. MEMORIAL DAYS

1. Chauncey M. Depew, "Decoration Day Speech at the Academy of Music in New York, 30 May 1879," in *Orations, Addresses and Speeches of Chauncey Depew*, vol. 1: *Birthday and Anniversary Addresses*, ed. John D. Champlin (New York: privately printed, 1910), 288–89.

2. For a fuller discussion of the connection between the rural cemetery movement and the invention of Memorial Day, see Ellen M. Litwicki, "Visions of America: Public Holidays and American Cultures, 1776–1900" (Ph.D. diss., University of Virginia, 1992), 259–67. On the rural cemetery movement, see Stanley French, "The Cemetery as Cultural Institution: The Establishment of Mount Auburn and the 'Rural Cemetery' Movement," in *Death in America*, ed. David E. Stannard (Philadelphia: Univer-

sity of Pennsylvania Press, 1975), 69–91; James J. Farrell, *Inventing the American Way of Death, 1830–1920* (Philadelphia: Temple University Press, 1980), 99–113; and Neil Harris, "The Cemetery Beautiful," in *Passing: The Vision of Death in America*, ed. Charles O. Jackson, Contributions in Family Studies, no. 2 (Westport, Conn.: Greenwood Press, 1977), 103–11.

3. *A History of the Origin of Memorial Day as Adopted by the Ladies' Memorial Association of Columbus, Georgia* (Columbus, Ga.: Thomas Gilbert for the Lizzie Rutherford Chapter of the Daughters of the Confederacy, 1898), 20–21; *In Memoriam Mary Walker Barney* (Richmond: Whittet and Shepperson, [1893]), 6–7. On the use of flowers, see Robert W. Habenstein and William M. Lamers, "The Pattern of Late Nineteenth-Century Funerals," in *Passing: The Vision of Death in America*, ed. Charles O. Jackson, Contributions in Family Studies, no. 2 (Westport, Conn.: Greenwood Press, 1977), 96–97; and Harris, "Cemetery Beautiful," 106–7.

4. Mrs. George T. Fry, "Memorial Day—Its Origin," *Confederate Veteran* 1 (May 1893): 149. Not surprisingly, this became a stock story of the day's origins. See, for example, "Our Memorial Day," *Confederate Veteran* 22 (May 1914): 195. A good discussion of the relationship between women, children, and mourning is found in Ann Douglas, "Heaven Our Home: Consolation Literature in the Northern United States, 1830–1880," in *Death in America*, ed. David E. Stannard (Philadelphia: University of Pennsylvania Press, 1975), 49–68.

5. *History of the Origin of Memorial Day, Columbus*, 17–25, 37–39.

6. Ibid., 5–7, 37. For the origins of southern ladies' memorial associations and Memorial Days, see *History of the Confederated Memorial Associations of the South*, rev. and authorized ed. (New Orleans: Graham Press for the Confederated Southern Memorial Association, 1904); Gaines M. Foster, *Ghosts of the Confederacy: Defeat, the Lost Cause, and the Emergence of the New South, 1865 to 1913* (New York: Oxford University Press, 1987),38–39; and Lee Ann Whites, *The Civil War as a Crisis in Gender: Augusta, Georgia, 1860–1890* (Athens: University of Georgia Press, 1995), 182–89.

7. Mrs. Charles J. Williams, letter, *Columbus (Georgia) Times*, 12 March 1866, reprinted in *History of the Origin of Memorial Day, Columbus*, 24–25.

8. Kate Mason Rowland, comp., "Notes Concerning Confederate Memorial Day and Other Southern Holidays," Holograph, ca. 1903, in Virginia Historical Society, Richmond; Foster, *Ghosts of the Confederacy*, 42.

9. *Chicago Tribune*, 26 May 1895, typescript copy, Chicago Holidays and Celebrations folder, Chicago Historical Society, Chicago. On the Boalsburg and Waterloo claims, see Conrad Cherry, "Two American Sacred Ceremonies: Their Implications for the Study of Religion in America," *American Quarterly* 21 (Winter 1969): 739–40.

10. Mrs. John A. Logan, quoted in "Origin of Memorial Day," *Southern Historical Society Papers* 37 (1909): 368; Logan's order is quoted in George W. Douglas, comp., *The*

American Book of Days (New York: H. W. Wilson, 1937), 294. Mrs. Logan also described her role in the origins of the federal holiday in an 1892 letter, reprinted in "The Confederate Memorial Day," *Confederate Veteran* 1 (January 1893): 20–21.

11. *Augusta (Georgia) Chronicle*, quoted in Ada Ramp Walden, "The First Memorial Day," *Confederate Veteran* 39 (March 1931): 117. On the connections between evangelicalism, "women's sphere," and benevolence and reform, see Mary P. Ryan, *Women in Public: Between Banners and Ballots, 1825–1880* (Baltimore: Johns Hopkins University Press, 1990), 39–42; and Nancy F. Cott, *The Bonds of Womanhood: "Woman's Sphere" in New England, 1780–1835* (New Haven: Yale University Press, 1977), 126–59. For discussions of women's roles on Memorial Day, see Foster, *Ghosts of the Confederacy*, 42–45; and Whites, *Civil War as a Crisis in Gender*, chap. 6.

12. Ladies' Hollywood Memorial Association, *To the Women of the South*, broadside, 1866, Virginia Historical Society, Richmond. On the establishment of the national cemetery system, see G. Kurt Piehler, *Remembering War the American Way* (Washington, D.C.: Smithsonian Institution Press, 1995), 50–52. The federal government took no responsibility for the care of Confederate graves until 1898; see Richard Severo and Lewis Milford, *The Wages of War: When America's Soldiers Came Home—From Valley Forge to Vietnam* (New York: Simon and Schuster, 1989), 134–35.

13. James Henry Gardner to Mary P. (Gardner) Florance, 1 June 1867, James Henry Gardner Papers, Virginia Historical Society, Richmond.

14. On women and mourning, see Douglas, "Heaven Our Home."

15. *Richmond Enquirer and Sentinel*, 2 May 1866; *Chicago Tribune*, 31 May 1890, 31 May 1892, 31 May 1893. For further information on northern women's roles on Memorial Day, see Nina Silber, *The Romance of Reunion: Northerners and the South, 1865–1900* (Chapel Hill: University of North Carolina Press, 1993), 59–60; and Cecilia Elizabeth O'Leary, *To Die For: The Paradox of American Patriotism* (Princeton: Princeton University Press, 1999), 91–107. O'Leary incorrectly suggests that the Women's Relief Corps created Memorial Day (91). On the Women's Relief Corps, see Stuart McConnell, *Glorious Contentment: The Grand Army of the Republic, 1865–1900* (Chapel Hill: University of North Carolina Press, 1992), 218–19.

16. "In Memoriam," *Harper's Weekly*, 31 May 1884, 341; May M. Anderson, "An Hour in Hollywood Cemetery," *Confederate Veteran* 4 (August 1896): 272; *History of the Origin of Memorial Day, Columbus*, 38; Kathryne E. Entler, "Memorial Day, June 3, in Los Angeles," *Confederate Veteran* 19 (September 1911): 421–22. For a discussion of the tradition of women as allegory, see Marina Warner, *Monuments and Maidens: The Allegory of the Female Form* (New York: Atheneum, 1985).

17. *Richmond Enquirer and Sentinel*, 14 May 1866; *Chicago Tribune*, 31 May 1900; "Decoration of Soldiers' Graves," *Harper's Weekly*, 20 June 1868, 388; *Chicago Tribune*, 31 May 1890.

18. *Tucson Arizona Daily Star*, 1 June 1890; Fred Eaton, "Way Out 'n the Prairie Kentry," *Youth's Companion*, 29 May 1890, 289–90.

19. "Decoration Day, 1900," *Harper's Weekly*, 2 June 1900, 508–9; Bertha Watson, "Popsie's Soldier," *Youth's Companion*, 25 May 1882, 217; "Mem'ry Day," *Youth's Companion*, 29 May 1890, 299.

20. *Tucson Arizona Weekly Citizen*, 6 June 1885; Henry Robinson Pollard, *Address Delivered before Oakwood Memorial Association, Richmond, Va., Saturday, May 7, 1910* (Richmond: Whittet and Shepperson, 1910), 5.

21. *Our Confederate Dead*, souvenir pamphlet of Ladies' Hollywood Memorial Association, Virginia Historical Society, Richmond, 1896; Mary H. Mitchell, *Hollywood Cemetery: The History of a Southern Shrine* (Richmond: Virginia State Library, 1985), 72–74; Mrs. B. A. C. Emerson, comp., *Historic Southern Monuments* (New York: Neale Publishing Co., 1911), 446–47. On other monuments erected under the auspices of the ladies' memorial associations, see Foster, *Ghosts of the Confederacy*, 36–46; and Whites, *Civil War as a Crisis in Gender*, 192–97.

22. *Richmond Dispatch*, 11 April 1870, 1 June 1870; *Our Confederate Dead*, 1896; Mitchell, *Hollywood Cemetery*, 85–87. For examples of such planning activity in Richmond, see *Richmond Dispatch*, 11 April 1870, 28 May 1870, 6 May 1875, 9 May 1885, 13 May 1885, 16 May 1890, and 9 May 1895.

23. *Address of Theodore W. Bean, of Norristown, Pennsylvania, Delivered at Seven Pines National Cemetery, on Memorial Day, May 30th, 1888, under the auspices of Phil Kearny Post No. 10, G.A.R. of Richmond, Virginia* (Richmond: n.p., 1888), 2; McConnell, *Glorious Contentment*, 218–19.

24. Lee Ann Whites suggests, in *Civil War as a Crisis in Gender* (chap. 6), that on Confederate Memorial Days women shored up the sagging masculinity of white southern men, and obscured their own more public role, by recasting the Confederate cause as the defense of southern women, children, and homes against northern aggressors.

25. *Tucson Arizona Weekly Citizen*, 6 June 1885; H. D. MacLachlan, "The Religious Aspect of Patriotism" (typescript of Memorial Day sermon preached in Richmond on 30 May 1909), 1, "Speeches, Addresses, Etc.," Lee Camp Records, Virginia Historical Society, Richmond; McConnell, *Glorious Contentment*, 79. On church services, see *Richmond Enquirer and Sentinel*, 11 May 1866; *Richmond Dispatch*, 7 May 1870, 11 May 1895; *Richmond Whig and Advertiser*, 3 June 1870; *Tucson Arizona Daily Star*, 28 May 1895; and Entler, "Memorial Day," 421–22.

26. *Our Confederate Dead*, souvenir pamphlet of Ladies' Hollywood Memorial Association, Virginia Historical Society, Richmond, 1916, 20. The general outline of Memorial Day exercises in this and the following paragraphs has been taken from the following reports: Entler, "Memorial Day"; *Front Royal Memorial Day Exercises 6-2-06*, broadside, Virginia Historical Society, Richmond; *History of the Origin of Memorial*

Day, Columbus, 38–39; *Chicago Tribune,* various post–Memorial Day issues between 1870 and 1900; *Richmond Dispatch,* various post–Memorial Day issues between 1870 and 1895; *Richmond Enquirer and Sentinel,* 2 May 1866, 11 May 1866; *Tucson Arizona Weekly Citizen,* 7 June 1884, 6 June 1885, 3 June 1893; *Tucson Arizona Daily Star,* 28 May 1887, 1 June 1890; *Tucson Citizen,* 29 May 1905.

27. *Chicago Tribune,* 31 May 1893; Leonora Rogers Schuyler, *Address Delivered before the Confederate Veteran Camp of New York at Mount Hope, New York,* 30 May 1914, pamphlet, Virginia Historical Society, Richmond; *Richmond Dispatch,* 31 May 1895; *Tucson Arizona Daily Star,* 1 June 1890.

28. *Richmond Dispatch,* 1 June 1870.

29. *Richmond Dispatch,* 2 June 1875, 3 June 1875; *Chicago Tribune,* 31 May 1885, 30 May 1886, 31 May 1890, 31 May 1892, 31 May 1893. For reference to the 1878 procession, see *Chicago Tribune,* 30 May 1952, in Holiday Clippings file, Chicago Historical Society.

30. *Chicago Tribune,* 31 May 1893, 30 May 1890; *Tucson Arizona Weekly Citizen,* 6 June 1885; *Richmond Dispatch,* 30 May 1895, 31 May 1895.

31. "Memorial Day," *Confederate Veteran* 2 (September 1894): 267.

32. Mrs. John H. Anderson, "Memorial Day," *Confederate Veteran* 40 (May 1932): 164.

33. *Richmond Dispatch,* 31 May 1870; "How It Began," *Chicago Tribune,* 30 May 1947, in Holiday Clippings file, Chicago Historical Society; Douglas, *American Book of Days,* 297; "Memorial Day Discrimination," *Confederate Veteran* 10 (August 1902): 348. Also see "Memorial Day—The South's Term," *Confederate Veteran* 1 (November 1893): 326; "Pathetic Memories. Don't Want Memorial and Decoration Days Merged," *Confederate Veteran* 10 (June 1902): 265. I have used the term "Memorial Day" rather than "Decoration Day" throughout this chapter for the sake of consistency and because veterans on both sides preferred it over Decoration Day.

34. "Honoring Our Dead Heroes," *Harper's Weekly,* 6 June 1868, 365–66; Douglas, *American Book of Days,* 295. Historians of the GAR have argued that it was Radical Republicans who were really behind the establishment of the federal Memorial Day; see, for example, McConnell, *Glorious Contentment,* 24–27, 193–200.

35. This incident is recounted in Severo and Milford, *Wages of War,* 131; *New York Times,* 3 June 1869, quoted in ibid., 158–59.

36. Jacob Engelbrecht, *The Diary of Jacob Engelbrecht,* ed. William R. Quynn, vol. 3: *The Civil War, 1858–1878* (Frederick, Md.: The Historical Society of Frederick County, 1976), 30 May 1871; *Chicago Tribune,* 30 May 1886; "Our Fallen Heroes," *Southern Historical Society Papers* 7 (1879): 376.

37. *Tucson Arizona Weekly Citizen,* 6 June 1885; Douglas, *American Book of Days,* 294; *Chicago Tribune,* 31 May 1885, 31 May 1893. On the pension issue, see Charles M. Leoser, "The Grand Army as a Pension Agency," *Forum,* July 1893, 522–31.

38. *Richmond Dispatch,* 21 May 1885; *Our Confederate Dead,* 1916, 17–18; Piehler, *Remembering War,* 76–77.

39. W. Lloyd Warner, *American Life: Dream and Reality* (Chicago: University of Chicago Press, 1953), 3; John Logan, "Address," *Memorial Day, May 30th and 31st, 1886, U.S. Grant Post, No. 327, Dept. of New York, G.A.R.,* souvenir booklet, Virginia Historical Society, Richmond, 23; *Richmond Enquirer and Sentinel,* 11 May 1866.

40. *Chicago Tribune,* 30 May 1886; Graham Daves, "The Causes of the War, 1861–65, and Events of Its First Year," *Southern Historical Society Papers* 32 (1904): 293.

41. Rev. Philip D. Stephenson, *The "Men of the Ranks": or, the Confederate Private as a Type and His Place in History* (pamphlet of address at Hollywood Cemetery, Richmond, Va., 29 May 1909), 4; Eaton, "Prairie Kentry," 290; *Chicago Tribune,* 31 May 1870; *Our Confederate Dead,* 1896. Also see Foster, *Ghosts of the Confederacy,* 129–31; Piehler, *Remembering War,* 53–56, 61; and Kirk Savage, *Standing Soldiers, Kneeling Slaves: Race, War, and Monument in Nineteenth-Century America* (Princeton: Princeton University Press, 1997), 162–208.

42. *Chicago Tribune,* 30 May 1886; *Address of Theodore W. Bean,* 8. On the class origins of the veterans and memorial associations, see particularly McConnell's study of the membership of three GAR posts, *Glorious Contentment,* 55–71, 81–82, 221–30; see also Foster, *Ghosts of the Confederacy,* 44, 109–12, 195–96.

43. *Chicago Tribune,* 31 May 1870; *Richmond Dispatch,* 21 May 1885. On the legalization of the holiday, see Douglas, *American Book of Days,* 296; and Paul H. Buck, *The Road to Reunion, 1865–1900* (Boston: Little, Brown and Co., 1937), 117–18.

44. Charles E. Adams, Diary, 4 vols., 1: 31 May 1886, 3: 30 May 1887, 30 May 1888, 4: 30 May 1889, box 64, document 258, Downs Collection, Henry Francis DuPont du Winterthur Library, Winterthur, Del.

45. *Tucson Arizona Weekly Citizen,* 9 May 1885; "Right Regard for Memorial Days," *Confederate Veteran* 12 (June 1904): 291; *Chicago Tribune,* 31 May 1895.

46. "The Blue and the Gray," *Harper's Weekly,* 9 June 1877, 438; *The Union: A Plea for Reconciliation, Being an Address by Hon. Roger A. Pryor, Delivered in the Academy of Music, Brooklyn, N.Y., on Decoration Day, May 30th, 1877* (Brooklyn: Eagle Job and Book Printing Department, 1877), 17–22.

47. Pryor, *The Union,* 4–5, 8–9, 10–12; Baker P. Lee, *Confederate Memorial Address Delivered at Elmwood Cemetery, Norfolk, Va., May 19, 1887* (Richmond: G. R. Tenser, 1887), 4; Depew, "Decoration Day Speech, 30 May 1879," 284.

48. *Address of Theodore W. Bean,* 10–12; *Address by General William Ruffin Cox Delivered before the Oakwood Memorial Association, Richmond, Va., May 10, 1911* (Richmond: F. J. Mitchell Printing, n.d.), 5.

49. On sentiment favoring forgetting the war, see, for example, Silber, *Romance of Re-*

union, 61. On the refocusing of the war story, see Foster, *Ghosts of the Confederacy*, 66–70; and McConnell, *Glorious Contentment*, 168–83.

50. McConnell, *Glorious Contentment*, 84–124; "Constitution and By-Laws for the United Confederate Veterans," *Confederate Veteran* 4 (May 1896): 68. For additional discussion of the GAR's difficulties in the 1870s, see Wallace Evan Davies, *Patriotism on Parade: The Story of Veterans' and Hereditary Organizations in America, 1783–1900* (Cambridge: Harvard University Press, 1955), 33–35, 190–93.

51. Minute Book, vol. 1, 27 April 1883, Grand Camp Confederate Veterans, R. E. Lee Camp, No. 1, Records, Virginia Historical Association, Richmond (hereafter cited as Lee Camp Minute Book).

52. The South Carolina regiment's visit to Boston is mentioned in *Memorial Day Oration by Erastus Edward Williamson of Hyde Park, Massachusetts, at Hampton, Virginia, May 30, 1876*, pamphlet, Virginia Historical Society, Richmond, 6–7. On the Wilkes Post's trip to Virginia and the Virginians' reciprocal visit, see Louis C. Gosson, *Post-Bellum Campaigns of the Blue and Gray, 1881–1882* (Trenton, N.J.: Naar, Day and Naar, 1882); *On to Richmond! Post No. 23, G.A.R., Dept. of New Jersey, October 16, 1881* (Trenton, N.J.: John L. Murphy, 1881). For other Lee Camp reunion activities, see Lee Camp Minute Book, vol. 1, 29 June 1883, 21 September 1883, 19 October 1883, 30 May 1884, 4 July 1884; vol. 2, 1 May 1885, 12 June 1885, 26 February 1886, 25 February 1887, 13 May 1887, 24 June 1887, 8 June 1888, 27 June 1888.

53. *Richmond Dispatch*, 1 June 1880, 21 May 1885; *Tucson Arizona Daily Star*, 30 May 1880; *Tucson Arizona Weekly Citizen*, 6 June 1885.

54. *Chicago Tribune*, 6 December 1885, 30 May 1886, 31 May 1890.

55. Lee Camp Minute Book, vol. 1, 17 May 1883, 29 May 1883; vol. 2, 19 March 1886, 28 May 1886, 4 June 1886; *Memorial Day, 1886, U. S. Grant Post*, 7, 14, 18–19.

56. Lee Camp Minute Book, vol. 2, 4 May 1888, 25 May 1888, 1 June 1888.

57. "Memorial Day—The South's Term," 326 (emphasis in original). On veterans refusing to join the United Confederate Veterans, see Foster, *Ghosts of the Confederacy*, 108–14.

58. For examples of invitations to and from other Confederate groups, see Lee Camp Minute Book, vol. 1, 6 June 1884; vol. 2, 29 May 1885, 28 May 1886; vol. 3, 9 May 1890, 23 May 1890, 15 May 1891, 13 May 1892; vol. 4, 12 May 1893, 30 May 1893, 30 May 1896; and vol. 5, 30 May 1898, 18 May 1900. I found no reference to participation in any GAR exercises in the 1890s in the minute books.

59. Lee Camp Minute Book, vol. 4, 27 April 1894; vol. 5, 30 July 1897. The camp later bitterly opposed a proposed semicentennial commemoration of the war's end in Richmond, declaring that its members would support a "strictly Southern celebration of progress in fifty years, but all are opposed to any proposition which will invite

veterans of the Northern armies to Richmond" (Lee Camp Minute Book, vol. 8, 16 May 1913).

60. *Richmond Dispatch*, 11 May 1890.

61. *Chicago Tribune*, 30 May 1886; *Address of President Roosevelt at Arlington, Memorial Day, May 30, 1902*, pamphlet, Virginia Historical Society, Richmond, 6–7.

62. Susan C. Soderberg, "Maryland's Civil War Monuments," *The Historian* 58 (Spring 1996): 536; "Confederate Dead at Arlington Decorated for the First Time," *The "Lost Cause"* 9 (June 1903): 72–73, box 11, folder "Confederate Dead, Arlington Memorial Day Services," Samuel Edwin Lewis Papers, Virginia Historical Society, Richmond; Silber, *Romance of Reunion*, 93–196. Foster also examines the popularity of the myth of the Lost Cause in *Ghosts of the Confederacy*, 79–159. For literary reconciliation themes, see, for example, Anderson, "An Hour in Hollywood Cemetery"; A. J. Leland, "Reunited," *Youth's Companion*, 29 May 1890, 294–95; and Sarah Orne Jewett, "Decoration Day," in *A Native of Winby and Other Tales* (Boston: Houghton, Mifflin, 1893), 39–64.

63. *Richmond Dispatch*, 30 May 1895.

64. *Richmond Dispatch*, 30 May 1890; Kirk Savage, "The Politics of Memory: Black Emancipation and the Civil War Monument," in *Commemorations: The Politics of National Identity*, ed. John R. Gillis (Princeton: Princeton University Press, 1994), 132–33. For a discussion of the 1858 unveiling of Richmond's Washington monument, see Litwicki, "Visions of America," 113–18.

65. *Chicago Tribune*, 30 May 1890; *Richmond Planet*, 31 May 1890.

66. *Richmond Dispatch*, 30 May 1890; Amos W. Wright, "The Lee Monument at Richmond," *Harper's Weekly*, 14 June 1890, 470.

67. *Chicago Tribune*, 3 May 1895, 4 May 1895, 31 May 1895.

68. *Chicago Tribune*, 30 May 1895, 4 May 1895; "Our Monument in Chicago," *Confederate Veteran* 3 (June 1895): 176–77.

69. *Chicago Tribune*, 30 May 1895, 31 May 1895.

70. *Richmond Dispatch*, 21 May 1885, 31 May 1890.

71. *Oration of General John A. Logan, Commander-in-Chief of Grand Army of the Republic, Delivered upon the Occasion of the Decoration of Union Soldiers' Graves, at the National Cemetery, Arlington, Va., on Memorial Day, May 30, 1870* (Washington, D.C.: Office of the G.A. Journal, 1870), 4; Savage, "Politics of Memory," 135–36, 139–40; Piehler, *Remembering War*, 56–57; Foster, *Ghosts of the Confederacy*, 23–24.

72. "The Address of Hon. John Lamb, Delivered at Ashland, Va., on Memorial Day, Saturday, May 26, 1906," *Southern Historical Society Papers* 34 (1906): 58; "The Blue and the Gray," *Harper's Weekly*, 6 June 1885, 354; *Chicago Tribune*, 31 May 1895. For examples of Union veterans downplaying slavery, see *Tucson Arizona Weekly Citizen*, 6 June 1885; Depew, "Decoration Day Speech, 30 May 1879," 280–84; and *Address of Theodore W. Bean*, 4–5.

73. Piehler, *Remembering War*, 56–57; Savage, "Politics of Memory," 136. On white oratory, see, for example, *Oration Delivered by Hon. George C. Hazleton on Decoration Day, at Arlington, Va., May 29, 1880* (Washington, D.C.: National Republican Printing House, 1880), 13–15. Kirk Savage discusses the racial implications of enshrining in monuments the white common soldier as hero of the war in *Standing Soldiers, Kneeling Slaves*, 174–76, 180–81, 186–93.

74. Booker T. Washington, "Address at the Unveiling of the Robert Gould Shaw Monument," in *Orations from Homer to William McKinley*, vol. 25, ed. Mayo W. Hazeltine (New York: P. F. Collier and Son, 1902), 10864. On the Shaw monument, see Savage, *Standing Soldiers, Kneeling Slaves*, 193–207.

75. *Address of Theodore W. Bean*; T. B. Edgington, "The Race Problem in the South— Was the Fifteenth Amendment a Mistake?" *Southern Historical Society Papers* 17 (1889): 23, 24, 27, 32.

76. See the editorial from the *Memphis Daily Advocate* appended to Edgington, "Race Problem," 32–33; Stephenson, *Men of the Ranks*, 9–10.

77. Clement A. Evans, "Our Confederate Memorial Day," *Confederate Veteran* 4 (July 1896): 223.

78. For example, see *Address by General William Ruffin Cox*, 9.

79. Rev. R. A. Goodwin, "Memorial Sermon," *Southern Historical Society Papers* 37 (1909): 345; Douglas S. Freeman, "Address—Memorial Exercises, May 10th, 1916, Oakwood Cemetery, Richmond, Va.," *Southern Historical Society Papers*, n.s., 3 (September 1916): 15.

80. "Memorial Day at Savannah, Ga.," *Confederate Veteran* 3 (May 1895): 131; Edgington, "Race Problem," 24–26. Nina Silber discusses this "cult of Anglo-Saxonism" in *Romance of Reunion*, 143–56.

81. *Richmond Dispatch*, 31 May 1890. See also *Richmond Planet*, 24 May 1890, 8 June 1895, 28 May 1898, 4 June 1898; *Richmond Times-Dispatch*, 31 May 1905, 30 May 1910. For an example of nonsegregated federal exercises, see *Richmond Dispatch*, 31 May 1870. On the segregation of GAR posts, see McConnell, *Glorious Contentment*, 213–18; and Davies, *Patriotism on Parade*, 267–70.

82. *Chicago Tribune*, 31 May 1885, 30 May 1886, 31 May 1895; *Chicago Defender*, 1 June 1912.

83. *Chicago Tribune*, 30 May 1886; *Chicago Defender*, 1 June 1912.

84. *Richmond Planet*, 31 May 1890.

2. EMANCIPATION DAYS

1. *Richmond Dispatch*, 2 January 1866.
2. Ibid.
3. Ibid.
4. Ibid.

5. This growing scholarship includes Geneviève Fabre, "African-American Commemorative Celebrations in the Nineteenth Century," in *History and Memory in African-American Culture*, ed. Geneviève Fabre and Robert O'Meally (New York: Oxford University Press, 1994), 72–91; Elizabeth Rauh Bethel, *The Roots of African-American Identity: Memory and History in Free Antebellum Communities* (New York: St. Martin's Press, 1997); Shane White, "'It Was a Proud Day': African Americans, Festivals, and Parades in the North, 1741–1834," *Journal of American History* 81 (June 1994): 13–50; William B. Gravely, "The Dialectic of Double-Consciousness in Black American Freedom Celebrations, 1808–1863," *Journal of Negro History* 67 (Winter 1982): 302–17; and Leonard I. Sweet, "The Fourth of July and Black Americans in the Nineteenth Century: Northern Leadership Opinion within the Context of the Black Experience," *Journal of Negro History* 61 (July 1976): 256–75. Fewer works examine post-emancipation celebrations. See Mitchell Kachun, "'The Faith That the Dark Past Has Taught Us': African-American Commemorations in the North and West and the Construction of a Usable Past 1808–1915" (Ph.D. diss., Cornell University, 1997); and William H. Wiggins Jr., *O Freedom! Afro-American Emancipation Celebrations* (Knoxville: University of Tennessee Press, 1987).

6. *Elevator*, 15 January 1869, quoted in Mitchell Kachun, "A Belief in Their Own Possibilities: African-American Historical Orations, 1863–1913" (paper presented at the Great Lakes History Conference, Grand Rapids, Mich., 7 October 1995), 4; James Weldon Johnson, "Fifty Years," *New York Times*, 1 January 1913.

7. *Richmond Planet*, 12 July 1890, 18 October 1890.

8. Fabre, "African-American Commemorative Celebrations," 86–87; "The Negro Celebration in Washington," *Harper's Weekly*, 12 May 1866, 300; *Richmond Dispatch*, 2 January 1866. For Juneteenth, see Wiggins, *O Freedom!* My usage of the terms "official" and "vernacular" is based on John Bodnar, *Remaking America: Public Memory, Commemoration, and Patriotism in the Twentieth Century* (Princeton: Princeton University Press, 1992), 13–20.

9. This argument is suggested by Kirk Savage, *Standing Soldiers, Kneeling Slaves: Race, War, and Monument in Nineteenth-Century America* (Princeton: Princeton University Press, 1997), 65.

10. *Richmond Dispatch*, 6 July 1880. On other black celebrations in Richmond, see, for example, *Richmond Dispatch*, 2 January 1868, 3 January 1870, 3 January 1871, 2 January 1872, 6 July 1875, 22 February 1870, 23 February 1875, and 24 February 1880; *Richmond Daily Whig*, 2 January 1867; and *New York Times*, 4 April 1866.

11. *Richmond Times*, 4 July 1866, quoted in Robert Pettus Hay, "Freedom's Jubilee: One Hundred Years of the Fourth of July, 1776–1876" (Ph.D. diss., University of Kentucky, 1967), 268–69. On the postwar absence of celebration by white Southerners, see Hay, "Freedom's Jubilee," 267–73.

12. *Richmond Daily Whig,* 2 January 1867; *Richmond Dispatch,* 2 January 1868.

13. *Richmond Dispatch,* 3 January 1870; Peter J. Rachleff, *Black Labor in the South: Richmond, Virginia, 1865–1890,* Class and Culture Series (Philadelphia: Temple University Press, 1984), 41, 61–62. On Walker and Virginia's "redeemers," see C. Vann Woodward, *Reunion and Reaction: The Compromise of 1877 and the End of Reconstruction,* rev. ed. (Boston: Little, Brown and Co., 1966), 41.

14. *Richmond Planet,* 18 October 1890; *Richmond Dispatch,* 17 October 1890. On the 3 April holiday, see *New York Times,* 4 April 1866; and Rachleff, *Black Labor,* 39–41, 49. I could find no mention of this celebration in the Richmond press before the 1890s, but that is probably because the white papers rarely reported on strictly black events, and the black *Richmond Planet* did not exist in the early postwar era. On the Fifteenth Amendment celebrations, see Rachleff, *Black Labor,* 65, 68, 87–88, 127.

15. *Richmond Planet,* 11 October 1890; Rachleff, *Black Labor,* 93–96; C. Vann Woodward, *Origins of the New South, 1877–1913,* new ed., A History of the South, ed. Wendell Holmes Stephenson and E. Merton Coulter, vol. 9 (n.p.: Louisiana State University Press for the Littlefield Fund for Southern History of the University of Texas, 1971), 220. Woodward notes that Richmond hosted an Afro-American League convention in April 1890.

16. *Richmond Planet,* 11 October 1890.

17. *Richmond Planet,* 18 October 1890.

18. Ibid.; *Richmond Dispatch,* 18 October 1890.

19. *Richmond Planet,* 18 October 1890.

20. Ibid.; *Richmond Times,* 17 October 1890. On the accusations against Harrison and on Lily-white Republicanism, see Woodward, *Origins of the New South,* 219–20, 461–64.

21. *Richmond Planet,* 18 October 1890; *Richmond Times,* 17 October 1890.

22. *Richmond Dispatch,* 11 October 1890; *Richmond Times,* 12 October 1890; *Richmond Planet,* 18 October 1890.

23. *Richmond Dispatch,* 12 October 1890, 16 October 1890; *Richmond Times,* 12 October 1890, 16 October 1890.

24. *Richmond Dispatch,* 18 October 1890, 7 October 1890, 18 March 1890.

25. *Richmond Planet,* 11 October 1890; *Richmond Dispatch,* 18 October 1890. I have been unable to determine whether women did, indeed, vote. Only the white newspapers mentioned this incident. All of the main speakers and delegates appear to have been male, which would not have been unusual at that time.

26. *Richmond Planet,* 11 October 1890.

27. *Richmond Times,* 18 October 1890; *Richmond Dispatch,* 16 October 1890, 17 October 1890, 18 October 1890.

28. "The Thirty-Third Anniversary of the Great Emancipation Proclamation, September 22, '96," at Alexandria, Va., broadside, Virginia Historical Society, Richmond.

29. *Richmond Planet*, 11 October 1890, 11 February 1905, 23 March 1918. On the variety of dates celebrated by African Americans, see Wiggins, *O Freedom!*, xvi–xvii.

30. *New York Times*, 1 January 1913; "The Emancipation Jubilee," *Nation*, 9 January 1913, 26–27; *Daily Jewish Courier*, 6 January 1913, in the Chicago Public Library Omnibus Project, comp. and trans., *The Chicago Foreign Language Press Survey* (Chicago, 1942), section III.B.3, "Holidays."

31. David Glassberg, *American Historical Pageantry: The Uses of Tradition in the Early Twentieth Century* (Chapel Hill: University of North Carolina Press, 1990), 132–33; Kachun, "A Belief in Their Own Possibilities," 8–9; Cecilia Elizabeth O'Leary, *To Die For: The Paradox of American Patriotism* (Princeton: Princeton University Press, 1999), 200–203.

32. *Chicago Defender*, 6 January 1912, 17 February 1912.

33. *Chicago Defender*, 15 February 1913.

34. Ibid.

35. Ibid.

36. Kirk Savage, "The Politics of Memory: Black Emancipation and the Civil War Monument," in *Commemorations: The Politics of National Identity*, ed. John R. Gillis (Princeton: Princeton University Press, 1994), 139–40.

3. LABOR'S DAYS

1. *Workingman's Advocate*, 7 July 1866.

2. *Workingman's Advocate*, 1 January 1870, 30 April 1870, 2 February 1874. On the Colored National Labor Union in Richmond, see Peter J. Rachleff, *Black Labor in the South: Richmond, Virginia, 1865–1890*, Class and Culture Series (Philadelphia: Temple University Press, 1984), 61–65, 193–94.

3. David R. Roediger, *The Wages of Whiteness: Race and the Making of the American Working Class*, rev. ed. (London: Verso, 1999), 175–76. Roediger goes so far as to assert that the abolition of slavery "made the eight-hour movement itself possible" (173–74).

4. Ibid., 168–78; Melton Alonza McLaurin, *The Knights of Labor in the South*, Contributions in Labor History, no. 4 (Westport, Conn.: Greenwood Press, 1978), 131–38.

5. On the labor movement in late nineteenth-century America, see David Montgomery, *The Fall of the House of Labor: The Workplace, the State, and American Labor Activism, 1865–1925* (Cambridge: Cambridge University Press, 1987). Works that address particular segments of the labor movement include Bruce C. Nelson, *Beyond the Martyrs: A Social History of Chicago's Anarchists, 1870–1900*, Class and Culture Series (New Brunswick, N.J.: Rutgers University Press, 1988); Leon Fink, *Workingmen's Democracy: The Knights of Labor and American Politics* (Urbana: University of Illinois Press, 1983); McLaurin, *The Knights of Labor in the South*; and Rachleff, *Black Labor*.

6. James R. Barrett, "Americanization from the Bottom Up: Immigration and the Re-making of the Working Class in the United States, 1880–1930," *Journal of American History* 79 (December 1992): 1009–10. In *Wages of Whiteness*, Roediger points out that the bars to black entrance into skilled crafts reinforced the white supremacist views of white workers (178).

7. McLaurin, *The Knights of Labor in the South*; Rachleff, *Black Labor*, chaps. 8–10.

8. Nelson, *Beyond the Martyrs*, 28, 50.

9. Philip S. Foner, *May Day: A Short History of the International Workers' Holiday, 1886–1986* (New York: International Publishers, 1986), 12, 10–15. For accounts of eight-hour meetings, see *Workingman's Advocate*, 21 April 1866 and other issues in 1866 and 1867.

10. *Chicago Tribune*, 2 May 1867. Antebellum trade unions had fought successfully to re-duce working hours from 12 to 10 in many trades; see Foner, *May Day*, 8–9. On the artisan processions, see Sean Wilentz, "Artisan Republican Festivals and the Rise of Class Conflict in New York City, 1788–1837," in *Working-Class America: Essays on Labor, Community, and American Society*, ed. Michael Frisch and Daniel J. Walkowitz, The Working Class in American History (Urbana: University of Illinois Press, 1983), 37–77; and Susan G. Davis, *Parades and Power: Street Theatre in Nineteenth-Century Philadelphia* (Philadelphia: Temple University Press, 1986; Berkeley: University of California Press, 1988), 113–53.

11. *Chicago Tribune*, 2 May 1867.

12. Ibid.

13. Ibid.

14. *Chicago Tribune*, 3 May 1867; Foner, *May Day*, 13–14.

15. For examples of such occasions, see *Workingman's Advocate*, 27 November 1869, 19 October 1872, 26 October 1872, 16 November 1872, 18 January 1873, 8 February 1873, 28 June 1873, and 6 May 1876; Nelson, *Beyond the Martyrs*, 127–52.

16. *Workingman's Advocate*, 7 July 1866. On the rowdy Fourth in antebellum Philadelphia and the efforts of unions to redirect it, see Davis, *Parades and Power*, 42–45.

17. *Chicago Tribune*, 5 July 1876; *Workingman's Advocate*, 12 August 1876.

18. *Chicago Tribune*, 4 July 1876; Philip S. Foner, ed., *We, the Other People* (Urbana: University of Illinois Press, 1976), 99–100. The liberty cap quote is from *The New York Socialist*, 15 July 1876, and is quoted by Foner in *We, the Other People*, 99.

19. Workingmen's Party of Illinois, "Declaration of Independence," quoted in Foner, *We, the Other People*, 100, 102; *Chicago Tribune*, 4 July 1876.

20. Ira Steward, "A Second Declaration of Independence," quoted in Foner, *We, the Other People*, 117–18.

21. *Chicago Daily Socialist*, 26 April 1902, 25 March 1905, 16 March 1909. For more information on the commune festivals in Chicago, see Nelson, *Beyond the Martyrs*, 142–46.

22. Jonathan Grossman, "Who Is the Father of Labor Day?" *Labor History* 14 (Fall 1973): 617–18; Theodore F. Watts, *The First Labor Day Parade, Tuesday, September 5, 1882: Media Mirrors to Labor's Icons* (Silver Spring, Md.: Phoenix Rising, 1983), 28, 26–33; Michael Kazin and Steven J. Ross, "America's Labor Day: The Dilemma of a Workers' Celebration," *Journal of American History* 78 (March 1992): 1299–1302.

23. Watts, *First Labor Day Parade*, 1, 26–33, 56–61; Grossman, "Father of Labor Day." For McGuire's claims, see Peter J. McGuire, "Labor Day—Its Birth and Significance," *American Federationist* 4 (October 1897): 183.

24. For a description of the celebration, see Watts, *First Labor Day Parade*, 41–61.

25. Ibid., 59; Nelson, *Beyond the Martyrs*, 46–47.

26. Grossman, "Father of Labor Day," 621–22.

27. *Chicago Tribune*, 6 September 1885, 8 September 1885. On the founding of the Central Labor Union and its rivalry with the Trades and Labor Assembly, see Nelson, *Beyond the Martyrs*, 40–44.

28. *Chicago Tribune*, 6 September 1885, 8 September 1885.

29. *Chicago Tribune*, 7 September 1885, 8 September 1885.

30. *Chicago Tribune*, 8 September 1885, 7 September 1885.

31. *Chicago Tribune*, 7 September 1885, 8 September 1885.

32. *Chicago Tribune*, 8 September 1885.

33. *Chicago Tribune*, 7 September 1885. Franklin Rosemont discusses the popular image of the anarchist in "A Bomb-Toting, Long-Haired, Wild-Eyed Fiend: The Image of the Anarchist in Popular Culture," in *Haymarket Scrapbook*, ed. Dave Roediger and Franklin Rosemont (Chicago: Charles H. Kerr Publishing, 1986), 203–12. Also see Carl Smith, *Urban Disorder and the Shape of Belief: The Great Chicago Fire, the Haymarket Bomb, and the Model Town of Pullman* (Chicago: University of Chicago Press, 1995), 149–54.

34. *Chicago Tribune*, 6 September 1885; Nelson, *Beyond the Martyrs*, 46–48. On the role of socialists in the American Federation of Labor, see Gerald N. Grob, *Workers and Utopia: A Study of Ideological Conflict in the American Labor Movement, 1865–1900*, Northwestern University Studies in History, no. 2 ([Evanston, Ill.]: Northwestern University Press, 1961), 163–81.

35. Nelson, *Beyond the Martyrs*, 178; Foner, *May Day*, 15–18. For a discussion of May Day as Moving Day in New York City, see Kenneth A. Scherzer, *The Unbounded Community: Neighborhood Life and Social Structure in New York City, 1830–1875* (Durham, N.C.: Duke University Press, 1992), 19–48.

36. "Appeal to All Trade and Labor Unions," 1 February 1886, quoted in Foner, *May Day*, 19.

37. *Chicago Tribune*, 2 May 1886; Nelson, *Beyond the Martyrs*, 178–83.

38. *Chicago Tribune*, 4 May 1886.

39. *Chicago Tribune*, 2 May 1886, 4 May 1886.

40. Foner, *May Day*, 21–22, 27–28; Philip S. Foner, "The Polish-American Martyrs of the First May Day," in *Haymarket Scrapbook*, ed. Dave Roediger and Franklin Rosemont (Chicago: Charles H. Kerr Publishing, 1986), 88–90.

41. Haymarket defendants Michael Schwab, August Spies, Adolph Fisher, George Engel, and Louis Lingg were all born in Germany, and Samuel Fielden emigrated from England. The events of 3 and 4 May are both too well known and too complex to bear retelling here. The best overall account is Paul Avrich, *The Haymarket Tragedy* (Princeton, N.J.: Princeton University Press, 1984). Also see Smith's chapters on Haymarket in *Urban Disorder*, and Nelson, *Beyond the Martyrs*, 184–200.

42. *Chicago Tribune*, 10 November 1890, 26 June 1893, 11 November 1895; Voltairine de Cleyre, "Our Martyred Comrades" (speech delivered in Philadelphia, 17 November 1900), in *The First Mayday: The Haymarket Speeches, 1895–1910*, introduction by Paul Avrich (Orkney, U.K.: Cienfuegos Press; New York: Libertarian Book Club, 1980), 17; Smith, *Urban Disorder*, 170. On the commune festival, see, for example, *Eight-Hour Herald*, 13 February 1896.

43. *Chicago Tribune*, 23 February 1889; Foner, *May Day*, 40.

44. *Chicago Tribune*, 5 July 1889, 3 September 1889, 23 February 1890; Foner, *May Day*, 40.

45. Foner, *May Day*, 42–44; "How It Began," *World Marxist Review* 29 (May 1986): 16–17.

46. *Chicago Tribune*, 2 May 1890.

47. *Chicago Tribune*, 2 May 1890, 2 September 1890, 23 February 1890.

48. *Chicago Tribune*, 2 May 1890, 2 September 1890.

49. Foner, *May Day*, 45–56; *Richmond Dispatch*, 2 May 1890. On the American Federation of Labor and May Day, see, for example, "May and Eight Hours," *American Federationist* 3 (May 1896): 50–51; and "May 1, 1898—Prepare for It," *American Federationist* 4 (May 1897): 52.

50. *Chicago Tribune*, 2 May 1890, 2 May 1891.

51. Grossman, "Father of Labor Day," 621–22; "When Labor Day Became Law," *American Federationist* 9 (September 1902): 536.

52. *Chicago Daily Socialist*, 30 August 1909, 29 August 1903. Kazin and Ross note in "America's Labor Day" (1303) that because many employers refused to give workers the holiday, Labor Day became "a virtual one-day general strike in many cities."

53. *Chicago Daily Socialist*, 29 April 1911.

54. *Chicago Tribune*, 4 September 1900. Also see Kazin and Ross, "America's Labor Day," 1308.

55. *Chicago Tribune*, 3 September 1895, 7 September 1886, 2 May 1891.

56. *Chicago Tribune*, 2 May 1891, 7 September 1886, 2 September 1890, 4 September 1898; *Chicago Daily Socialist*, 3 May 1910.

57. *Chicago Tribune*, 4 September 1898, 3 September 1895; *Tucson Citizen*, 4 September 1905; *Richmond Dispatch*, 2 September 1890, 4 September 1900.

58. *Tucson Citizen*, 4 September 1905; *Chicago Tribune*, 3 September 1895, 2 May 1891; "Labor Day Observance," *American Federationist* 3 (October 1896): 171; *Knights of Labor*, 11 September 1886.

59. On artisan craft enactments in Philadelphia's Grand Federal Procession of 1788, see Davis, *Parades and Power*, 117–25.

60. *Knights of Labor*, 14 August 1886.

61. *Knights of Labor*, 11 September 1886; *Richmond Dispatch*, 31 August 1890. On the Gold Dust Twins and other uses of African Americans in advertising in this era, see Grace Elizabeth Hale, *Making Whiteness: The Culture of Segregation in the South, 1890–1940* (New York: Pantheon Books, 1998), 162–64, 166–67.

62. *Chicago Tribune*, 6 September 1886, 7 September 1886.

63. *Tucson Citizen*, 4 September 1905. On the deemphasis of production in the emerging consumer culture, see William Leach, *Land of Desire: Merchants, Power, and the Rise of a New American Culture* (New York: Random House, 1993), 147–50; and Susan Strasser, *Satisfaction Guaranteed: The Making of the American Mass Market* (Washington, D.C.: Smithsonian Institution Press, 1995), 15–16.

64. *Chicago Tribune*, 7 September 1886, 5 September 1893.

65. *Chicago Tribune*, 2 September 1890, 5 September 1892.

66. *Chicago Tribune*, 2 May 1895, 2 September 1895; *Chicago Daily Socialist*, 3 May 1910; Foner, *May Day*, 71, 79.

67. *Chicago Daily Socialist*, 3 May 1910; *Chicago Tribune*, 2 May 1891.

68. *Chicago Tribune*, 2 September 1890, 4 September 1898.

69. *Chicago Tribune*, 2 September 1890, 4 September 1900.

70. *Chicago Tribune*, 19 September 1892, 5 September 1892; *Chicago Daily Socialist*, 29 August 1903.

71. *Chicago Daily Socialist*, 30 August 1902, 19 April 1902, 6 September 1902, 1 August 1903.

72. *Richmond Dispatch*, 4 September 1900; *Chicago Tribune*, 7 September 1886, 2 September 1895, 3 September 1895, 2 May 1891, 4 September 1898, 4 September 1900; *Chicago Daily Socialist*, 23 August 1902, 7 September 1910, 6 September 1910.

73. *Chicago Daily Socialist*, 7 September 1910. On the ethnicity of members of Chicago's trade unions, the Knights of Labor, the Socialist Labor Party, and the International Working People's Association in the mid-1880s, see Nelson, *Beyond the Martyrs*, 29 (table 2.1), 87 (table 4.3).

74. *Chicago Tribune*, 4 September 1900; *Nashville Banner*, 2 September 1892. On this development, also see Kazin and Ross, "America's Labor Day," 1306–8.

75. *Chicago Tribune*, 6 September 1887; Charles E. Adams, Diary, 4 vols., 3: 5 September 1887, box 64, document 258, Downs Collection, Henry Francis DuPont du Winterthur Library, Winterthur, Del.; *Richmond Dispatch*, 31 August 1890, 2 September 1890; *Tucson Citizen*, 30 August 1905.

76. *Chicago Daily Socialist*, 3 September 1909, 8 September 1909, 6 September 1910.
77. *Chicago Daily Socialist*, 14 February 1910, 19 July 1910; *Chicago Tribune*, 2 September 1890; *Richmond Dispatch*, 3 September 1895; *Richmond Times-Dispatch*, 5 September 1910, 6 September 1910.

4. ETHNIC HOLIDAYS

1. *Dziennik Zwiazkowy*, 19 December 1911, in the Chicago Public Library Omnibus Project, comp. and trans., *The Chicago Foreign Language Press Survey* (Chicago, 1942), section III.B.3, "Holidays" (hereafter cited as *CFLPS*).
2. Kathleen Neils Conzen, David A. Gerber, Ewa Morawska, George E. Pozzetta, and Rudolph J. Vecoli, "The Invention of Ethnicity: A Perspective from the U.S.A.," *Journal of American Ethnic History* 12 (Fall 1992): 3–41. Matthew Frye Jacobson provides a comprehensive examination of how immigrant nationalists built loyalties to the homeland in *Special Sorrows: The Diasporic Imagination of Irish, Polish, and Jewish Immigrants in the United States* (Cambridge: Harvard University Press, 1995).
3. On the construction of nationalism, the best starting points are Benedict Anderson, *Imagined Communities: Reflections on the Origins and Spread of Nationalism* (London: Verso, 1983); and Eric J. Hobsbawm, *Nations and Nationalism since 1780: Programme, Myth, Reality* (Cambridge: Cambridge University Press, 1990). Also helpful on the creation of a unique national heritage is David Lowenthal, "Identity, Heritage, and History," in *Commemorations: The Politics of National Identity*, ed. John R. Gillis (Princeton: Princeton University Press, 1994), 41–57.
4. Conzen, Gerber, Morawska, Pozzetta, and Vecoli, "Invention of Ethnicity," 5–6; April R. Schultz, *Ethnicity on Parade: Inventing the Norwegian American through Celebration* (Amherst: University of Massachusetts Press, 1994), 103–7.
5. Hobsbawm, *Nations and Nationalism*, 117–22; John Bodnar, *Remaking America: Public Memory, Commemoration, and Patriotism in the Twentieth Century* (Princeton: Princeton University Press, 1992), 15–16. On the middle-class nature of nationalism for particular ethnic groups, see Kerby A. Miller, "Class, Culture, and Immigrant Group Identity in the United States: The Case of Irish-American Ethnicity," in *Immigration Reconsidered: History, Society, and Politics*, ed. Virginia Yans-McLaughlin (New York: Oxford University Press, 1990), 96–129; Kathleen Neils Conzen, "Ethnicity as Festive Culture: Nineteenth-Century German America on Parade," in *The Invention of Ethnicity*, ed. Werner Sollors (New York: Oxford University Press, 1989), 44–76; Victor Greene, *For God and Country: The Rise of Polish and Lithuanian Ethnic Consciousness in America, 1860–1910* (Madison: State Historical Society of Wisconsin, 1975); and Schultz, *Ethnicity on Parade*. On the middle-class nature of these organizations, see John Bodnar, *The Transplanted: A History of Immigrants in Urban America* (Blooming-

ton: Indiana University Press, 1985), 120–30; and Conzen, "Ethnicity as Festive Culture," 49–59.

6. Jacobson, *Special Sorrows*, 57–64; Sally M. Miller, ed., *The Ethnic Press in the United States: A Historical Analysis and Handbook* (New York: Greenwood Press, 1987), xv.

7. Greene, *For God and Country*, 10–12.

8. Hobsbawm, *Nations and Nationalism*, 124–26. As Olivier Zunz has pointed out, the relationship between class and ethnicity remains largely unexamined ("American History and the Changing Meaning of Assimilation," *Journal of American Ethnic History* 4 [Spring 1985]: 53–72). Also see Bodnar, *The Transplanted*, 119–20.

9. Roland L. Guyotte and Barbara M. Posadas, "Celebrating Rizal Day: The Emergence of a Filipino Tradition in Twentieth-Century Chicago," in *Feasts and Celebrations in North American Ethnic Communities*, ed. Ramón Gutiérrez and Geneviève Fabre (Albuquerque: University of New Mexico Press, 1995), 111–27; *The Reform Advocate*, 17 April 1891, CFLPS.

10. Eric Hobsbawm discusses this process of appropriation in the development of Swiss nationalism in "Introduction: Inventing Traditions," in *The Invention of Tradition*, ed. Eric J. Hobsbawm and Terence Ranger (Cambridge: Cambridge University Press, 1983), 6–7. Also see Hobsbawm, *Nations and Nationalism*, 103–4; and Bodnar, *The Transplanted*, 46–49.

11. The reference to "German national games" was found in *Richmond Dispatch*, 7 October 1890, which describes "chicken-pulling" (the German name was *handseldagen*) as a game wherein "a live rooster and goose is [sic] placed under an inverted flower pot." Blindfolded children then attempted to hit the pot with a stick, thereby winning "the prize that is under it." On the Irish sports, see Michael F. Funchion, comp., *Irish American Voluntary Organizations* (Westport, Conn.: Greenwood Press, 1983), s.v. "Gaelic Athletic Association," by Patrick Hennessy. On the Highland games, see Rowland Tappan Berthoff, *British Immigrants in Industrial America, 1790–1950* (Cambridge: Harvard University Press, 1953), 151–52, 167–68. Hugh Trevor-Roper presents a fascinating analysis of the invention of the Highland tradition in "The Invention of Tradition: The Highland Tradition of Scotland," in *Invention of Tradition*, ed. Eric J. Hobsbawm and Terence Ranger (Cambridge: Cambridge University Press, 1983), 15–41.

12. On the link between the development of national languages and nationalism, see Hobsbawm, *Nations and Nationalism*, 103–8, 110–19; and Anderson, *Imagined Communities*, 41–49. On the revival and national symbolism of Gaelic and Hebrew, see Hobsbawm, *Nations and Nationalism*, 54, 106–7, 110, 112–13; Funchion, *Irish American Voluntary Organizations*, s.v. "Gaelic League"; and Rivka Shpak Lissak, *Pluralism and Progressives: Hull House and the New Immigrants, 1890–1919* (Chicago: University of Chicago Press, 1989), 83–87.

13. *Skandinaven*, 18 May 1911, CFLPS; *Richmond Times-Dispatch*, 18 March 1905.

14. *Scandia*, 17 May 1912, CFLPS; *Dziennik Zwiazkowy*, 2 May 1908, CFLPS; Norman Davies, *Heart of Europe: A Short History of Poland*, corrected edition (Oxford: Oxford University Press, 1986), 251, 310–11.

15. Tony Bennett, *The Birth of the Museum: History, Theory, Politics* (London: Routledge, 1995), 149; Hobsbawm, *Nations and Nationalism*, 73–74; Davies, *Heart of Europe*, 168–69, 311, 331–36; Funchion, *Irish American Voluntary Organizations*, s.v. "Ancient Order of Hibernians in America"; Greene, *For God and Country*, 21–23.

16. *Skandinaven*, 4 April [17 May?] 1910, CFLPS; *Chicago Tribune*, 18 March 1895.

17. *Chicago Tribune*, 1 December 1900. On the gymnastics movement, see Eric Pumroy and Katja Rampelmann, "Historical Overview of the Turner Movement in the United States," in *Research Guide to the Turner Movement in the United States*, comp. Eric Pumroy and Katja Rampelmann, Bibliographies and Indexes in American History, no. 33 (Westport, Conn.: Greenwood Press, 1996), xvii–xxvii; and Donald E. Pienkos, *One Hundred Years Young: A History of the Polish Falcons of America, 1887–1987* (Boulder, Colo.: East European Monographs, distributed by Columbia University Press, 1987).

18. Guyotte and Posadas,"Celebrating Rizal Day," 111; Anderson, *Imagined Communities*, 132.

19. *Dziennik Chicagoski*, 5 January 1894, 25 April 1894, CFLPS; *El Fronterizo*, 24 September 1887.

20. *Chicago Tribune*, 18 March 1895; Funchion, *Irish American Voluntary Organizations*, s.v. "United Irish Societies of Chicago," by John Corrigan; *Greek Star*, 3 April 1908, CFLPS.

21. *Chicago Tribune*, 5 September 1887; *Dziennik Chicagoski*, 27 April 1894, CFLPS.

22. *Daily Jewish Courier*, 21 July 1919, CFLPS; *Chicago Tribune*, 18 May 1890; *Las Dos Repúblicas*, 23 September 1877 (author's translation); *El Fronterizo*, 24 September 1887.

23. *El Fronterizo*, 24 September 1887, 10 September 1887 (author's translation); *Denní Hlasatel*, 6 July 1915, CFLPS; *Chicago Tribune*, 28 October 1892, CFLPS.

24. *Sunday Jewish Courier*, 18 May 1919, CFLPS; *Dziennik Chicagoski*, 12 May 1894, CFLPS; *Dziennik Zwiazkowy*, 4 December 1916, CFLPS.

25. *Dziennik Zwiazkowy*, 6 December 1916, CFLPS; *Skandinaven*, 18 May 1911, CFLPS; *Dziennik Chicagoski*, 3 January 1895, CFLPS.

26. *Chicago Record Herald*, 18 May 1905, CFLPS; *Dziennik Zwiazkowy*, 11 October 1917, CFLPS. On bourgeois codes of conduct in public spaces, see Bennett, *Birth of the Museum*, 27–28, 51–53.

27. For a full account of this conflict, see Ellen M. Litwicki,"From *Patrón* to *Patria*: The Nationalization of *Mexicano* Culture in Late Nineteenth-Century Tucson," *Cañon* 4 (Fall 1998): 31–56.

28. *Las Dos Repúblicas*, 9 September 1877 (author's translation); *Tucson Arizona Daily Star*, 29 August 1880.

29. *El Fronterizo*, 24 September 1887 (author's translation); *Tucson Arizona Daily Star*, 14 September 1890; Arizona Territorial Legislature, *Journals of the Sixteenth Legislative Assembly of the Territory of Arizona, 1891* (Phoenix: Herald Book and Job Office, 1891), Council Proceedings, 20 January 1891, 22 January 1891, 29 January 1891, 6 February 1891. On the adverse relationship between gambling and bourgeois morality, see Ann Fabian, *Card Sharps, Dream Books, and Bucket Shops: Gambling in 19th-Century America* (Ithaca, N.Y.: Cornell University Press, 1990), chap. 1. John Findlay has argued that attacks on western gaming emerged as frontier towns took on the trappings of "civilization," most particularly meaning bourgeois morality (*People of Chance: Gambling in American Society from Jamestown to Las Vegas* [New York: Oxford University Press, 1986], 79–100).

30. In 1887, for example, *El Fronterizo* published a list of contributors and the amounts of their donations (24 September 1887). This summary is based on my reading of holiday accounts in *El Fronterizo, Las Dos Repúblicas, Tucson Arizona Daily Star*, and *Tucson Arizona Weekly Citizen*, between 1871 and 1900. Lists of *junta* members were found in *Las Dos Repúblicas*, 26 August 1877 and 31 August 1878; and in *El Fronterizo*, 26 September 1884, 20 August 1887, and 10 August 1889. Occupational data were drawn from Thomas E. Sheridan, *Los Tucsonenses: The Mexican Community in Tucson 1854–1941* (Tucson: University of Arizona Press, 1986), 94–97, 100–102, 109, 114–17; and *Tucson and Tombstone General and Business Directory, for 1883 and 1884* (Tucson: Cobler and Co., 1883; microfilm 5449 by New Haven, Conn.: Research Publications, 1975).

31. *Tucson Arizona Daily Star*, 17 September 1887, 17 September 1879; *El Fronterizo*, 24 September 1887 (author's translation); *Las Dos Repúblicas*, 16 September 1877 (author's translation). Some liberals had even proposed naming an heir of Montezuma II to be emperor, and the Mexican shield they adopted featured the eagle and serpent of Aztec legend. See Victor Alba, "Mexico's Several Independences," in *Mexico: From Independence to Revolution, 1810–1910*, ed. W. Dirk Raat (Lincoln: University of Nebraska Press, 1982), 14–15.

32. In Mexico bourgeois community leaders transformed local fiestas into more wholesome paeans to bourgeois values and capitalist progress; see, for example, Steven Bunker, "From 'Where Is My Boy Tonight?' to 'The Great Fiesta': The Santa Rita Fiesta in Porfirian Chihuahua" (paper presented at the annual meeting of the Rocky Mountain Council for Latin American Studies, Fort Worth, Tex., February 1994). In the United States religious feasts remained particularly vibrant among Italian Americans. See, for example, Robert Anthony Orsi, *The Madonna of 115th Street: Faith and Community in Italian Harlem, 1880–1950* (New Haven: Yale University Press, 1985).

33. *Chicago Tribune*, 3 May 1891.

34. Ibid.

35. Ibid.; *Dziennik Chicagoski*, 13 May 1891, CFLPS.

36. *Chicago Tribune*, 3 May 1891; *Dziennik Chicagoski*, 6–8 May 1891, CFLPS; *Illinois Staats-Zeitung*, 5 May 1891, CFLPS.

37. *Chicago Tribune*, 3 May 1891. On the demise of the 3 May constitution, see Davies, *Heart of Europe*, 308–11.

38. *Dziennik Chicagoski*, 10 May 1892, CFLPS. The best discussion of the religionist-nationalist debate within American Polonia, and particularly in Chicago, is Greene's in *For God and Country*, 66–142. Also see John J. Bukowczyk, *And My Children Did Not Know Me: A History of the Polish-Americans* (Bloomington: Indiana University Press, 1987), 45–48. The descriptive terms are Greene's (10–11).

39. *Dziennik Chicagoski*, 24 April 1891, CFLPS. The *Zgoda* critique was discussed in *Dziennik Chicagoski*; I was unable to find the original *Zgoda* article.

40. *Dziennik Chicagoski*, 13 May 1891, 6–8 May 1891, CFLPS. The Polish National Alliance criticized the quality of the Catholic schools and sought to have Polish offered in public schools. See Lissak, *Pluralism and Progressives*, 135–36; Bodnar, *The Transplanted*, 157–58.

41. *Dziennik Chicagoski*, 2 December 1895, 27 November 1895, CFLPS.

42. *Denni Hlasatel*, 4 June 1915, 6 July 1915, 7 July 1915, CFLPS; Stephan Thernstrom, ed., *Harvard Encyclopedia of American Ethnic Groups* (Cambridge: Harvard University Press, Belknap Press, 1980), s.v. "Czechs," by Karen Johnson Freeze.

43. *Chicago Tribune*, 17 March 1867, 19 March 1867, 18 March 1870. On the Young Ireland Rebellion and the Fenians, see Funchion, *Irish American Voluntary Organizations*, s.v. "Fenian Brotherhood," by James W. Hurst.

44. *Chicago Tribune*, 5 March 1878; Funchion, *Irish American Voluntary Organizations*, s.v. "Clan na Gael," "United Irish Societies"; Thomas J. Rowland, "Irish-American Catholics and the Quest for Respectability in the Coming of the Great War, 1900–1917," *Journal of American Ethnic History* 15 (Winter 1996): 3–31.

45. *Chicago Tribune*, 18 March 1885; Funchion, *Irish American Voluntary Organizations*, s.v. "Ancient Order of Hibernians." On the Catholic domination of St. Patrick's Day, see *Chicago Tribune*, 18 March 1870, 18 March 1890, 17 March 1895, and 18 March 1895. Colleen McDannell discusses the clergy's role in redirecting male leisure and spirituality and its effect on St. Patrick's Day celebrations in "'True Men as We Need Them': Catholicism and the Irish-American Male," *American Studies* 27 (1986): 19–36.

46. *Chicago Tribune*, 14 July 1871. On this and other Boyne Day battles, also see Berthoff, *British Immigrants*, 189–93.

47. *Skandinaven*, 18 May 1911, CFLPS; *Scandia*, 17 June 1911, CFLPS.

48. *Skandinaven*, 20 May 1900, CFLPS. For examples of the separate Irish celebrations, see *Chicago Tribune*, 18 March 1890 and 5 March 1895. On the split within the republican movement, see Funchion, *Irish American Voluntary Organizations*, "Clan na Gael"

and "Ancient Order of Hibernians"; Michael F. Funchion, "The Political and Nationalist Dimensions," in *The Irish in Chicago*, ed. Lawrence J. McCaffrey, Ellen Skerrett, Michael F. Funchion, and Charles Fanning (Urbana: University of Illinois Press, 1987), 61–97.

49. *Chicago Tribune*, 3 May 1891; *Denní Hlasatel*, 6 July 1915, CFLPS; *Illinois Staats-Zeitung*, 30 May 1871, CFLPS. My conclusions on the lack of unions in ethnic holiday processions are based on my reading of holiday accounts in Chicago, Richmond, and Tucson newspapers between the 1870s and 1910s.

50. *Chicago Daily Socialist*, 15 March 1902, 22 April 1905, 6 May 1905, 13 January 1906, 20 January 1906, 27 January 1906, 27 April 1910, 28 April 1910; *Forward*, 19 April 1920, 1 May 1921, CFLPS.

51. *Il Proletario* (Philadelphia), 21 July 1907, CFLPS.

52. *La Parola Dei Socialisti*, 10 July 1909, CFLPS.

53. *La Parola Dei Socialisti*, 27 September 1913, CFLPS; *Chicagoer Arbeiter-Zeitung*, 1 May 1889, CFLPS.

54. *Dziennik Chicagoski*, 2 December 1895, CFLPS.

55. See, for example, *Tucson Arizona Daily Citizen*, 15 September 1900; *Tucson Citizen*, 18 September 1905 and 12 September 1920; and *El Tucsonense*, 14 September 1918 and 14 September 1920.

56. *Svornost*, 7 July 1880, CFLPS; *Denní Hlasatel*, 6 August 1906, CFLPS.

57. *Richmond Dispatch*, 13 September 1895, 7 October 1890.

58. *Chicago Tribune*, 18 March 1895; Resolution of Thanks, Irish Fellowship Club to President Taft, 2 April 1910, photocopy, and Line of March, 17 March 1910, typescript, Roger T. Faherty Papers, box 1, folder 1, Chicago Historical Society, Chicago.

59. Speech of Michael J. Faherty at Irish Fellowship Club's St. Patrick's Day Celebration, 17 March 1910, typescript, Faherty Papers, box 1, folder 1; *Richmond Dispatch*, 7 October 1890.

60. *Richmond Times-Dispatch*, 18 March 1910; *Skandinaven*, 20 May 1915, CFLPS.

61. *Skandinaven*, 18 May 1911, CFLPS; *Chicago Hebrew Institute Observer*, no. 6, 1913/14, quoted in Lissak, *Pluralism and Progressives*, 87.

62. *Chicago Tribune*, 4 May 1894; *El Fronterizo*, 18 September 1885 (author's translation).

63. *Tucson Arizona Daily Star*, 18 September 1887; *El Fronterizo*, 24 September 1887 (author's translation); *Skandinaven*, 4 April [17 May?] 1910, CFLPS.

64. Lissak, *Pluralism and Progressives*, 136–38.

65. *Skandinaven*, 20 May 1915, 9 July 1878, CFLPS; *Dziennik Zwiazkowy*, 15 June 1908, CFLPS.

66. *Sunday Jewish Courier*, 22 February 1914, CFLPS. On the centennial in Chicago, see *Chicago Tribune*, 4 July 1876 and 5 July 1876. For a more extensive analysis of ethnic celebrations of American holidays, see Ellen M. Litwicki, "'Our Hearts Burn with

Ardent Love for Two Countries': Ethnicity and Assimilation at Chicago Holiday Celebrations, 1876–1918," *Journal of American Ethnic History* 19 (Spring 2000): 3–34.

67. *L'Italia,* 27 June 1920, CFLPS.

68. See, for example, *Dziennik Chicagoski,* 13 February 1896, CFLPS; *Dziennik Zwiazkowy,* 10 February 1917, CFLPS; and *Chicago Tribune,* 5 July 1890 and 4 July 1895.

69. Schultz, *Ethnicity on Parade,* 104–7.

70. *Dziennik Zwiazkowy,* 15 June 1908, CFLPS; *Dziennik Chicagoski,* 9 May 1896, CFLPS; *Chicago Tribune,* 5 July 1890.

71. *Denní Hlasatel,* 31 May 1915, CFLPS.

72. *Tucson Arizona Daily Star,* 18 September 1887. For a similar comment, see ibid., 17 September 1890. None of the addresses, editorials, or holiday articles I have seen, whether the work of Mexican or European Americans, so much as mentioned the war between the United States and Mexico in the 1840s, even when recounting Mexico's history.

73. *Dziennik Chicagoski,* 4 May 1894, CLFPS; *Chicago Tribune,* 5 July 1889.

5. PATRIOTIC HOLIDAYS AND CIVIC EDUCATION

1. *Chicago Tribune,* 31 May 1889; William J. Adelman, "The True Story behind the Haymarket Police Statue," in *Haymarket Scrapbook,* ed. Dave Roediger and Franklin Rosemont (Chicago: Charles H. Kerr Publishing, 1986), 167–68; Carl Smith, *Urban Disorder and the Shape of Belief: The Great Chicago Fire, the Haymarket Bomb, and the Model Town of Pullman* (Chicago: University of Chicago Press, 1995), 170.

2. *Chicago Tribune,* 31 May 1889; Smith, *Urban Disorder,* 126; Adelman, "The True Story behind the Haymarket Police Statue," 167; Franklin Rosemont, "A Bomb-Toting, Long-Haired, Wild-Eyed Fiend: The Image of the Anarchist in Popular Culture," in *Haymarket Scrapbook,* ed. Dave Roediger and Franklin Rosemont (Chicago: Charles H. Kerr Publishing, 1986), 205; Bruce C. Nelson, *Beyond the Martyrs: A Social History of Chicago's Anarchists, 1870–1900,* Class and Culture Series (New Brunswick, N.J.: Rutgers University Press, 1988), 184–86, 188–89. On Medill's antilabor proclivities, see Stephen Longstreet, *Chicago, 1860–1919* (New York: David McKay Co., 1973), 232–38.

3. *Chicago Tribune,* 26 June 1893; William J. Adelman, "The Haymarket Monument at Waldheim," in *Haymarket Scrapbook,* ed. Dave Roediger and Franklin Rosemont (Chicago: Charles H. Kerr Publishing, 1986), 171.

4. Lucy E. Parsons, *The Industrial Worker,* 1 May 1912, in *Haymarket Scrapbook,* ed. Dave Roediger and Franklin Rosemont (Chicago: Charles H. Kerr Publishing, 1986), 183; Voltairine de Cleyre, "November Eleventh, Twenty Years Ago" (speech delivered in New York, 11 November 1907), in *The First Mayday: The Haymarket Speeches, 1895–1910,*

introduction by Paul Avrich (Orkney, UK: Cienfuegos Press; New York: Libertarian Book Club, 1980), 39. For examples of commemorations, see *Chicago Tribune*, 10 November 1890 and 12 November 1895; and Jay Fox, "Martyrs' Day in Chicago," *Free Society*, 5 December 1897, in *Haymarket Scrapbook*, ed. Dave Roediger and Franklin Rosemont (Chicago: Charles H. Kerr Publishing, 1986), 186–87.

5. *Chicago Tribune*, 1 July 1890, 3 July 1890, 4 July 1890, 31 May 1894, 30 May 1895, 31 May 1895, 4 July 1895, 5 July 1895; *Richmond Dispatch*, 4 July 1895, 5 July 1895; *Tucson Arizona Daily Star*, 6 July 1895; *Tucson Citizen*, 4 July 1905. On the diversity of late nineteenth-century celebrations, see Ellen M. Litwicki, "Visions of America: Public Holidays and American Cultures, 1776–1900" (Ph.D. diss., University of Virginia, 1992), 132–67; and David Glassberg, *American Historical Pageantry: The Uses of Tradition in the Early Twentieth Century* (Chapel Hill: University of North Carolina Press, 1990), 20–26.

6. Smith, *Urban Disorder*, 15. On the formation of the late nineteenth-century elite, see E. Digby Baltzell, *The Protestant Establishment: Aristocracy and Caste in America* (New York: Random House, 1964), 1–21, 110–39. On the reshaping of public behavior in this period, see Paul Boyer, *Urban Masses and Moral Order in America, 1820–1920* (Cambridge: Harvard University Press, 1978), 121–87; Lawrence W. Levine, *Highbrow Lowbrow: The Emergence of Cultural Hierarchy in America* (Cambridge: Harvard University Press, 1988), 184–200; Tony Bennett, *The Birth of the Museum: History, Theory, Politics* (London: Routledge, 1995), 27–28, 51–53; and James Gilbert, *Perfect Cities: Chicago's Utopias of 1893* (Chicago: University of Chicago Press, 1991), 28–40.

7. "Constitution Day," *Century*, December 1887, 327.

8. Ibid.; Eric J. Hobsbawm, "Mass-Producing Traditions: Europe, 1870–1914," in *The Invention of Tradition*, ed. Eric J. Hobsbawm and Terence Ranger (Cambridge: Cambridge University Press, 1983), 263–64. Apparently Constitution Day did make a comeback at the hands of patriotic organizations in the wake of World War I; see Richard M. Fried, *The Russians Are Coming! The Russians Are Coming! Pageantry and Patriotism in Cold-War America* (New York: Oxford University Press, 1998), 7. The difficulty of fitting the Constitution into celebratory forms has been apparent most recently in the contrast between the muted celebration of the bicentennial of the Constitution and the extravaganzas staged for the bicentennial of independence and the centennial of the Statue of Liberty.

9. *The Chicago Clubs Illustrated* (Chicago: Lanward Publishing Co., 1888), 55. On the composition of this elite in Chicago, see Smith, *Urban Disorder*, 13–15; and Gilbert, *Perfect Cities*, 36–43. I was able to find biographical information for fifty-one men who served on the committees organizing one or more of these celebrations. Of these men, thirty-nine were native born and eleven were foreign born (mostly German and Irish). For those for whom religious affiliations could be determined, six-

teen were Protestant, two were Catholic, and four were Jewish. Of those whose political affiliations were listed, twenty were Republicans and six were Democrats. Of
these men, twenty-one were the president or owner of their companies; nine were
financiers, nine were attorneys, and eleven were in retail or wholesale merchandising.
Almost half (twenty-four) belonged to the Union League Club. Biographical information was found in *The Biographical Dictionary and Portrait Gallery of Representative
Men of Chicago, Wisconsin, and the World's Columbian Exposition* (Chicago: American
Biographical Publishing Co., 1895); John J. Flinn, ed., *The Hand-Book of Chicago Biog-
raphy* (Chicago: Standard Guide Co., 1893); German Press Club of Chicago, comp.,
Prominent Citizens and Industries of Chicago (Chicago: German Press Club, 1901);
Charles Ffrench, ed., *Biographical History of the American Irish in Chicago* (Chicago:
American Biographical Publishing Co., 1897); and *Centennial History of the City of
Chicago, Its Men and Institutions* (Chicago: Inter Ocean, 1905).

10. Flinn, *Hand-Book of Chicago Biography*, s.v. "Hutchinson, Charles"; "Chicago Biographies and Miscellaneous Articles from the *Chicago Tribune* 1900–01," bound typescript, Newberry Library, Chicago; *Biographical Dictionary*, s.v. "Keith, Elbridge." Paul
Boyer discusses the "civic-uplift" zeal that swept American cities in the 1890s in *Urban
Masses*, 162–66. On cultural philanthropy in Chicago in the late nineteenth century,
see Kathleen D. McCarthy, *Noblesse Oblige: Charity and Cultural Philanthropy in Chicago,
1849–1929* (Chicago: University of Chicago Press, 1982), 64–67, 75–77, 84–95.

11. On the relationship between the elite and the middle class in late nineteenth-century
Chicago, see Gilbert, *Perfect Cities*, 4–11; and Smith, *Urban Disorder*, 13.

12. *Chicago Tribune*, 23 February 1887; "Holidays," *North American Review*, April 1857,
353–54, 363. On the Law and Order League, see Alfred T. Andreas, *History of Chicago*,
vol. 3, *From the Fire of 1871 until 1885* (Chicago: A. T. Andreas, 1886; reprint, New York:
Arno Press, 1975), 288–89; and Smith, *Urban Disorder*, 108.

13. *Chicago Tribune*, 23 February 1887; *Union League Club. Exercises in Commemoration of the
Birthday of Washington, February 22, 1889* (Chicago: P. F. Pettibone and Co., 1889), 49.

14. Adelman, "The True Story behind the Haymarket Police Statue," 167; *Centennial History of the City of Chicago*, 266–67.

15. *The Nation's Birthday: Chicago's Centennial Celebration of Washington's Inauguration, April
30, 1889* (Chicago: Slason Thompson and Co., 1890), 4, 11, 5.

16. Ibid., 21.

17. Ibid., 14 (emphasis in original), 16–17. For descriptions of the exercises held in various schools, see ibid., 107–53; and *Chicago Tribune*, 1 May 1889.

18. *Nation's Birthday*, 146, 111.

19. Ibid., 159–68.

20. Ibid., 285–86; *Chicago Tribune*, 1 May 1889.

21. *Chicago Tribune*, 1 May 1889.

22. *Nation's Birthday* lists all the committees and their members (317–25). Occupational data were found in *The Lakeside Directory of Chicago, 1889* (Chicago: Chicago Directory Co., 1889).

23. *Nation's Birthday,* 6–7.

24. Ibid., 8, 10. The book does not provide an accounting of individual subscribers, making it impossible to tell how many small subscriptions came from working-class or ethnic Chicagoans.

25. Ibid., 105, 167; *Chicago Tribune,* 1 May 1889.

26. *Nation's Birthday,* 183–84.

27. Ibid., 131.

28. Ibid., 214, 137, 199.

29. Ibid., 211, 167, 248–49. Occupational data on speakers were determined from titles and from the *Lakeside Directory, 1889.*

30. *Nation's Birthday,* 245, 106.

31. Ibid., 237.

32. *Chicagoer Arbeiter-Zeitung,* 1 May 1889, in the Chicago Public Library Omnibus Project, comp. and trans., *The Chicago Foreign Language Press Survey* (Chicago, 1942), section III.B.3, "Holidays" (hereafter cited as *CFLPS*); *Chicago Tribune,* 1 May 1889. Chicago's total population in 1890 was 1,099,850. The adult population (twenty-one and over) was estimated at about 60 percent of the total, based on figures from *School Census of the City of Chicago, 1884* and *Report of the School Census Taken May, 1908.*

33. *Nation's Birthday,* 146, 153; *Chicago Tribune,* 1 May 1889, 2 May 1889.

34. On the competition for the exposition, see Robert W. Rydell, *All the World's a Fair: Visions of Empire at American International Expositions, 1876–1916* (Chicago: University of Chicago Press, 1984), 42; and Finis Farr, *Chicago: A Personal History of America's Most American City* (New Rochelle, N.Y.: Arlington House, 1973), 166. The celebration was held on 21 October rather than 12 October because New York had decided to stage a huge celebration on the former date. The incensed directors persuaded Congress to change the official date of the anniversary to 21 October, the actual anniversary of Columbus's landfall by the Gregorian calendar (*World's Fair Notes,* issued by the Department of Publicity and Promotion, World's Columbian Exposition, 12 August 1892; *Statutes at Large,* 52nd Congress, Session 1, chap. 374 [1892]). Unlike Washington's Birthday, which had earlier been changed to the new calendar date of 22 February, the change of date for Columbus Day did not stick.

35. *Chicago Tribune,* 21 October 1892; *Dedicatory and Opening Ceremonies of the World's Columbian Exposition,* Memorial Volume (Chicago: Stone, Kastler and Painter, 1893), 245–46.

36. *Chicago Tribune,* 21 October 1892, 24 September 1892.

37. *Chicago Tribune,* 21 October 1892. Of the forty-six men on the committee on ceremonies, only one was not also on the exposition's board of directors. A list of board
and committee members is found in *Dedicatory and Opening Ceremonies,* 294. Occupational data on the members were drawn from *Biographical Dictionary;* German
Press Club, *Prominent Citizens and Industries;* Flinn, *Hand-Book of Chicago Biography;*
Ffrench, *Biographical History of the American Irish;* and *The Lakeside Directory of Chicago,
1892* (Chicago: R. R. Donnelly and Sons, 1892).

38. On these protests, see Rydell, *All the World's a Fair,* 52–53. At the time of the protests,
Ida B. Wells-Barnett was known as Ida B. Wells. She married Ferdinand L. Barnett
in 1895.

39. *Chicago Tribune,* 19 September 1892. The vote was 119 to 40.

40. *Chicago Tribune,* 15 February 1888, 12 February 1900, 13 February 1900. For other accounts of Lincoln celebrations in Chicago, see *Chicago Tribune,* 13 February 1889,
13 February 1890, 13 February 1892, and 13 February 1895.

41. Francis G. Blair, comp., *The One Hundredth Anniversary of the Birth of Abraham Lincoln*
(Springfield: Illinois State Journal Co., 1908), 3; Nathan William MacChesney, ed.,
Abraham Lincoln: The Tribute of a Century, 1809–1909 (Chicago: A. C. McClurg and
Co., 1910), 4–5, 9.

42. MacChesney, *Abraham Lincoln,* xxv, xxiii; *Tucson Citizen,* 12 February 1909.

43. *Richmond Times-Dispatch,* 13 February 1909. Virginia had made Lee's birthday a state
holiday in 1890, for instance; *Richmond Dispatch,* 22 February 1890. For celebrations
of Confederate heroes in Virginia, see *Richmond Dispatch,* 20 January 1891, 20 January
1895, and 20 January 1900; and *Richmond Times-Dispatch,* 20 January 1905, 4 June 1905,
20 January 1910, and 4 June 1910.

44. "President Abraham Lincoln," *Confederate Veteran* 17 (April 1909): 153–55.

45. *Richmond Times-Dispatch,* 13 February 1909; MacChesney, *Abraham Lincoln,* 6.

46. Rev. J. W. E. Bowen, "The Liberation of the Negro," quoted in MacChesney, *Abraham Lincoln,* 91–98.

47. William J. Calhoun, "The Negro's Place in National Life," quoted in MacChesney,
Abraham Lincoln, 107–9.

48. Calhoun, "The Negro's Place," 105–7.

49. Rev. A. J. Carey, "The Other Side of the Question," quoted in MacChesney, *Abraham
Lincoln,* 111.

50. *Chicago Daily Socialist,* 4 January 1909, 12 February 1909.

51. *Chicago Daily Socialist,* 15 February 1909.

52. Blair, *One Hundredth Anniversary,* 4.

53. "Columbus Day," *Youth's Companion,* 18 August 1892, 412; Lucille N. Graf, "Pledge to
the Flag," *American Mercury,* July 1956, 28–30.

54. "National School Celebration of Columbus Day," *Youth's Companion,* 8 September

1892, 446–47; *Youth's Companion*, 19 May 1892, 256, 17 November 1892, 608; Graf's "Pledge to the Flag" contains a melodramatic tale of the writing of the pledge.

55. *Nation's Birthday*, 101, 167.

56. *Chicago Tribune*, 23 February 1890, 23 February 1895, 22 February 1900, 23 February 1900; *Union League Club, Exercises in Commemoration of the Birthday of Washington, February 22, 1890* (Chicago: S. A. Maxwell and Co., [1890]).

57. *Tucson Arizona Daily Star*, 28 April 1889.

58. Cecilia Elizabeth O'Leary, *To Die For: The Paradox of American Patriotism* (Princeton: Princeton University Press, 1999), 6, chaps. 9–10. On these various groups, also see Stuart McConnell, "Reading the Flag: A Reconsideration of the Patriotic Cults of the 1890s," in *Bonds of Affection: Americans Define Their Patriotism*, ed. John Bodnar (Princeton: Princeton University Press, 1996), 102–19; Stuart McConnell, *Glorious Contentment: The Grand Army of the Republic, 1865–1900* (Chapel Hill: University of North Carolina Press, 1992); Wallace Evan Davies, *Patriotism on Parade: The Story of Veterans' and Hereditary Organizations in America, 1783–1900* (Cambridge: Harvard University Press, 1955); Michael Kammen, *Mystic Chords of Memory: The Transformation of Tradition in American Culture* (New York: Alfred A. Knopf, 1991), 204–5, 218, 244–46; David B. Tyack, *The One Best System: A History of American Urban Education* (Cambridge: Harvard University Press, 1974), 229–55; and Henry G. Hemenway, "An Analysis of Civic Education in American Secondary Schools, 1890–1916" (Ph.D. diss., University of Nebraska, 1969).

59. *Youth's Companion*, 29 August 1889, 429.

60. Davies, *Patriotism on Parade*, 242; *Chicago Tribune*, 30 May 1890, 31 May 1894, 30 May 1900, 30 May 1895.

61. *Tucson Arizona Weekly Citizen*, 1 March 1890; *Youth's Companion*, 25 December 1890, 713, and 9 October 1890, 521. On the schoolhouse flag movement, see O'Leary, *To Die For*, 176–80; McConnell, *Glorious Contentment*, 227–28; McConnell, "Reading the Flag," 103; Davies, *Patriotism on Parade*, 218–20; and Wilbur Zelinsky, *Nation into State: The Shifting Symbolic Foundations of American Nationalism* (Chapel Hill: University of North Carolina Press, 1989), 202–3.

62. George T. Balch, *Methods of Teaching Patriotism in the Public Schools* (New York: D. Van Nostrand, 1890), xxxv, 9, 11–13, 17–18, 26, 32–35; *Youth's Companion*, 2 July 1891, 376. On Balch, see O'Leary, *To Die For*, 151–55.

63. Davies, *Patriotism on Parade*, 218, 353–55; "Father of Flag Day Honored at Wisconsin Home," *Chicago Tribune*, 15 June 1946, Holiday Clippings file, Chicago Historical Society; *Chicago Tribune*, 18 June 1893, 14 June 1894. Although Cigrand was later dubbed the "father of Flag Day," there were other contenders for the title. Another story of the holiday's origins credited Louise Dalton, a United Daughter of the Confederacy and Daughter of the American Revolution, who lobbied for the bill prohibiting the

desecration of the flag. See L. Byrd Mock, "Founder of National Flag Day," *Confederate Veteran* 25 (May 1917): 237.

64. *Chicago Tribune*, 17 June 1894.

65. March Brothers, *A Catalogue of Thanksgiving Exercises, Christmas Goods, and Requisites for the February Holidays* (Lebanon, Ohio, 1902), 1, 30.

66. Horace G. Brown, "Observance of Historic Days at School," *Education* 32 (November 1911): 147–52; Constance D'Arcy MacKay, *Patriotic Plays and Pageants for Young People* (New York: Henry Holt and Co., 1912), 3, iii.

67. Alice J. Preston, "Washington Exercise," in "Friday Exercises," *Normal Instructor* 17 (February 1908): 26.

68. March Brothers, *Catalogue*, 25; Edith Cameron, "Little Hatchet Drill," in *Arizona Special Days*, pamphlet issued by C. O. Case, Superintendent of Public Instruction, State of Arizona (Arizona: n.p., 1915), 26; Lillian M. Jones, "How About It?" in "Entertainment for February Holidays," *Normal Instructor and Primary Plans* 25 (February 1916): 62.

69. Constance D'Arcy MacKay, "Lincoln Cabin Scene," in "Music and Entertainment," *Normal Instructor* 21 (February 1912): 33. For an example of the storekeeper tale, see "Abe Lincoln's Honesty," in Robert Haven Schauffler, ed., *Lincoln's Birthday* (New York: Moffatt, Yard and Co., 1918), 17–18.

70. Margrete Petersen, "Dances and Recitations for Washington's Birthday," *Normal Instructor and Primary Plans* 25 (February 1916): 63; "February Blackboard Reading Lesson," *Normal Instructor* 17 (February 1908): 25; Alice Cook Fuller, "A Colonial Tea Party," in "Friday Exercises," *Normal Instructor* 17 (February 1908): 28.

71. Charles R. Skinner, ed., *Manual of Patriotism for Use in the Public Schools of the State of New York* (Albany, N.Y.: n.p., 1904), 205–6, 213, 220–21; "Memorial Day Exercises," *Normal Instructor* 10 (May 1901): 25.

72. *Memorial Day Annual 1912* (Richmond: n.p., 1912), 66, 91, 92–93; Kate Pleasants Minor, "The Origin and Meaning of Memorial Day," in *Memorial Day Annual 1912* (Richmond: n.p., 1912), 88.

73. Robert Haven Schauffler, ed., *Flag Day* (New York: Moffat, Yard and Co., 1917), 211–12; Skinner, *Manual of Patriotism*, 35.

74. *Chicago Tribune*, 17 June 1894, 16 June 1895; "A Flag Exercise," in Case, *Arizona Special Days*, 5; Jane A. Stewart, "Flag Day Exercise," *Normal Instructor* 17 (June 1908): 28–29; "The Living Flag," in Schauffler, *Flag Day*, 211; Sallie M. Stillman, "A Drill for Flag Day or Closing Day," *Normal Instructor and Primary Plans* 25 (June 1916): 57.

75. Mary L. Kniskern, "A Lesson on the Flag," *Normal Instructor* 10 (May 1901): 26.

76. *Nation's Birthday*, 104.

77. *Chicago Tribune*, 13 February 1900.

78. MacKay, *Patriotic Plays and Pageants*, 38–43.

79. Lee F. Hanmer, "Holiday Celebrations," *Journal of Education* 75 (28 March 1912): 346.
80. *Nation's Birthday*, 153.
81. *Denní Hlasatel*, 14 October 1912, CFLPS; *Saloniki*, 24 February 1917, CFLPS. The actual Havlíček anniversary had been in July, but because schoolchildren were then on vacation, the Freethinkers worried that they were not reaping the benefit of the nationalist celebration.
82. *Chicagoer Arbeiter-Zeitung*, 1 May 1889, CFLPS.
83. J. L. McCreery, "Little Abe's Flag Day," *Chicago Daily Socialist*, 24 June 1905.
84. Lawrence W. Levine discusses the relationship between the decline of oratory and the rise of visual entertainment in *Highbrow Lowbrow*, 46–47.

6. HOLIDAYS AND THE PROGRESSIVE SEARCH FOR COMMUNITY

1. Mrs. Isaac L. [Dr. Julia Barnett] Rice, "Hoodlumism in Holiday Observance," *Forum*, April 1909, 317–22.
2. For a discussion of the divergent interests, goals, and approaches of these groups, see Paul Boyer, *Urban Masses and Moral Order in America, 1820–1920* (Cambridge: Harvard University Press, 1978), 175–90; and David Glassberg, *American Historical Pageantry: The Uses of Tradition in the Early Twentieth Century* (Chapel Hill: University of North Carolina Press, 1990), 30–40, 52–67.
3. "Beautiful Towns and Villages," *Youth's Companion*, 24 April 1890, 224.
4. Robert Haven Schauffler, ed., *Arbor Day* (New York: Moffat, Yard and Co., 1917), [xii–xiii], 9–10, 13–14; George W. Douglas, comp., *The American Book of Days* (New York: H. W. Wilson, 1937), 221–22; *Arbor and Bird Day, Illinois, 1906*, circular no. 79 (Springfield: Illinois State Journal Co., 1906), 11.
5. J. Sterling Morton to C. A. Babcock, 23 April 1894, in U.S. Department of Agriculture, Division of Biological Survey, *Bird Day in the Schools*, circular no. 17 [1896], 1; ibid., 4–5; *Arbor and Bird Day, Illinois, 1910*, circular no. 47 (n.p., 1910), 5.
6. Schauffler, *Arbor Day*, [xvii], 67, 32; *Youth's Companion*, 24 April 1890, 223.
7. Illinois Arbor Day Proclamation by Governor Joseph W. Fifer, 24 March 1892, Newberry Library, Chicago; *Arbor and Bird Day, Illinois, 1906*, 7–8.
8. Birdsey G. Northrup, "Arbor Day in the Schools," in Schauffler, *Arbor Day*, 14–15.
9. George William Curtis, "A New Holiday," in Schauffler, *Arbor Day*, 7; U.S. Department of Agriculture, *Bird Day in the Schools*, 2; Edward M. Deems, comp., *Holy Days and Holidays* (New York: Funk and Wagnalls, 1902; reprint, New York: Gale Research Co., 1968), 529; *Arbor and Bird Day, Illinois, 1906*, 9. Also see "Arbor Day," *Journal of Education* 75 (7 March 1912): 267.
10. *Tucson Citizen*, 6 February 1924, Holiday Clippings file, Arizona Historical Society, Tucson; Curtis, "A New Holiday," 8.

11. Caroline H. Stanley, "Arbor Day," *Journal of Education* 75 (7 March 1912): 267; Mary Day Bancroft, "An Arbor Day Dialogue," in "Arbor Day," *Journal of Education* 73 (23 February 1911): 209, 214; Mary V. Myers, "The Birds of Killingworth," in "Bird Day Plays and Recitations," *Normal Instructor and Primary Plans* 25 (March 1916): 60.

12. Schauffler, *Arbor Day*, 314–15; "Bird Day Plays and Recitations," 60; *Illinois Arbor and Bird Days 1919*, circular no. 134 (n.p., 1919), 17–21; Daisy L. Horton, "Arbor Day," *Normal Instructor* 21 (April 1912): 34–35.

13. "New York State Programme, 1889," in Schauffler, *Arbor Day*, 359–60; "Arbor Day Exercises for All Grades," *Normal Instructor and Primary Plans* 25 (March 1916): 57.

14. Deems, *Holy Days and Holidays*, 525; *Tucson Arizona Daily Citizen*, 6 February 1891; *Tucson Citizen*, 5 February 1909; *Arizona Arbor Day 1916* (Phoenix: McNeil Co., 1916), 23.

15. *Tucson Arizona Daily Star*, 4 February 1905; Schauffler, *Arbor Day*, 46.

16. William H. Burnham, "Every-Day Patriotism," *Outlook* 90 (7 November 1908): 535; Horace G. Brown, "Observance of Historic Days at School," *Education* 32 (November 1911): 148 (emphasis in original).

17. Constance D'Arcy MacKay, *Patriotic Plays and Pageants for Young People* (New York: Henry Holt and Co., 1912), 4 (emphasis in original). On the transformation of civic education, see Henry G. Hemenway, "An Analysis of Civic Education in American Secondary Schools, 1890–1916" (Ph.D. diss., University of Nebraska, 1969), 15–16, 38–52.

18. Percival Chubb, *Festivals and Plays in Schools and Elsewhere* (New York: Harper and Bros., 1912), 237, 41.

19. Ibid., 6, 11, 20–21, xviii; "Holiday Celebrations," *Journal of Education* 75 (16 May 1912): 550.

20. Charles Horton Cooley, *Social Organization: A Study of the Larger Mind* (New York: Charles Scribner's Sons, 1909), 26–27, 33, 38; Rev. William Norman Hutchins, "Moral Values in National Holidays," *Biblical World* 49 (March 1917), 168. My discussion of progressive ideas about community has been informed by Jean B. Quandt, *From the Small Town to the Great Community: The Social Thought of Progressive Intellectuals* (New Brunswick, N.J.: Rutgers University Press, 1970); R. Jackson Wilson, *In Quest of Community: Social Philosophy in the United States, 1860–1920* (New York: John Wiley and Sons, 1968); and Boyer, *Urban Masses*, 225–31.

21. John Dewey, *The School and Society* (Chicago: University of Chicago Press, 1900), 44, 27.

22. Charles Horton Cooley, *Social Process* (New York: Charles Scribner's Sons, 1918), 76, 74; George Creel, "The Hopes of the Hyphenated," *Century*, January 1916, in *Social History of American Education*, vol. 2, *1860 to the Present*, ed. Rena L. Vassar (Chicago: Rand McNally and Co., 1965), 223.

23. Creel, "Hopes of the Hyphenated," 224.

24. Ibid.; Luther Halsey Gulick, *A Philosophy of Play* (New York: Charles Scribner's

Sons, 1920), 242, 263; Luther Halsey Gulick, *Folk and National Dances*, reprinted from the *Proceedings of the Second Annual Playground Congress* for the Playground Association of America and the Russell Sage Foundation, no. 64 (New York: n.p., 1908), 4, 9; Quandt, *Small Town to Great Community*, 152–53. On the playground movement, see Dominick Cavallo, *Muscles and Morals: Organized Playgrounds and Urban Reform, 1880–1920* (Philadelphia: University of Pennsylvania Press, 1981).

25. Chubb, *Festivals and Plays*, 116, 94–96; Glassberg, *American Historical Pageantry*, 124–50.

26. Cooley, *Social Process*, 278, 280. Cooley approved of the restrictions on Asian immigration for the same reason.

27. Bancroft, "Arbor Day Dialogue," 209, 214.

28. Lee F. Hanmer, "Holiday Celebrations," *Journal of Education* 75 (28 March 1912): 346; Boyer, *Urban Masses*, 256.

29. Constance D'Arcy MacKay, *Patriotic Drama in Your Town* (New York: Henry Holt and Co., 1918), 25, 13; Barr Ferree, "Elements of a Successful Parade," *Century*, July 1900, 457; Robert Withington, *English Pageantry: An Historical Outline*, vol. 2 (Cambridge: Harvard University Press, 1920), 235; Mary Porter Beegle and Jack Randall Crawford, *Community Drama and Pageantry* (New Haven: Yale University Press, 1916), 35, 27, 31–34.

30. Ferree, "Elements of a Successful Parade," 458, 459; Chubb, *Festivals and Plays*, 228–29; Charles Rollinson Lamb, "Some Practical Suggestions," *Century*, July 1900, 463–64.

31. MacKay, *Patriotic Drama*, 13–14; Chubb, *Festivals and Plays*, 10–11, xx.

32. Percival Chubb, quoted in A. Georgette Bowden-Smith, "National Holidays," *Living Age*, 22 January 1910, 246; Gulick, *Folk and National Dances*, 14.

33. Luther H. Gulick, "The Vacant Fourth," *Survey*, 3 July 1909, 482, quoted in Roy Rosenzweig, *Eight Hours for What We Will: Workers and Leisure in an Industrial City, 1870–1920* (Cambridge: Cambridge University Press, 1983), 153. Rosenzweig argues that the movement also constituted a bourgeois attack on working-class and immigrant methods of celebration (153–57).

34. George Augustus Sala, *My Diary in America in the Midst of War*, 2nd ed., vol. 1 (London: Tinsley Brothers, 1865), 345, 348; Samuel Canby Rumford, "Life along the Brandywine between 1880–1895," document 341, Downs Collection, Henry Francis DuPont du Winterthur Library, Winterthur, Del., 28; *Youth's Companion*, 12 June 1890, 327.

35. Rice, "Hoodlumism in Holiday Observance," 320; *Chicago Tribune*, 2 July 1911; "In an Editorial Way," *Ladies' Home Journal*, July 1908, 3; Raymond W. Smilor, "Creating a National Festival: The Campaign for a Safe and Sane Fourth, 1903–1916," *Journal of American Culture* 2 (Winter 1980): 611–22.

36. "The New Patriotism," *Journal of Education* 75 (22 February 1912): 211; Hanmer, "Holiday Celebrations," 345–46; Smilor, "Creating a National Festival," 617.

37. Percy MacKaye, "The New Fourth of July," *Century*, July 1910, 394–96; Glassberg, *American Historical Pageantry*, 172.

38. MacKaye, "New Fourth," 396 (emphasis in original).

39. Glassberg, *American Historical Pageantry*, 63–64; Withington, *English Pageantry*, vol. 2, 241.

40. Henry Crittenden Morris to Trustees of the Sane Fourth Association, 1 July 1909; Sane Fourth Association pamphlet [1909]; both in Henry Crittenden Morris Papers, box 2, folder 9, Chicago Historical Society, Chicago.

41. Marquis Eaton to Henry Crittenden Morris, 14 June 1910 (emphasis in original); Mimeograph from Marquis Eaton, 24 June 1910; Marquis Eaton to Charles E. Beals, 27 June 1910 (emphasis in original); all Morris Papers, box 2, folder 9.

42. *Chicago Daily Socialist*, 24 February 1910, 5 July 1910, 24 June 1910.

43. Marquis Eaton, "Report of the President to the Trustees of the Sane Fourth Association" [1911], Morris Papers, box 2, folder 9.

44. *Chicago Tribune*, 2 July 1911, 3 July 1911, 5 July 1911. Curiously for a purported celebration of American independence, the Pain spectacle was advertised to conclude with a display of "Coronation Fireworks" in honor of England's George V.

45. Eaton, "Report of President"; *Chicago Tribune*, 5 July 1911.

46. *Dziennik Zwiazkowy*, 5 July 1911, in the Chicago Public Library Omnibus Project, comp. and trans., *The Chicago Foreign Language Press Survey* (Chicago, 1942), section III.B.3, "Holidays" (hereafter cited as *CFLPS*); *Chicago Tribune*, 5 July 1911; *Denní Hlasatel*, 5 July 1911, *CFLPS*.

47. *Chicago Daily Socialist*, 5 July 1911.

48. Eaton, "Report of the President"; Marquis Eaton to Henry Crittenden Morris, 19 June 1912; James Edgar Brown to Morris, 28 June 1912; all in Morris Papers, box 2, folder 9.

49. Marquis Eaton to Chicago Association of Commerce, 2 November 1914, Morris Papers, box 2, folder 9; West Chicago Park Commissioners, *Forty-Seventh Annual Report, 1915* (Chicago, 1915), 89.

50. Marquis Eaton to Henry Crittenden Morris, 27 June 1913, Morris Papers, box 2, folder 9; Smilor, "Creating a National Festival," 617, 620–21; "The New Patriotism," 211. Roy Rosenzweig casts a dissenting vote, contending in *Eight Hours for What We Will* that in Worcester bonfires replaced firecrackers, actually increasing fire danger (162).

51. Beegle and Crawford, *Community Drama*, 31; "The Standardization of Holidays," *Independent*, 29 June 1914, 546.

52. Hanmer, "Holiday Celebrations," 347.

53. *New York Times*, 1 January 1913.
54. MacKay, *Patriotic Drama*, 36, 40, 44; Beegle and Crawford, *Community Drama*, 33.
55. "Chicago's Spirit Shown by City Christmas Tree," uncited newspaper, 17 December 1913, in Clip book, Charles L. Hutchinson Papers, Newberry Library, Chicago.
56. Everett B. Mero, "The Value of Holidays in the Building of Citizenship," *American City* 9 (October 1913): 323, 326. On the legalization of Columbus Day, see Douglas, *American Book of Days*, 530–31. Columbus Day did not become a federal holiday until 1934.
57. Mero, "Value of Holidays," 323, 325; Withington, *English Pageantry*, vol. 2, 245–48.
58. Mero, "Value of Holidays," 326–27.
59. *Anniversary Exercises West Park No. 2, Washington's Birthday, Wednesday, February 22, 1911* (Chicago: Charles W. Lehmann, 1911); *Anniversary Exercises 1911, West Park No. 2*, souvenir program. On the development of Chicago's neighborhood parks in the progressive era, see *A Breath of Fresh Air: Chicago's Neighborhood Parks of the Progressive Reform Era, 1900–1925*, the catalog of an exhibit at the Grand Army of the Republic Museum, Chicago Public Library Cultural Center (n.p.: Lake County Press, 1989). On the progressive view of these parks, see Boyer, *Urban Masses*, 236–42. The neighborhood park remains largely unexplored by historians.
60. "Citizenship Receptions," *School and Society* 1 (19 June 1915): 880–81; Edward George Hartmann, *The Movement to Americanize the Immigrant* (New York: AMS Press, 1967), 108–21.
61. *Survey*, 31 July 1915, 390.
62. *New York Times*, 3 July 1915, 6 July 1915.
63. *New York Times*, 4 July 1915, 5 July 1915, 6 July 1915.
64. Louis Weinberg, "Celebrating Independence," *New Republic*, 17 July 1915, 278.
65. Ibid., 278–79.
66. *Abendpost*, 12 October 1914, 28 January 1915, CFLPS.
67. *El Tucsonense*, 2 September 1916; *Tucson Citizen*, 27 August 1918, 1 September 1918.
68. *Dziennik Zwiazkowy*, 30 November 1914, 28 January 1918, CFLPS.
69. *Dziennik Zwiazkowy*, 14 June 1917, 3 May 1918, 11 May 1917, CFLPS. For an example of a speaker urging Poles to join the Polish rather than the American army, see *Dziennik Zwiazkowy*, 28 January 1918, CFLPS.
70. *Denní Hlasatel*, 4 August 1917, CFLPS.
71. *Chicago Defender*, 28 September 1918.
72. *Chicago Defender*, 28 September 1918, 22 June 1918.
73. *Chicago Defender*, 16 February 1918, 22 June 1918.
74. *Chicago Defender*, 22 June 1918.
75. *Chicago Defender*, 5 October 1918, 16 February 1918. Of course the governor failed to mention the evening's other honoree, Frederick Douglass.

76. *Chicago Tribune*, 14 June 1918, 15 June 1918.

77. Hartmann, *Movement to Americanize*, 200–208; Stephen Vaughn, *Holding Fast the Inner Lines: Democracy, Nationalism, and the Committee on Public Information* (Chapel Hill: University of North Carolina Press, 1980), 120.

78. *Sunday Jewish Courier*, 23 June 1918, CFLPS; *Denní Hlasatel*, 30 June 1918, CFLPS. On the celebration program, see *Chicago Tribune*, 2 July 1918, 4 July 1918.

79. *New York Times*, 5 July 1918.

80. Ibid.

81. Ibid.

82. *Chicago Tribune*, 5 July 1918; *Denní Hlasatel*, 5 July 1918, CFLPS; *Loxias*, 11 July 1918, CFLPS.

83. *Denní Hlasatel*, 25 June 1918, 5 July 1918, CFLPS; *Chicago Tribune*, 3 July 1918; *Loxias*, 11 July 1918, CFLPS; *Chicago Defender*, 13 July 1918.

84. *Chicago Tribune*, 4 July 1918, 3 July 1918.

85. *Chicago Tribune*, 3 July 1918.

86. *Sunday Jewish Courier*, 23 June 1918, CFLPS.

87. *New York Times*, 5 July 1918; Glassberg, *American Historical Pageantry*, 224. The *Times* did note that "eighteen Haitians in civilian clothes" brought up the rear of the parade.

88. *New York Times*, 5 July 1918.

89. "Standardization of Holidays."

CONCLUSION

1. *Richmond Times-Dispatch*, 12 November 1918; *Tucson Citizen*, 12 November 1918.

2. *Tucson Citizen*, 12 November 1918, 30 October 1920, 10 November 1920, 11 November 1920, 12 November 1920.

3. John Dos Passos, *1919* (Boston: Houghton Mifflin, 1932; New York: New American Library, 1969), 462–67.

4. *Denní Hlasatel*, 25 October 1922, in the Chicago Public Library Omnibus Project, comp. and trans., *The Chicago Foreign Language Press Survey* (Chicago, 1942), section III.B.3, "Holidays" (hereafter cited as *CFLPS*); *Chicago Italian Chamber of Commerce*, 19 November 1922, CFLPS. On Czech-Slovak Independence Day celebrations, see *Denní Hlasatel*, 29 October 1920, 27 October 1921, 29 October 1921, 1 November 1922, CFLPS.

5. *Chinese Daily Times*, 13 October 1935, CFLPS; *Sonntagpost*, 11 April 1926, CFLPS; *Abendpost*, 17 September 1934, CFLPS. John Bodnar examines ethnic celebrations in this period in *Remaking America: Public Memory, Commemoration, and Patriotism in the Twentieth Century* (Princeton: Princeton University Press, 1992), 41–77.

6. Michael Kazin and Steven J. Ross, "America's Labor Day: The Dilemma of a Workers'

Celebration," *Journal of American History* 78 (March 1992): 1313–19; Richard M. Fried, *The Russians Are Coming! The Russians Are Coming! Pageantry and Patriotism in Cold-War America* (New York: Oxford University Press, 1998), 12–18, 51–66.

7. Dunkirk and Buffalo, New York, for example, both celebrate Juneteenth. See *Dunkirk (N.Y.) Observer*, 29 May 1999; *Buffalo News*, 20 June 1999. On the King holiday, see "King Day: Official at Last," *Newsweek* (20 January 1986): 22. The first official celebration was not held until 1986.

8. *New York Times*, 19 February 1991, A16, national edition; *St. Louis Post-Dispatch*, 30 May 1999. On the Monday holiday law, see "Holidays: Better on Monday," *Time* (5 July 1968): 40; and "Whatever Happened to . . . the Plan for More Monday Holidays," *U.S. News and World Report* (1 September 1969): 5. For examples of recent Memorial Day exercises, see *Buffalo News*, 1 June 1999; and *Dunkirk (N.Y.) Observer*, 1 June 1999. Although the Monday holiday legislation is fairly recent, there were calls for this change as early as 1912. See R. H. Weevil, "The Holiday Calendar: Can We Improve It?" *Survey* (17 February 1912), 1756–57.

9. Christine Cecilia Wagner, "Rediscovering Memorial Day: Politics, Patriotism, and Gender" (Ph.D. diss., Syracuse University, 1992); Renee E. Warren, "No Promised Land in AZ," *Black Enterprise* (February 1991): 16.

10. *New York Times*, 13 February 1993, A25, 23 February 1993, B3.

11. *New York Times*, 1 March 1993, B3; 2 March 1993, B3; 18 March 1993, A1, West Coast edition. In the latest round of this conflict, New York senatorial candidate Hillary Rodham Clinton marched on 5 March 2000 in an early St. Patrick's Day parade in Queens, which allowed gay and lesbian organizations to participate. No doubt her opponent, Rudolph Giuliani, will be conspicuous at the AOH's annual procession (*Buffalo News*, 6 March 2000).

12. *New York Times*, 18 March 1993, A14, West Coast edition.

INDEX

Boldface page numbers indicate illustrations